MUSIC
for
EAR TRAINING

Chord Progression w̄ I & V

-Listen for bass motion

-Fill in Sup. and B Voices First

-Listen for chord Quality - Major or Major-Minor 7th

-Remember Voice leading Principles

MUSIC
for
EAR TRAINING

FOURTH EDITION

Michael Horvit   Timothy Koozin   Robert Nelson

Moores School of Music, University of Houston

Software production team

Joel Love	Samuel Hunter
Bryan Bilocura	Jaemi Loeb
Timothy Rolls	Timothy Nord
Jill Bays-Purtill	Kristine Woldy
Shanta Childers	Crystal Visco

Software design

Timothy Koozin

SCHIRMER
CENGAGE Learning™

Australia • Brazil • Japan • Korea • Mexico • Singapore • Spain • United Kingdom • United States

SCHIRMER
CENGAGE Learning

Music for Ear Training
Fourth Edition
Michael Horvit, Timothy Koozin,
Robert Nelson

Publisher: Clark Baxter

Assistant Editor: Elizabeth Newell

Managing Media Editor: Katie Schooling

Marketing Program Manager: Gurpreet Saran

Content Project Manager: Rosemary Winfield

Art Director: Faith Brosnan

Manufacturing Planner: Mary Beth Hennebury

Rights Acquisition Specialist: Amanda Groszko

Production Service: MPS Limited

Cover Designer: Wing-ip Ngan, Inkdesign, Inc.

Cover Image: Mike Kemp / Getty Images;
Datacraft Co. Ltd. / Getty Images

Compositor: MPS Limited

For product information and technology assistance, contact us at
**Cengage Learning Customer & Sales Support,
1-800-354-9706.**

For permission to use material from this text or product,
submit all requests online at **www.cengage.com/permissions**.

Further permissions questions can be emailed to
permissionrequest@cengage.com.

Library of Congress Control Number: 2012933601

Student Edition:
ISBN-13: 978-0-8400-2981-2
ISBN-10: 0-8400-2981-0

Schirmer
20 Channel Center Street
Boston, MA 02210
USA

Cengage Learning is a leading provider of customized learning solutions with office locations around the globe, including Singapore, the United Kingdom, Australia, Mexico, Brazil and Japan. Locate your local office at **international.cengage.com/region**.

Cengage Learning products are represented in Canada by Nelson Education, Ltd.

For your course and learning solutions, visit **www.cengage.com**.

Purchase any of our products at your local college store
or at our preferred online store **www.cengagebrain.com**.

Instructors: Please visit **login.cengage.com** and log in to access instructor-specific resources.

Printed in the United States of America
1 2 3 4 5 6 7 16 15 14 13 12

Contents

Getting Started   *xvii*

What's New in Music for Ear Training, Version 4.0   *xvii*

Suggestions to the Instructor   *xviii*

Suggestions to the Student   *xx*

UNIT 1

Intervals, Triads, and Scales   1

Major and Minor Seconds: QUIZ No. 1   1
                          QUIZ No. 2   2

Major and Minor Thirds: QUIZ No. 1   3
                         QUIZ No. 2   4

Perfect and Augmented Fourths: QUIZ No. 1   5
                                QUIZ No. 2   6

Perfect and Diminished Fifths: QUIZ No. 1   7
                                QUIZ No. 2   8

All Perfect Intervals and Tritones: QUIZ No. 1   9
                                     QUIZ No. 2   10

Major and Minor Sixths: QUIZ No. 1   11
                         QUIZ No. 2   12

Major and Minor Sevenths: QUIZ No. 1   13
                           QUIZ No. 2   14

All Intervals: QUIZ No. 1   15
                QUIZ No. 2   16

Major and Minor Triads: QUIZ No. 1   17
                         QUIZ No. 2   18

Introducing Diminished Triads: QUIZ No. 1   19
                                QUIZ No. 2   20

Introducing Augmented Triads: QUIZ No. 1   21

QUIZ No. 2   22

Major and Minor Scales: QUIZ No. 1   23

QUIZ No. 2   24

UNIT 2

Rhythmic Dictation: Simple Meters   25

Rhythmic Dictation: QUIZ No. 1   28

QUIZ No. 2   29

QUIZ No. 3   30

Melodic Dictation: Seconds, Thirds, and Fourths   31

Preliminary Exercises   31

Melodies   34

Melodic Dictation: QUIZ No. 1   37

QUIZ No. 2   38

QUIZ No. 3   39

QUIZ No. 4   40

UNIT 3

Melodic Dictation: Fifths, Sixths, and Octaves   41

Preliminary Exercises   41

Melodies   44

Melodic Dictation: QUIZ No. 1   47

QUIZ No. 2   48

QUIZ No. 3   49

QUIZ No. 4   50

Harmonic Dictation: Four-Part Settings of the Tonic Triad   51

Harmonic Dictation: QUIZ No. 1   53

QUIZ No. 2   54

QUIZ No. 3   55

UNIT 4

Rhythmic Dictation: 2:1 Subdivisions of the Beat   56

Rhythmic Dictation: QUIZ No. 1   59

QUIZ No. 2   60

QUIZ No. 3   61

Melodic Dictation: The Tonic Triad and Dominant Seventh   62

Preliminary Exercises   62

Melodies   64

Melodic Dictation: QUIZ No. 1   68

                                                 QUIZ No. 2   69

                                                 QUIZ No. 3   70

                                                 QUIZ No. 4   71

Harmonic Dictation: The Tonic Triad and Dominant Seventh   73

   Basic Progressions   73

   Phrase-Length Exercises   82

   Harmonic Dictation: QUIZ No. 1   85

                                                 QUIZ No. 2   86

                                                 QUIZ No. 3   87

                                                 QUIZ No. 4   88

UNIT 5

Rhythmic Dictation: 4:1 Subdivision of the Beat, Anacruses   89

   Rhythmic Dictation: QUIZ No. 1   92

                                                 QUIZ No. 2   93

                                             QUIZ No. 3   95

Melodic Dictation: Primary Triads and the Dominant Seventh   97

   Preliminary Exercises   97

   Melodies   98

   Melodic Dictation: QUIZ No. 1   102

                                                 QUIZ No. 2   103

                                             QUIZ No. 3   104

                                             QUIZ No. 4   105

Harmonic Dictation: Primary Triads and the Dominant Seventh; Cadential Tonic Six-Four   106

   Basic Progressions   106

     Primary triads and the dominant seventh   106

     Cadential tonic six-four   108

   Phrase-Length Exercises   110

   Harmonic Dictation: QUIZ No. 1   113

                                                 QUIZ No. 2   114

                                             QUIZ No. 3   115

                                             QUIZ No. 4   116

UNIT 6

Rhythmic Dictation: Dots and Ties   117

   Rhythmic Dictation: QUIZ No. 1   120

                                                 QUIZ No. 2   121

                                             QUIZ No. 3   123

Melodic Dictation: Minor Mode   125

   Preliminary Exercises   125

   Melodies   126

   Melodic Dictation: QUIZ No. 1   130
                        QUIZ No. 2   131
                        QUIZ No. 3   132
                        QUIZ No. 4   133

Harmonic Dictation: Minor Mode; First Inversion of Triads   135

   Basic Progressions   135

     Minor mode   135

     First inversion of triads   136

   Phrase-Length Exercises   139

   Harmonic Dictation: QUIZ No. 1   143
                        QUIZ No. 2   144
                        QUIZ No. 3   145
                        QUIZ No. 4   147

UNIT 7

Melodic Dictation: The Supertonic Triad   149

   Preliminary Exercises   149

   Melodies   150

   Melodic Dictation: QUIZ No. 1   154
                        QUIZ No. 2   155
                        QUIZ No. 3   156
                        QUIZ No. 4   158

Harmonic Dictation: The Supertonic Triad; Inversions of V7   160

   Basic Progressions   160

     Supertonic triad   160

     Inversions of V7   162

   Phrase-Length Exercises   164

   Harmonic Dictation: QUIZ No. 1   167
                        QUIZ No. 2   169
                        QUIZ No. 3   171
                        QUIZ No. 4   173

UNIT 8

Rhythmic Dictation: Compound Meter   175

   Rhythmic Dictation: QUIZ No. 1   178
                        QUIZ No. 2   179
                        QUIZ No. 3   180

Melodic Dictation: All Diatonic Triads   181

    Preliminary Exercises   181

    Melodies   183

    Melodic Dictation: QUIZ No. 1   186

                    QUIZ No. 2   187

                    QUIZ No. 3   188

                    QUIZ No. 4   190

Harmonic Dictation: All Diatonic Triads   192

    Basic Progressions   192

    Phrase-Length Exercises   197

    Harmonic Dictation: QUIZ No. 1   200

                    QUIZ No. 2   201

                    QUIZ No. 3   202

                    QUIZ No. 4   204

UNIT 9

Rhythmic Dictation: Triplets and Duplets   206

    Rhythmic Dictation: QUIZ No. 1   209

                    QUIZ No. 2   210

                    QUIZ No. 3   211

Melodic Dictation: Supertonic and Leading Tone Sevenths   212

    Preliminary Exercises   212

    Melodies   213

    Melodic Dictation: QUIZ No. 1   218

                    QUIZ No. 2   219

                    QUIZ No. 3   220

                    QUIZ No. 4   222

Harmonic Dictation: Supertonic and Leading Tone Sevenths   224

    Basic Progressions   224

    Phrase-Length Exercises   229

    Harmonic Dictation: QUIZ No. 1   233

                    QUIZ No. 2   234

                    QUIZ No. 3   235

                    QUIZ No. 4   237

UNIT 10

Examples from Music Literature   239

    1. Johann Sebastian Bach.   Minuet in G   239

    2. Johann Sebastian Bach.   *Aus meines Herzens Grunde* (chorale)   240

    3. Johann Sebastian Bach.   *Wir glauben all' an einen Gott* (chorale)   240

4. Ludwig van Beethoven.   Six Variations on *Nel cor più non mi sento*   241

5. Friedrich Kuhlau.   Sonatina Op. 88, No. 3, Mvt. III   241

6. Wolfgang Amadeus Mozart.   String Quintet, K. 581, Mvt. IV   242

QUIZ No. 1   243

Joseph Haydn.   Sonata in D Major, Hob. XVI:33, Menuetto con
Variazioni   243

QUIZ No. 2   244

John Farmer.   *Fair Phyllis* (chorale)   244

QUIZ No. 3   245

Wolfgang Amadeus Mozart.   String Quartet, K. 80, Mvt. III, Trio   245

UNIT 11

Rhythmic Dictation: Syncopation   246

Rhythmic Dictation: QUIZ No. 1   249
QUIZ No. 2   250
QUIZ No. 3   252

Melodic Dictation: Non-Dominant Seventh Chords   253

Preliminary Exercises   253

Melodies   254

Melodic Dictation: QUIZ No. 1   258
QUIZ No. 2   259
QUIZ No. 3   260
QUIZ No. 4   262

Harmonic Dictation: Non-Dominant Seventh Chords   264

Basic Progressions   264

Phrase-Length Exercises   267

Harmonic Dictation: QUIZ No. 1   270
QUIZ No. 2   271
QUIZ No. 3   272
QUIZ No. 4   274

UNIT 12

Melodic Dictation: Scalar Variants, Modal Borrowing, Decorative
Chromaticism   276

Preliminary Exercises   276
Scalar variants   276
Modal borrowing   277
Decorative chromaticism   278

Melodies   281

Melodic Dictation: QUIZ No. 1 285

QUIZ No. 2 286

QUIZ No. 3 287

QUIZ No. 4 289

Harmonic Dictation: Scalar Variants, Modal Borrowing 290

Basic Progressions 290

Scalar variants 290

Modal borrowing 292

Phrase-Length Exercises 295

Harmonic Dictation: QUIZ No. 1 300

QUIZ No. 2 302

QUIZ No. 3 304

QUIZ No. 4 306

UNIT 13

Melodic Dictation: Secondary Dominants 308

Preliminary Exercises 308

Melodies 310

Melodic Dictation: QUIZ No. 1 314

QUIZ No. 2 315

QUIZ No. 3 317

Harmonic Dictation: Secondary Dominants 319

Basic Progressions 319

Phrase-Length Exercises 322

Harmonic Dictation: QUIZ No. 1 326

QUIZ No. 2 328

QUIZ No. 3 330

UNIT 14

Examples from Music Literature 332

1. Johann Sebastian Bach. *Herr, wie du willst, so shick's mit mir* (chorale) 332

2. Johann Sebastian Bach. *Jesu, meiner Seelen Wonne* (chorale) 332

3. Johann Sebastian Bach. *Wer nur den lieben Gott läßt walten* (chorale) 332

4. Johann Sebastian Bach. Minuet in G Minor 333

5. Edward MacDowell. *To a Wild Rose*, Op. 51, No. 1 333

6. Carl Maria von Weber. German Dance 334

7. Frederic Chopin. Valse, Op. 69, No. 1 334

8. Wolfgang Amadeus Mozart. String Quartet, K. 158, mvt. I 335

9. Joseph Haydn. Divertimento in D 336

10. Ludwig van Beethoven. String Quartet, Op. 18, No. 6, mvt. I 337

QUIZ No. 1   338

   1. Johann Sebastian Bach.   *Jesu, meiner Seelen Wonne* (chorale)   338

   2. Johann Sebastian Bach.   *Es woll' uns Gott genadig sein* (chorale)   338

QUIZ No. 2   339

   1. Ludwig van Beethoven.   *Romanze* from Sonatina in G   339

   2. Frederic Chopin.   Prelude, Op. 28, No. 7   339

QUIZ No. 3   340

   Joseph Haydn.   Divertimento in G, Hob. II:3   340

UNIT 15

Melodic Dictation: Modulation to Closely Related Keys   341

   Melodies   341

   Melodic Dictation: QUIZ No. 1   346

                      QUIZ No. 2   347

                      QUIZ No. 3   349

Harmonic Dictation: Modulation to Closely Related Keys   350

   Phrase-Length Exercises   350

   Harmonic Dictation: QUIZ No. 1   355

                       QUIZ No. 2   357

                       QUIZ No. 3   359

UNIT 16

Rhythmic Dictation: Quintuple Meter   361

   Preliminary Exercises   361

   Comprehensive Exercises   362

   Rhythmic Dictation: QUIZ No. 1   365

                    QUIZ No. 2   366

                    QUIZ No. 3   368

Melodic Dictation: The Neapolitan Sixth Chord, Augmented Sixth Chords, and Modulation to Distantly Related Keys   369

   Preliminary Exercises   369

   Melodies   371

   Melodic Dictation: QUIZ No. 1   375

                      QUIZ No. 2   377

                      QUIZ No. 3   379

Harmonic Dictation: The Neapolitan Sixth Chord, Augmented Sixth Chords, Enharmonic Modulation   381

   Basic Progressions   381

   Phrase-Length Exercises   384

Harmonic Dictation: QUIZ No. 1   388

QUIZ No. 2   390

QUIZ No. 3   392

UNIT 17

Examples from Music Literature   394

   1. Johann Sebastian Bach.   *Ach Gott, vom Himmel sieh' darein* (chorale)   394

   2. Johann Sebastian Bach.   *Befiehl du deine Wege* (chorale)   394

   3. Johann Sebastian Bach.   *Ach Gott, wie manches Herzeleid* (chorale)   395

   4. Johann Sebastian Bach.   *Hilf, Herr Jesu, lass gelingen* (chorale)   396

   5. Johann Sebastian Bach.   Bourrée, French Overture   397

   6. Jeremiah Clarke.   Jigg   398

   7. Antonio Diabelli.   Rondino   399

   8. Joseph Haydn.   Sonata, Hob. XVI:27, mvt. III   399

   9. Ludwig van Beethoven.   Bagatelle, Op. 119, No. 1   400

  10. Ludwig van Beethoven.   Minuet in G Major, WoO 10, No. 2   400

  11. Mikail Ivanovich Glinka.   Waltz, Op. 39, No. 15   401

  12. Franz Schubert.   Scherzo in B-flat   401

  13. Joseph Haydn.   Divertimento, Hob. II:18, mvt. III, Trio   402

  14. Ludwig van Beethoven.   Quartet, Op. 18, No. 1, mvt. III   403

  15. Ludwig van Beethoven.   Quartet, Op. 18, No. 4, mvt. III   404

  16. Ludwig van Beethoven.   Quartet, Op. 18, No. 4, mvt. IV   405

  17. Wolfgang Amadeus Mozart.   Quartet, K. 421, mvt. III   406

  18. Wolfgang Amadeus Mozart.   Quartet, K. 170, mvt. I   407

QUIZ No. 1   409

   1. Johann Sebastian Bach.   *Befiehl du deine Wege* (chorale)   409

   2. Domenico Scarlatti.   Sonata, Longo 83   409

   3. Joseph Haydn.   Sonata, Hob. XVI:37, mvt. III   410

   4. Ludwig van Beethoven.   Sonata "Pathetique," Op. 13, mvt. III   410

QUIZ No. 2   411

   1. Johann Sebastian Bach.   *Meine Seel' erhebt den Herren* (chorale)   411

   2. Ludwig van Beethoven.   Sonata, Op. 14, No. 1, mvt. II   412

   3. Johannes Brahms.   Waltz, Op. 39, No. 15   412

   4. Ludwig van Beethoven.   Quartet, Op. 18, No. 2, mvt. III, Trio   413

QUIZ No. 3   414

   1. Johann Sebastian Bach.   *Jesu, meine Freude* (chorale)   414

   2. Robert Schumann.   "Important Event," *Scenes from Childhood,* Op. 15, No. 6   415

   3. Edvard Grieg.   Rigaudon, Op. 40, No. 5, Trio   415

   4. Ludwig van Beethoven.   Quartet, Op. 18, No. 3, mvt. III   416

UNIT 18

Rhythmic Dictation: Irregular Meters   417

    Rhythmic Dictation: QUIZ No. 1   420

        QUIZ No. 2   421

Melodic Dictation: Diatonic Modes   422

    Melodic Dictation: QUIZ No. 1   426

        QUIZ No. 2   428

Harmonic Dictation: Diatonic Modes   429

    Harmonic Dictation: QUIZ No. 1   433

        QUIZ No. 2   435

UNIT 19

Rhythmic Dictation: Changing Meters   437

    Rhythmic Dictation: QUIZ No. 1   440

        QUIZ No. 2   441

Part Music Dictation: Pandiatonicism   442

    Part Music Dictation: QUIZ No. 1   450

        QUIZ No. 2   453

UNIT 20

Rhythmic Dictation: Syncopation Including Irregular and Mixed Meters   455

    Rhythmic Dictation: QUIZ No. 1   458

        QUIZ No. 2   459

Melodic Dictation: Extended and Altered Tertian Harmony   461

    Melodic Dictation: QUIZ No. 1   465

        QUIZ No. 2   467

Harmonic Dictation: Extended and Altered Tertian Harmony   469

    Harmonic Dictation: QUIZ No. 1   473

        QUIZ No. 2   475

UNIT 21

Melodic Dictation: Exotic Scales   477

    Melodic Dictation: QUIZ No. 1   482

        QUIZ No. 2   483

Part Music Dictation: Exotic Scales   485

    Part Music Dictation: QUIZ No. 1   489

        QUIZ No. 2   491

UNIT 22

Melodic Dictation: Quartal Harmony   492

    Melodic Dictation: QUIZ No. 1   496
                       QUIZ No. 2   498

Part Music Dictation: Quartal Harmony   500

    Part Music Dictation: QUIZ No. 1   503
                        QUIZ No. 2   505

UNIT 23

Part Music Dictation: Polyharmony and Polytonality   507

    Part Music Dictation: QUIZ No. 1   514
                        QUIZ No. 2   517

UNIT 24

Melodic Dictation: Interval Music   520

    Preliminary Exercises   520

    Melodies   523

    Melodic Dictation: QUIZ No. 1   527
                       QUIZ No. 2   529

UNIT 25

Melodic Dictation: Serial Music   531

    Melodic Dictation: QUIZ No. 1   534
                     QUIZ No. 2   535

UNIT 26

Examples from Music Literature   536

    Part 1: Modality, pandiatoniscism, free tertian, jazz   536

        1. Béla Bartók, Evening in the Country   536

        2. Igor Stravinsky, Vivo   537

        3. Ernst Bloch, Waves, mm. 71–78   537

        4. Claude Debussy, Prelude VIII, mm. 24–28   538

        5. Claude Debussy, Sarabande, mm. 23–29   538

        6. Igor Stravinsky, *L'Histoire du Soldat*, "Marche Royale"   539

QUIZ No. 1   540

    1. Carlos Chávez, Prelude No. 2   540

    2. Claude Debussy, Rêverie, mm. 51–58   540

    3. Igor Stravinsky, *L'Histoire du Soldat,* Petit Choral   541

    4. Bronislau Kaper, Green Dolphin Street   541

Part 2: Scalar and chordal techniques, polytonality   542

    1. Béla Bartók, Forty-four Violin Duets, No. 33, Harvest Song   542

    2. Bela Bartók, Sketches, II (See-saw . . .)   542

    3. Béla Bartók, Sketches, V (Roumanian Folk Song)   543

    4. John Alden Carpenter, Danza, mm. 193–198   543

    5. Ángel Lasala, Trío No. 1, I, mm. 77–82   544

QUIZ No. 2   545

    1. Béla Bartók, Bear Dance   545

Part 3: Interval music, free atonality, and serialism   546

    1. Igor Stravinsky, Symphony of Psalms, II   546

    2. Béla Bartók, Music for Strings, Percussion, and Celesta, I   546

    3. Arnold Schoenberg, Three Songs   546

    4. Luigi Dallapiccola, Goethe Lieder, Mvt. 2   546

    5. Roger Sessions, Sonata for Violin   547

    6. Arnold Schoenberg, Drei Klavierstück, Op. 11, No. 1   547

    7. Anton Webern, Symphony, Op. 21, II, Variationen, Thema   548

QUIZ No. 3   549

    1. Edgard Varèse, Octandre, I   549

    2. Ernst Krenek, Suite for Violoncello Solo   549

    3. Luigi Dallapiccola, Quaderno Musicale di Annalibera, I   549

Getting Started

1. Create your online user account at **CengageBrain.com**, following the instructions on the card included with your book. Do not lose the access code printed on the card. Only registered users have full access to the Website.

2. Begin your online practice immediately at **MusicForEarTraining.com**. You can also download the **MusicET** application to your computer for practice without an Internet connection. Refer to the "Downloads and Help" page at the Website for more information.

What's New in Music for Ear Training, Version 4.0

- New streaming audio for all music listening examples, rendered with the highest-quality instrumental timbres sampled from all the principal instruments of the orchestra. Listening exercises at the **MusicForEarTraining.com** Website are compatible with popular Web browsers for computers and mobile tablets.

- The dual option of listening either with digital audio online or with the downloadable software application and internal computer sound.

- No CD drive is needed for off-line listening. The downloadable application replaces and updates content on the third edition CD-ROM, in a format newly optimized for current Windows and Macintosh systems.

- New Web-based preliminary exercises for intervals, chords, and scales to help students acquire strong listening skills in music fundamentals. Contextual listening examples provide opportunities to hear intervals and chords in musical contexts with scales, melodies, and varied instrumental timbres. An online record tracks the student's progress.

- A new unit of music literature examples for twentieth-century techniques, with excerpts for dictation from works by major modern composers including Debussy, Bartok, Stravinsky, Schoenberg, and others.

Suggestions to the Instructor

Create your online user account as an instructor at **CengageBrain.com**. Your registration authorizes full access to the *Music for Ear Training* Website at **MusicForEarTraining.com**.

These listening exercises for dictation with accompanying workbook are intended as supplements to a course in Ear Training.

Often, there is not sufficient class time to provide students with the reinforcing experiences necessary to develop the tools to take music dictation with ease, assurance, and fluency. The ability to write down music after hearing it is an extremely important skill that benefits the musician in numerous ways. It enhances one's aural acuity both as a performer and listener and makes all musical experiences more vivid and comprehensible.

This interactive material provides each individual student with the equivalent of a private ear-training tutor. Each student may proceed at his or her own pace. Examples and portions of examples can be listened to as often as necessary for each individual to master the material. Isolated lines in four-part examples and right-hand or left-hand parts in keyboard textures can be selected as listening options. *It is important, however, that the student develop the ability to take down dictation accurately within a limited number of replays*, possibly four, or other number recommended by the instructor.

The Website at **MusicForEarTraining.com** delivers musical listening examples rendered with the highest-quality orchestral and keyboard sampled sounds while the downloadable software application provides opportunity for the student to work without an Internet connection using computer internal sound. The layout of the workbook is designed in parallel with the listening examples, so that the student can write dictation directly onto the appropriate page. Formatted staves with time and key signatures and bar lines are provided for each example. Answers for all practice dictation examples are immediately available on-screen using either the Web interface or the downloadable application. Answers for the quizzes at the end of each chapter are available only to the teacher in the Instructor's Edition of the workbook.

All of the material in *Music for Ear Training* is cumulative. Each chapter builds upon those that have preceded it. We have included the following types of material for dictation:

1. **Rhythmic exercises** are played on a single pitch and provide practice with specific rhythmic problems.

2. **Melodic exercises** are composed in a musical way and deal with specific scalar, harmonic, and rhythmic material. In most chapters, preliminary as well as full-length exercises are provided.

3. **Harmonic exercises** are played in four-voice texture, either choral or keyboard. They focus on particular chordal vocabulary. In most chapters, preliminary as well as full-length exercises are provided.

4. **Quizzes** are included in each chapter after the exercises in each of the above topics.

5. **Music from the literature**. At strategic points throughout *Music for Ear Training*, chapters containing cumulative examples from the literature in a variety of textures are included.

The number of exercises within each unit was dictated by the desire to present both a sufficient number of exercises and a few more challenging exercises for the advanced students. It is, of course, not necessary to do each and every exercise. The instructor may even wish to assign only certain exercises within the quizzes or may wish to mix items from the rhythmic, melodic, and harmonic exercises.

The Web-based Unit 1 listening exercises present intervals and chords in musical contexts with scales and melodies. The online record of activity maintained for each student may be useful as a guide in determining when students have acquired a foundation in the aural study of rudiments that will contribute to success in Unit 1 quizzes and the dictations that follow in later units. The downloadable **MusicET** application also gives the student the opportunity for virtually endless drill with intervals, qualities of triads, and scale types. The student is allowed to determine the range of intervals to hear from a single category—for example, major and minor thirds—up to all intervals. Similarly, the student may elect specific qualities of triads to hear. The practice drills are followed by quizzes that use the formatted sheets in the workbook. Students access the audio for the quizzes using either the Web interface or the downloaded application, as preferred. The interval quizzes are graded by interval type, but each quiz contains a section that is cumulative—that is, all intervals to that point are included and in all possible arrangements.

It is not necessary to do Unit 1 in any particular order. Scales can easily precede intervals, for example. Unit 1 should also be considered a resource unit, and students should be encouraged to return to it at any time for review drill, particularly on intervals and triad qualities.

New to this edition is Unit 26, Examples from Music Literature, which contains examples of the literature of the twentieth century. These excerpts exemplify the techniques presented in Units 18 through 25. Composers representing a wide variety of styles are included, ranging from Debussy to Stravinsky and Webern.

Music for Ear Training may be used conveniently with most of the sight singing texts currently available. It is designed in parallel with *Music for Sight Singing* by Thomas Benjamin, Michael Horvit, and Robert Nelson, sixth edition (Schirmer Books, 2013), and will work especially smoothly with the presentation of materials in that book.

The Instructor's Edition is laid out parallel to the Student Edition but with the answers to all of the exercises and quizzes included. The Roman numeral analyses provided for the common-practice examples follow the system used in Thomas Benjamin, Michael Horvit, and Robert Nelson, *Techniques and Materials of Music*, seventh edition (Schirmer, 2008), but instructors should feel free to substitute whatever system they prefer. Lead sheet (jazz) chord symbol usage is also far from uniform, and instructors may wish to specify how they want chords analyzed in Unit 20. Some serial melodies in Unit 25 show accidentals on every note; others use the traditional method. Enharmonic equivalents are occasionally indicated parenthetically, as with tritones in Unit 1. In other places, students may notate certain notes enharmonically, and the instructor will need to determine the correctness of these spellings.

Suggestions to the Student

The *Music for Ear Training* Website provides access to the audio and drills that you will use with the workbook. To gain entry, create your online user account at **CengageBrain.com**. You will need to enter the access code you received on a card included with this book. Simply follow the instructions on the card. After entering your registration information, you will automatically receive an email containing an encoded link that will allow you to gain entry to the *Music for Ear Training* Website. Clicking on the link in the email message will send you to the site as an authenticated user. You need to complete this process only once. For return visits, you can go directly to the *Music for Ear Training* Website at **MusicForEarTraining.com**.

The ability to hear and quickly comprehend any piece of music is a skill that is crucial to the musician. Having a "good ear" involves more than just playing or singing in tune. Traditionally, students acquire this skill through the discipline of aural dictation—listening to a musical example and then writing it down. Unfortunately, all too many students approach this facet of their musical studies with trepidation and anxiety. They may assume that only those musicians blessed with perfect pitch can do dictation. In fact, aural comprehension is a skill that can be acquired with diligent, structured practice. *Music for Ear Training* is designed to give the student an ample number of ear-training practice exercises that can be completed outside the classroom and at the student's own pace. The exercises are carefully graded to lead from simple isolated problems, such as interval recognition, all the way to the transcription of short pieces from the literature. You can compare your results with the correct solution by clicking on the "**Show Answer**" button.

Four categories of exercises appear throughout *Music for Ear Training*:

- Rhythmic dictation drills,

- Preliminary exercises for melodic dictation, which focus on particular musical patterns, and harmonic dictation, which focuses on chord progressions,

- Melodies and phrase-length harmonic exercises, and

- Music from the literature.

Exercises in interval, triad, and scale recognition are contained in the first unit. You can return to this unit for review at any time. As a rule, the preliminary exercises introduce a specific item, such as an interval or a chord, and help you to assimilate that item through drill. The melodies and phrase-length harmonic exercises are cumulative and serve to integrate the new items into the vocabulary previously presented. You can go back and review the interval and triad recognition drills from Unit 1 using the Website or downloaded software at any time. The units containing music from the literature will help you to gauge your progress. You will see how facility with the rhythmic, melodic, and harmonic exercises improves your understanding of the music that is the stuff of your day-to-day activities.

Quizzes are included for each unit of the workbook. These quizzes may be given in class or assigned as homework, and your instructor may ask you to submit them. The solutions for these quizzes are available only to your instructor.

Since aural dictation is often a new experience, it is easy to become overwhelmed. As an aid, we have incorporated at the beginning of most sets of exercises a number of suggestions and strategies for listening. You will also occasionally find specific suggestions preceding certain exercises. Here is a summary of all those general strategies; they will help you to focus your listening and correctly interpret what you hear.

These lists are not intended to exhaust all the possibilities. Your instructor will likely have additional suggestions, and you will discover other useful devices on your own. From time to time, additional suggestions will appear on the screen. These suggestions are intended to help you deal with a particular exercise, but make a note of them because they will come in handy for other exercises as well.

Rudiments

Unit 1 provides exercises for intervals, triads, and scales. The Web-based Unit 1 exercises present intervals and chords within musical contexts of scales and melodies. You can track your progress with an online record of your activity. The downloadable **MusicET** application allows you to control your practice session with a virtually unlimited number of examples. For intervals, you may elect to concentrate on just one size—say, seconds—or you may elect to listen to as broad a range of interval sizes as you wish. There are similar options with triads and scales. Unit 1 is a valuable resource unit, and you should use it for review at any time. For example, the melodic dictation exercises are graded by interval content, and you may wish to review the particular intervals before working on the melodies. Similarly, when seventh chords are introduced, you might wish to review sevenths.

Rhythmic Dictation

1. Define the time signature (how many beats per measure, simple or compound, and so on), and then listen to the complete exercise.

2. How is the meter defined? Do you hear long notes on strong beats and quicker notes on weak beats? Try tapping the beat as you listen to the example.

3. What is the most frequently occurring note value? Is it the beat unit or a division of the beat? How many different values are there?

4. Do you hear recurring patterns? Are there instances of any particular rhythmic device such as syncopation?

Melodic Dictation

1. Listen to the complete exercise.

2. Establish the key for yourself by listening to either the given scale or the tonic note. (Simply click on the buttons for the scale or the note.)

3. Does the music move by step or by skip? Are the skips large or small? Do consecutive skips arpeggiate a particular chord?

4. What is the shape, or curve, of the melody? It can be helpful to draw a simple graph of its design before writing down the actual pitches.

5. Listen for important structural pitches. These include the first and last pitches, cadential pitches, metric and agogic accents, and the highest and lowest pitches. Try sketching in these pitches first.

6. If you use solfège syllables or scale degree numbers in your singing, then writing these during dictation may also be a helpful strategy.

7. Listen for phrase and cadence structure. What is the form of the melody? Are there interior cadences? Do two phrases form a period? Remember to constantly apply what you have learned in your theory classes. The more you are aware of what is likely to be true, the more you will hear.

8. Do you hear a pattern in the music? This patterning may be rhythmic only, or it may involve both rhythm and pitch. Are patterns repeated or sequenced? Are there recurrences of musical ideas, particularly at the beginning of subsequent phrases?

9. As you listen to a melody, sketch simple symbols to indicate pitches and rhythms; that is, circles for whole and half notes and dots for shorter note values. Allow for proportional distances between note heads to represent values within a measure. Supply precise rhythmic values as a subsequent step, then notate what you hear in final form.

10. An excellent method of enhancing your ability to take melodic dictation is to write down melodies from memory. When taking a break in the practice room or library, think of a tune you already know. It may be a folk, children's, popular, or patriotic song. Pick a key and jot it down. This will strengthen your ability to get material you clearly have in your mind down on paper.

Harmonic Dictation

1. Listen to the complete exercise.

2. For phrase-length exercises, what kind of cadence(s) do you hear?

3. Chord progressions in the common-practice period follow predictable patterns. If you have identified one chord, consider the finite number of possibilities for chords that might logically follow. If you have identified the cadential chords, try working backwards.

4. Whether listening online or with the downloaded application, the interface allows you to isolate the individual voices. Be sure to use stereo headphones or speakers of good quality, since the online audio relies on stereo separation to isolate voices in some examples. Hearing the lines clearly will help in distinguishing between two chords that are somewhat interchangeable, such as IV and ii6.

Examples from Music Literature

These exercises present actual pieces of music. It should be possible to transcribe these pieces note-for-note. The following suggestions should prove helpful:

1. Listen to the complete exercise.

2. How would you characterize the texture of the music? Are there clear melodic lines? Most piano textures and ensemble textures will have prominent melodies. Focus on these lines that you will be able to isolate.

3. All examples, even those that are contrapuntal, will have obvious harmonic implications. In more homophonic pieces, the chord structures should be quite clear and easily heard as such. Although you will not be required to supply the Roman numerals, harmonic analysis can be a great aid in hearing the music.

4. What is the structure of the music? Do you clearly hear phrase and cadence? What are the cadence types?

Finally, the application will allow you to listen to any one exercise as many times as you wish, and early on in your work, this may be necessary. You should always try, however, to transcribe the music with as few hearings as possible. In most cases, four repetitions should be more than enough. As your skills develop, the number of hearings should decrease. You may elect at any time to see the solution to any of the exercises except for the quizzes. After comparing your solution with that on the screen, you may wish to listen one more time, concentrating on those places where you made mistakes.

The workbook provides you with staff paper already formatted with the correct number of measures for each example along with the key, time signatures, and any given pitches. You may find it useful to use scratch paper for your preliminary sketches, using the workbook only to enter your final version. The workbook pages are easily removed when exercises need to be handed in for evaluation by your instructor.

Unit 1

Intervals, Triads, and Scales

Use the practice drills online and in the MusicET application to prepare for these quizzes.

Major and Minor Seconds: QUIZ NO. 1

Melodic ascending

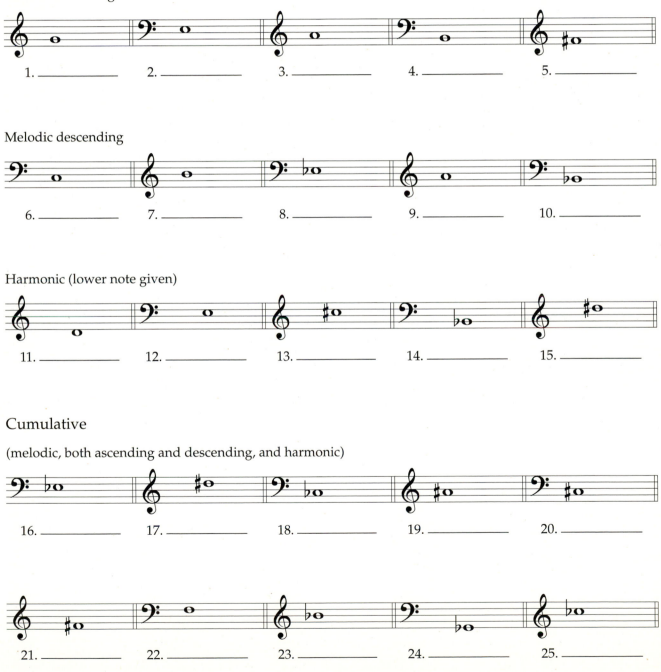

1. _____ 2. _____ 3. _____ 4. _____ 5. _____

Melodic descending

6. _____ 7. _____ 8. _____ 9. _____ 10. _____

Harmonic (lower note given)

11. _____ 12. _____ 13. _____ 14. _____ 15. _____

Cumulative

(melodic, both ascending and descending, and harmonic)

16. _____ 17. _____ 18. _____ 19. _____ 20. _____

21. _____ 22. _____ 23. _____ 24. _____ 25. _____

Major and Minor Seconds: QUIZ NO. 2

Melodic ascending

1. _____ 2. _____ 3. _____ 4. _____ 5. _____

Melodic descending

6. _____ 7. _____ 8. _____ 9. _____ 10. _____

Harmonic (lower note given)

11. _____ 12. _____ 13. _____ 14. _____ 15. _____

Cumulative

(melodic, both ascending and descending, and harmonic)

16. _____ 17. _____ 18. _____ 19. _____ 20. _____

21. _____ 22. _____ 23. _____ 24. _____ 25. _____

Major and Minor Thirds: QUIZ NO. 1

Thirds only

Melodic ascending

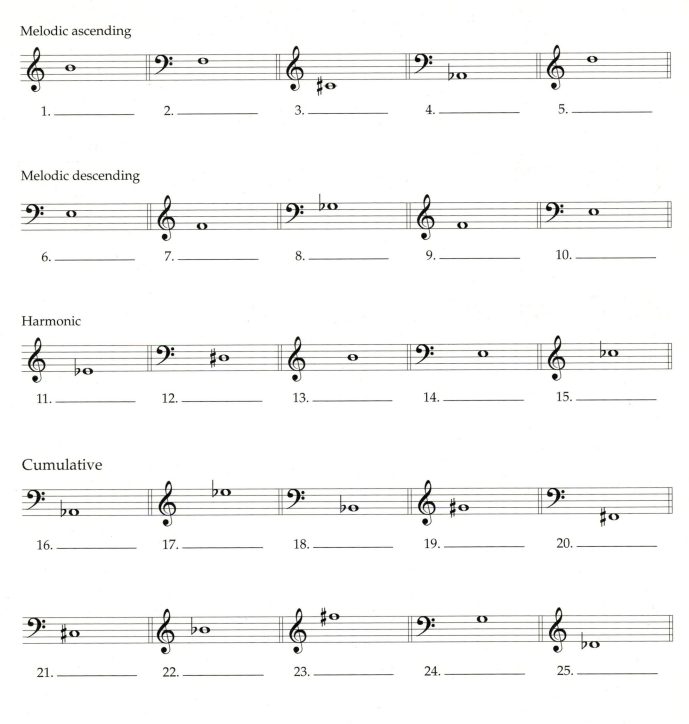

1. _____ 2. _____ 3. _____ 4. _____ 5. _____

Melodic descending

6. _____ 7. _____ 8. _____ 9. _____ 10. _____

Harmonic

11. _____ 12. _____ 13. _____ 14. _____ 15. _____

Cumulative

16. _____ 17. _____ 18. _____ 19. _____ 20. _____

21. _____ 22. _____ 23. _____ 24. _____ 25. _____

Major and Minor Thirds: QUIZ NO. 2

Thirds only

Melodic ascending

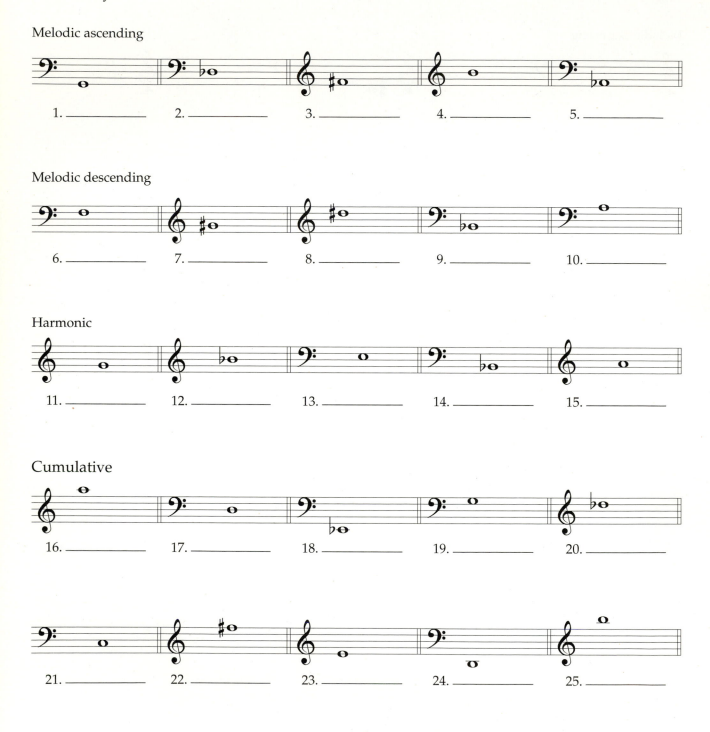

1. _____ 2. _____ 3. _____ 4. _____ 5. _____

Melodic descending

6. _____ 7. _____ 8. _____ 9. _____ 10. _____

Harmonic

11. _____ 12. _____ 13. _____ 14. _____ 15. _____

Cumulative

16. _____ 17. _____ 18. _____ 19. _____ 20. _____

21. _____ 22. _____ 23. _____ 24. _____ 25. _____

Class:

Professor:

Name: _____

Perfect and Augmented Fourths: QUIZ NO. 1

Fourths only

Melodic ascending

1. _____ 2. _____ 3. _____ 4. _____ 5. _____

Melodic descending

6. _____ 7. _____ 8. _____ 9. _____ 10. _____

Harmonic

11. _____ 12. _____ 13. _____ 14. _____ 15. _____

Cumulative

16. _____ 17. _____ 18. _____ 19. _____ 20. _____

21. _____ 22. _____ 23. _____ 24. _____ 25. _____

Perfect and Augmented Fourths: QUIZ NO. 2

Fourths only

Melodic ascending

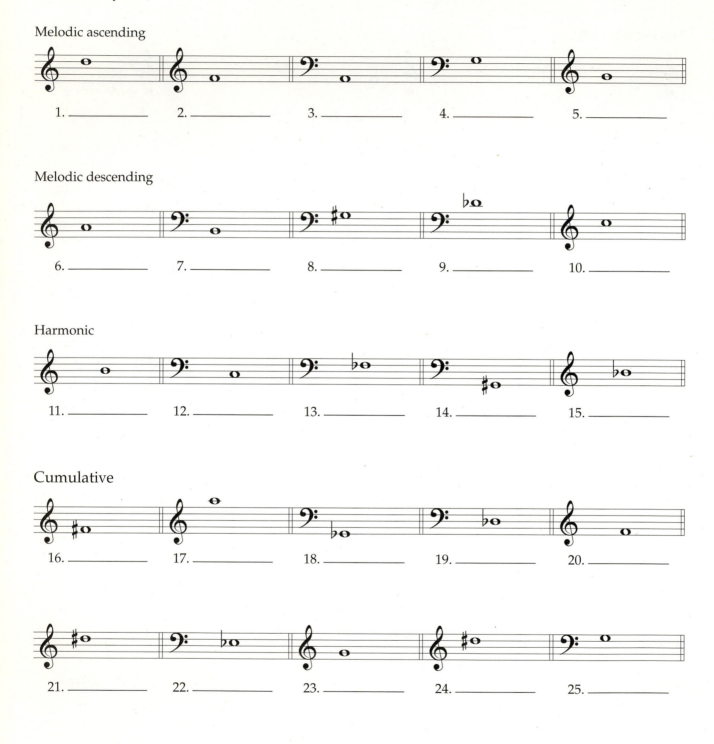

1. _____ 2. _____ 3. _____ 4. _____ 5. _____

Melodic descending

6. _____ 7. _____ 8. _____ 9. _____ 10. _____

Harmonic

11. _____ 12. _____ 13. _____ 14. _____ 15. _____

Cumulative

16. _____ 17. _____ 18. _____ 19. _____ 20. _____

21. _____ 22. _____ 23. _____ 24. _____ 25. _____

Perfect and Diminished Fifths: QUIZ NO. 1

Fifths only

Melodic ascending

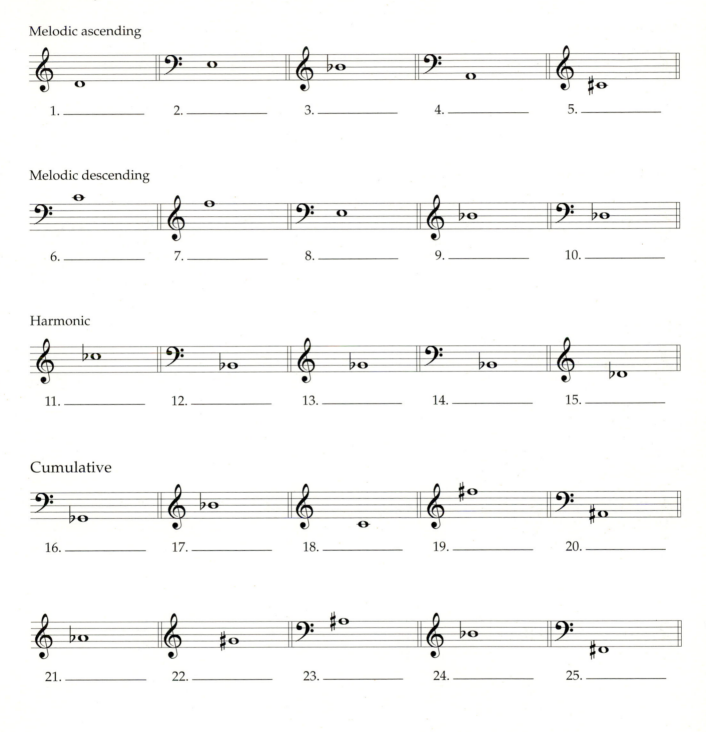

1. _____ 2. _____ 3. _____ 4. _____ 5. _____

Melodic descending

6. _____ 7. _____ 8. _____ 9. _____ 10. _____

Harmonic

11. _____ 12. _____ 13. _____ 14. _____ 15. _____

Cumulative

16. _____ 17. _____ 18. _____ 19. _____ 20. _____

21. _____ 22. _____ 23. _____ 24. _____ 25. _____

Class: _____

Name: _____

Professor: _____

Perfect and Diminished Fifths: QUIZ NO. 2

Fifths only

Melodic ascending

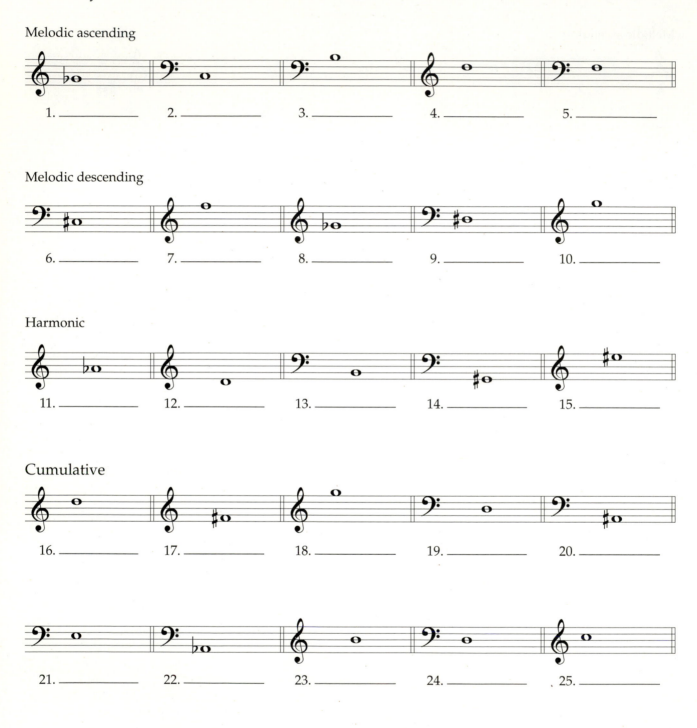

1. _____   2. _____   3. _____   4. _____   5. _____

Melodic descending

6. _____   7. _____   8. _____   9. _____   10. _____

Harmonic

11. _____   12. _____   13. _____   14. _____   15. _____

Cumulative

16. _____   17. _____   18. _____   19. _____   20. _____

21. _____   22. _____   23. _____   24. _____   25. _____

Class:

Professor:

Name: _____

All Perfect Intervals and Tritones: QUIZ NO. 1

Perfect intervals and tritones only

Melodic ascending

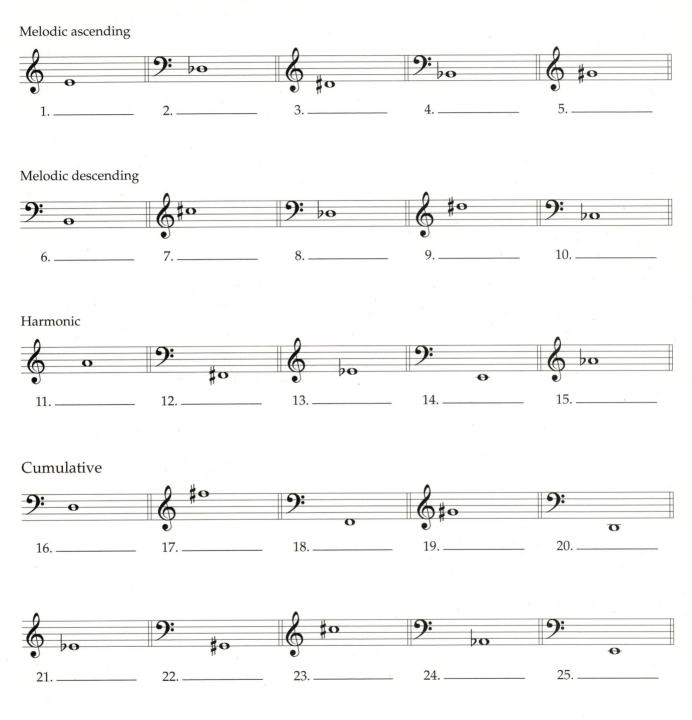

1. _____ 2. _____ 3. _____ 4. _____ 5. _____

Melodic descending

6. _____ 7. _____ 8. _____ 9. _____ 10. _____

Harmonic

11. _____ 12. _____ 13. _____ 14. _____ 15. _____

Cumulative

16. _____ 17. _____ 18. _____ 19. _____ 20. _____

21. _____ 22. _____ 23. _____ 24. _____ 25. _____

All Perfect Intervals and Tritones: QUIZ NO. 2

Perfect intervals and tritones only

Melodic ascending

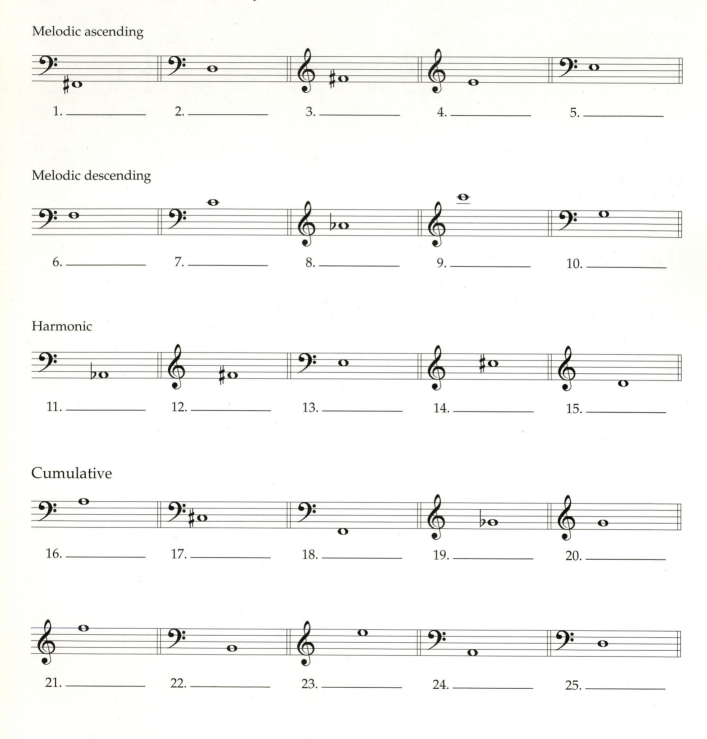

1. _____   2. _____   3. _____   4. _____   5. _____

Melodic descending

6. _____   7. _____   8. _____   9. _____   10. _____

Harmonic

11. _____   12. _____   13. _____   14. _____   15. _____

Cumulative

16. _____   17. _____   18. _____   19. _____   20. _____

21. _____   22. _____   23. _____   24. _____   25. _____

Major and Minor Sixths: QUIZ NO. 1

Sixths only

Melodic ascending

1. _____ 2. _____ 3. _____ 4. _____ 5. _____

Melodic descending

6. _____ 7. _____ 8. _____ 9. _____ 10. _____

Harmonic

11. _____ 12. _____ 13. _____ 14. _____ 15. _____

Cumulative

16. _____ 17. _____ 18. _____ 19. _____ 20. _____

21. _____ 22. _____ 23. _____ 24. _____ 25. _____

Major and Minor Sixths: QUIZ NO. 2

Sixths only

Melodic ascending

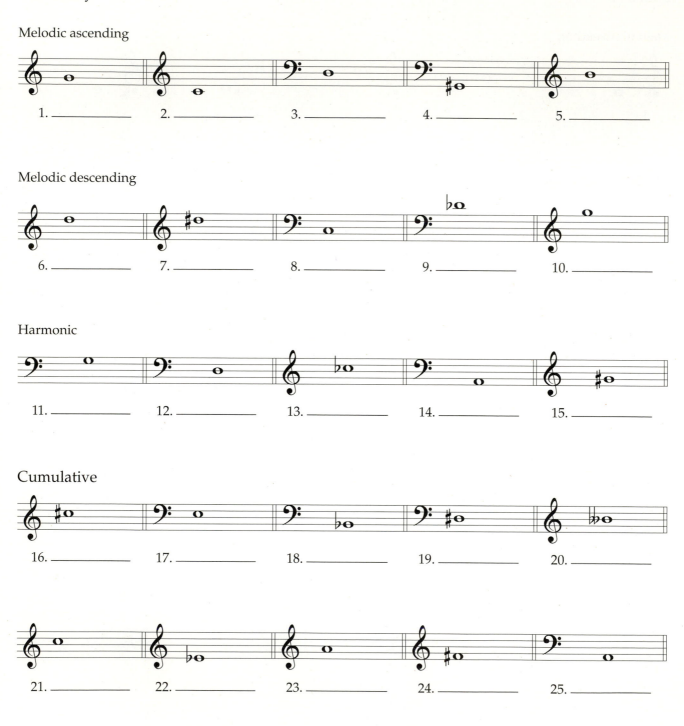

1. _____ 2. _____ 3. _____ 4. _____ 5. _____

Melodic descending

6. _____ 7. _____ 8. _____ 9. _____ 10. _____

Harmonic

11. _____ 12. _____ 13. _____ 14. _____ 15. _____

Cumulative

16. _____ 17. _____ 18. _____ 19. _____ 20. _____

21. _____ 22. _____ 23. _____ 24. _____ 25. _____

Major and Minor Sevenths: QUIZ NO. 1

Sevenths only

Melodic ascending

1. _____ 2. _____ 3. _____ 4. _____ 5. _____

Melodic descending

6. _____ 7. _____ 8. _____ 9. _____ 10. _____

Harmonic

11. _____ 12. _____ 13. _____ 14. _____ 15. _____

Cumulative

16. _____ 17. _____ 18. _____ 19. _____ 20. _____

21. _____ 22. _____ 23. _____ 24. _____ 25. _____

Major and Minor Sevenths: QUIZ NO. 2

Sevenths only

Melodic ascending

1. _____   2. _____   3. _____   4. _____   5. _____

Melodic descending

6. _____   7. _____   8. _____   9. _____   10. _____

Harmonic

11. _____   12. _____   13. _____   14. _____   15. _____

Cumulative

16. _____   17. _____   18. _____   19. _____   20. _____

21. _____   22. _____   23. _____   24. _____   25. _____

All Intervals: QUIZ NO. 1

1. _____ 2. _____ 3. _____ 4. _____ 5. _____

6. _____ 7. _____ 8. _____ 9. _____ 10. _____

11. _____ 12. _____ 13. _____ 14. _____ 15. _____

16. _____ 17. _____ 18. _____ 19. _____ 20. _____

21. _____ 22. _____ 23. _____ 24. _____ 25. _____

All Intervals: QUIZ NO. 2

1. _____ 2. _____ 3. _____ 4. _____ 5. _____

6. _____ 7. _____ 8. _____ 9. _____ 10. _____

11. _____ 12. _____ 13. _____ 14. _____ 15. _____

16. _____ 17. _____ 18. _____ 19. _____ 20. _____

21. _____ 22. _____ 23. _____ 24. _____ 25. _____

Major and Minor Triads: QUIZ NO. 1

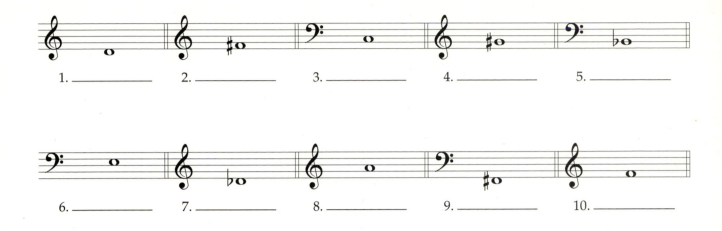

1. _____   2. _____   3. _____   4. _____   5. _____

6. _____   7. _____   8. _____   9. _____   10. _____

Name: _____

Major and Minor Triads: QUIZ NO. 2

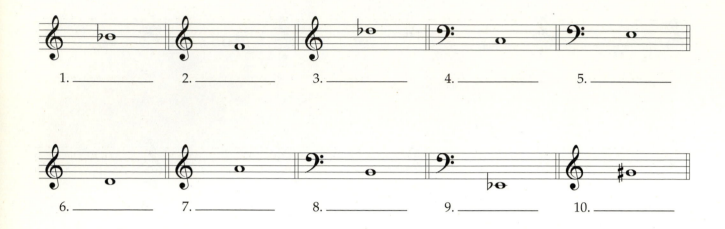

1. _____ 2. _____ 3. _____ 4. _____ 5. _____

6. _____ 7. _____ 8. _____ 9. _____ 10. _____

Introducing Diminished Triads: QUIZ NO. 1

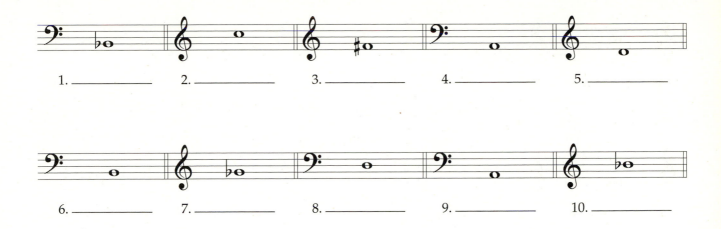

1. _____   2. _____   3. _____   4. _____   5. _____

6. _____   7. _____   8. _____   9. _____   10. _____

Introducing Diminished Triads: QUIZ NO. 2

1. _____ 2. _____ 3. _____ 4. _____ 5. _____

6. _____ 7. _____ 8. _____ 9. _____ 10. _____

Name: _____

Introducing Augmented Triads: QUIZ NO. 1

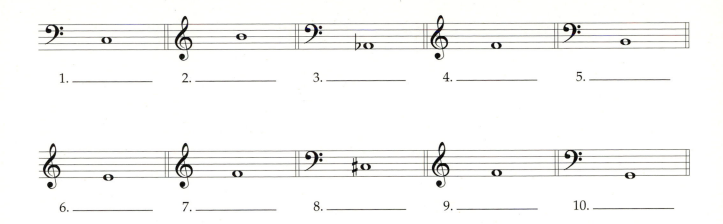

1. _____   2. _____   3. _____   4. _____   5. _____

6. _____   7. _____   8. _____   9. _____   10. _____

Class:

Professor:

Name: _____

Introducing Augmented Triads: QUIZ NO. 2

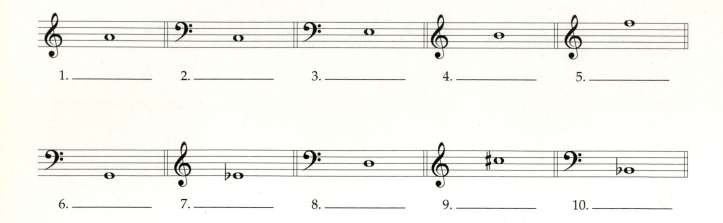

1. _____ 2. _____ 3. _____ 4. _____ 5. _____

6. _____ 7. _____ 8. _____ 9. _____ 10. _____

Major and Minor Scales: QUIZ NO. 1

1. _____

2. _____

3. _____

4. _____

5. _____

6. _____

7. _____

8. _____

9. _____

10. _____

Major and Minor Scales: QUIZ NO. 2

1. _____

2. _____

3. _____

4. _____

5. _____

6. _____

7. _____

8. _____

9. _____

10. _____

Unit 2

Rhythmic Dictation: Simple Meters

The goal of this unit is recognition of basic patterns in simple meters. The beat will be established by count-off clicks and the tempo may be adjusted. Listen first to each exercise while counting or tapping the beat. Which notes correspond to the beat? Which notes combine beats into larger values? Be aware of the number of beats per measure. Where do the longer values typically occur?

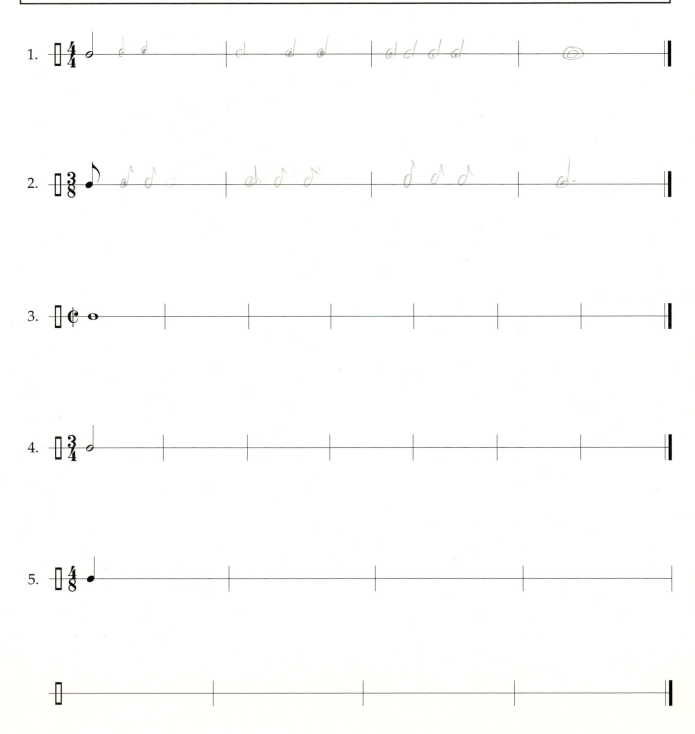

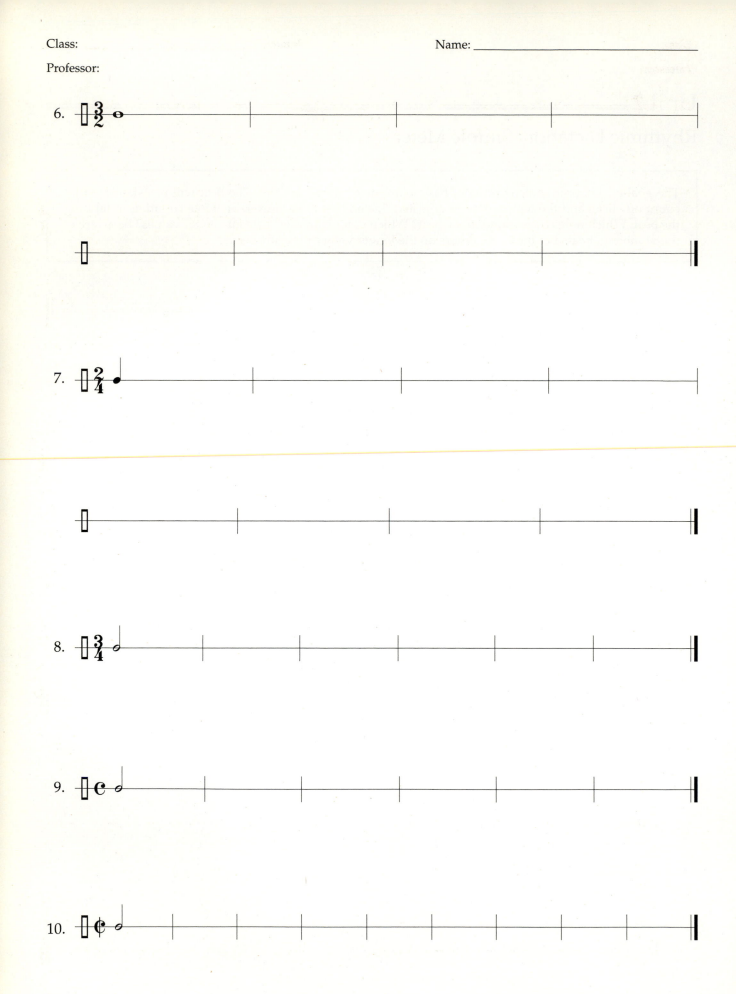

11.

12.

13.

14.

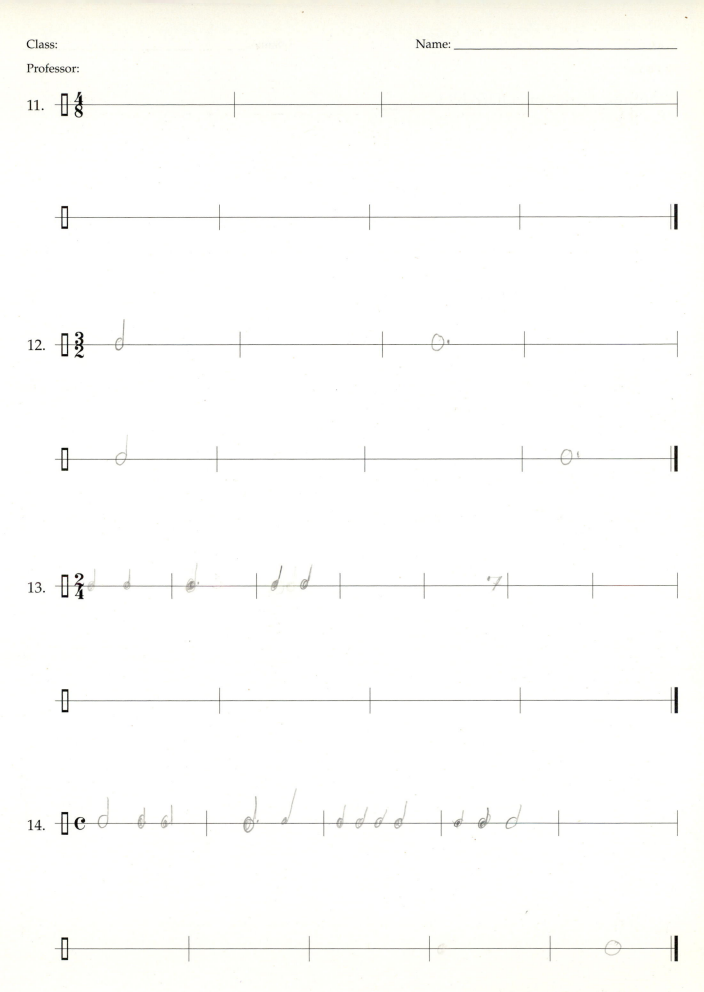

Rhythmic Dictation: QUIZ NO. 1

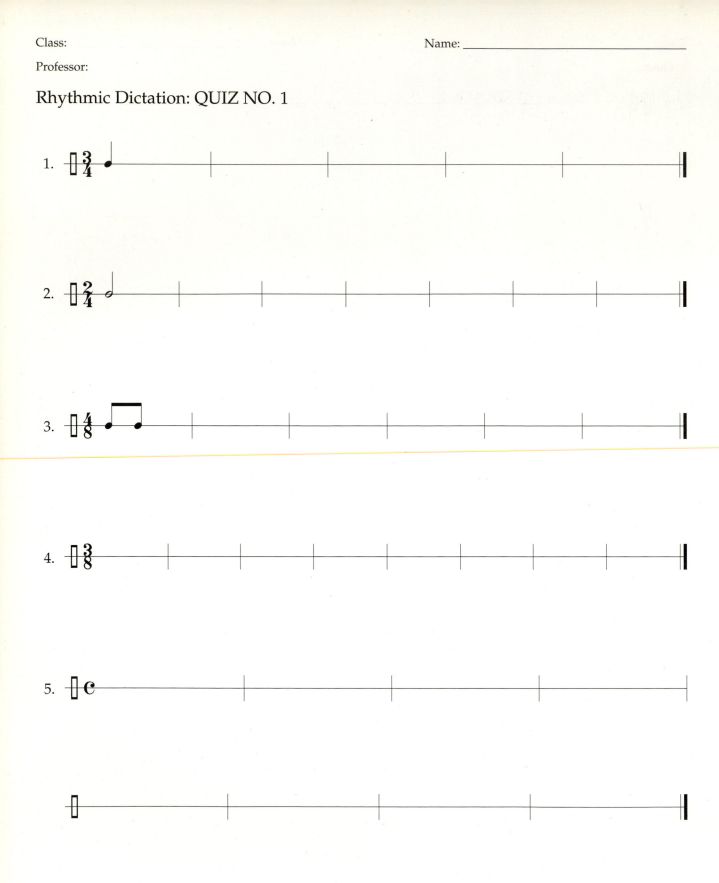

1. $\frac{3}{4}$

2. $\frac{2}{4}$

3. $\frac{4}{8}$

4. $\frac{3}{8}$

5. ¢

Name: _____

Rhythmic Dictation: QUIZ NO. 2

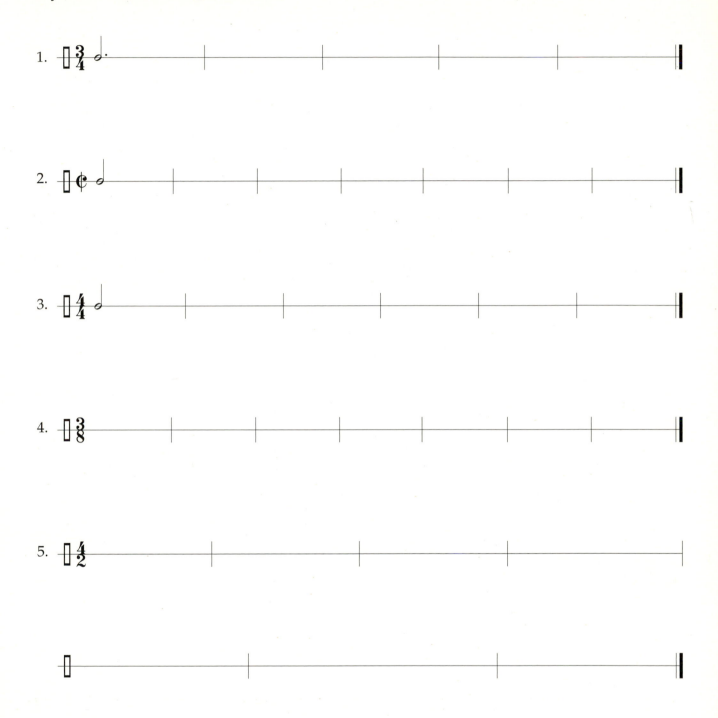

1. $\frac{3}{4}$

2. $\mathbf{C}$

3. $\frac{4}{4}$

4. $\frac{3}{8}$

5. $\frac{4}{2}$

Rhythmic Dictation: QUIZ NO. 3

1.

2.

3.

4.

5.

Melodic Dictation: Seconds, Thirds, and Fourths

Preliminary Exercises

7.

do mi re fa   mi fa so   la fa so mi   fa re do

8.

9.

10.

11.

12.

13.

14.

15.

16.

17.

18.

Melodies

This unit contains melodies that are entirely conjunct (stepwise) in motion as well as melodies containing skips of major or minor thirds and perfect fourths. Click the buttons to hear the provided tonic note and scale. Try first singing the appropriate scale to establish a point of reference. Then listen to the melody. Does the music move by step? Is the direction of the line up or down? What scale fragment occurs? What is the pattern of whole and half steps? Do you hear a skip? Concentrate on that interval. Sing the two notes and "fill in" the missing notes. This will tell you if the skip is a third or a fourth. Finally, write out the melody. If you are uncertain about some of the pitches, leave a blank or indicate alternatives. Listen again, filling in the blanks. When you feel confident you have "solved" the melody, listen one last time. Sing along, using syllables, to check your work.

Deliberamente

7.

Moderato

8.

Cantabile

9.

Tempo di Valse

10.

Andante

11.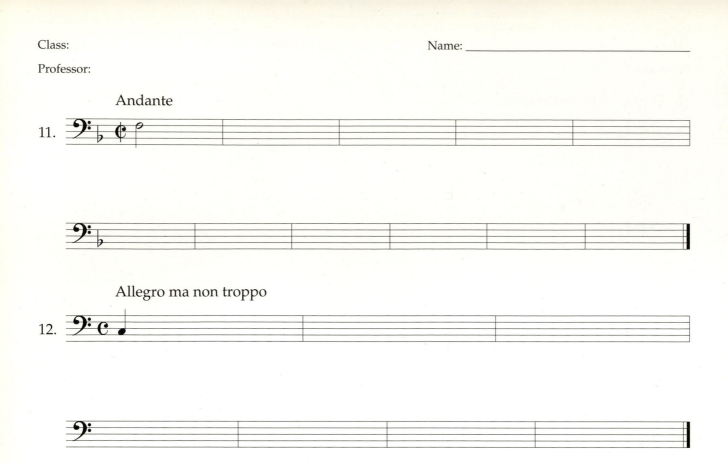

Allegro ma non troppo

12.

In the last two exercises, you will need to determine both the pitch and the rhythmic value of the first note.

Waltz

13.

Cantabile

14.

Class:

Professor:

Name: _____

Melodic Dictation: QUIZ NO. 1

Allegretto

1.

Andante

2.

Eroico

3.

Allegro

4.

Animato

5.

Melodic Dictation: QUIZ NO. 2

Class: _____ Name: _____

Professor: _____

Melodic Dictation: QUIZ NO. 3

Class: _____ Do Mi Sol | La Fa Re | Sol Fa Ti | Do Mi Sol Mi Do |

Professor: _____

Name: _____

Melodic Dictation: QUIZ NO. 4

In this quiz you will need to determine both the value and pitch of the initial note.

40   Unit 2

Unit 3

Melodic Dictation: Fifths, Sixths, and Octaves

Preliminary Exercises

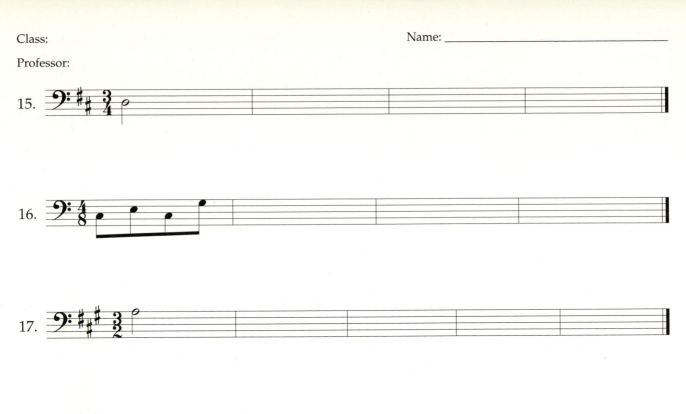

15.

16.

17.

18.

Melodies

These melodies introduce consecutive skips outlining the tonic triad and also introduce larger skips of fifths, sixths, and octaves. As before, establish the key by singing the scale. You may also wish to sing the tonic triad. Then listen to the melody. Is the motion by step or by skip? Are there consecutive skips outlining a triad? What is the lowest note? The highest? Isolate the arpeggiation and check with syllables. Check the larger skips by isolating the interval and "filling in" the missing notes.

Con moto

11.

Cantabile

12.

You will need to determine the first pitch for the last two exercises.

Andante

13.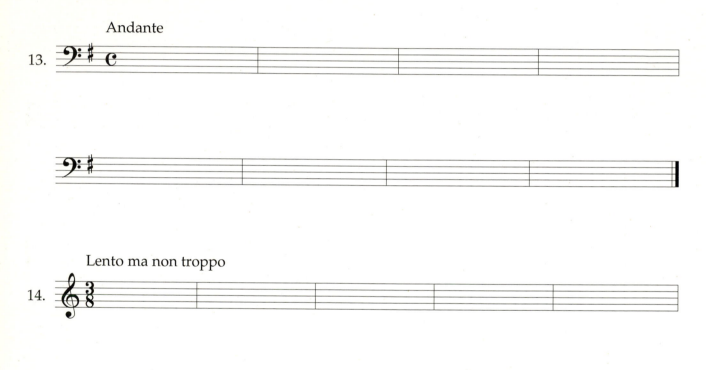

Lento ma non troppo

14.

Melodic Dictation: QUIZ NO. 1

Melodic Dictation: QUIZ NO. 2

Melodic Dictation: QUIZ NO. 3

Melodic Dictation: QUIZ NO. 4

Maestoso

1.

Andantino

2.

Spiritoso

3.

Allegretto

4.

Moderato

5.

Harmonic Dictation: Four-Part Settings of the Tonic Triad

The tonic triad is presented with all the possibilities of soprano-line motion. Since all the chords are in root position, you can easily fill in the bass line. Listen then for the direction of the soprano line. What is the melodic interval from one note to the next? Since the soprano will itself outline the tonic triad it should be easy to work out. Finally, fill in the inner voices, paying particular attention to the rules of part-writing.

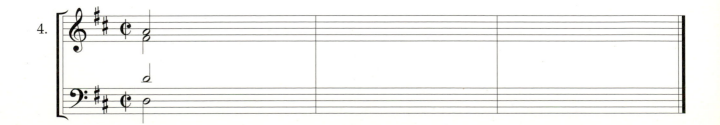

Class:

Professor:

Name: _____

5.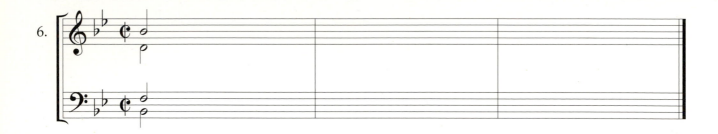

6.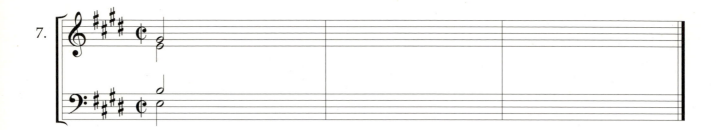

7.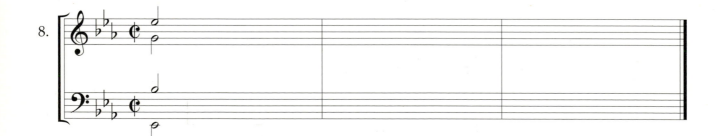

8.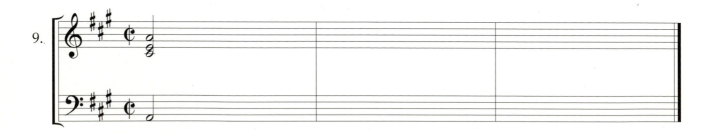

9.

Harmonic Dictation: QUIZ NO. 1

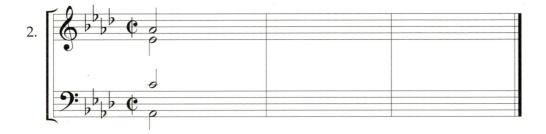

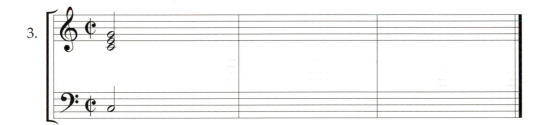

Harmonic Dictation: QUIZ NO. 2

1.

2.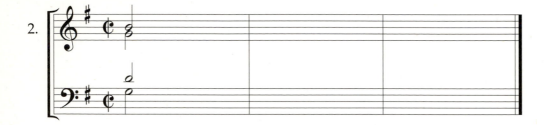

3.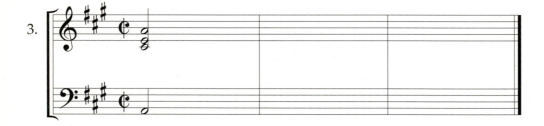

Harmonic Dictation: QUIZ NO. 3

1.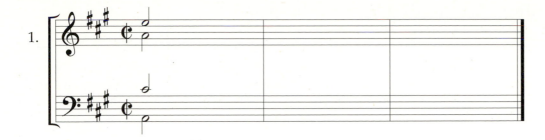

2.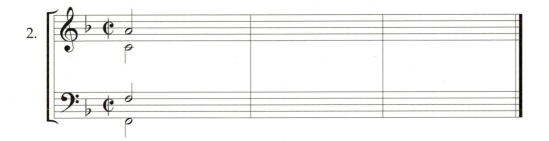

3.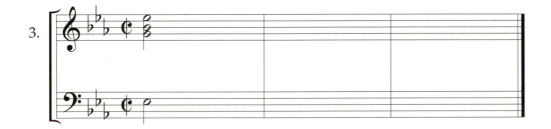

Unit 4

Rhythmic Dictation: 2:1 Subdivisions of the Beat

These exercises introduce simple divisions of the beat. As before, listen to the example while you count or tap the beat. Where is the beat divided? Where do multiple beat values occur? Sketch out your solution, then listen again while counting or tapping your solution. How does it compare? Correct any errors.

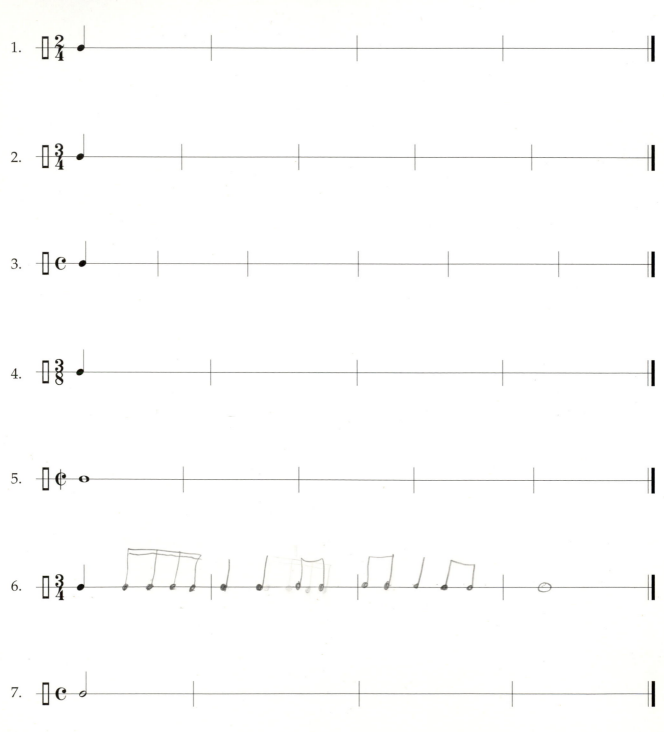

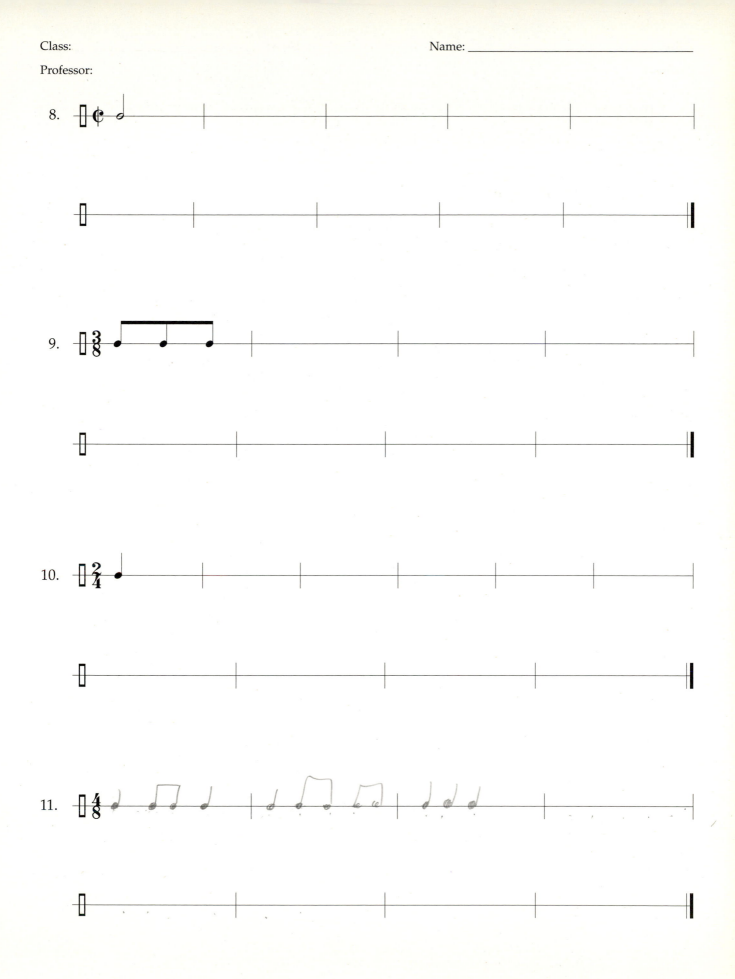

Name: _____

Rhythmic Dictation: QUIZ NO. 1

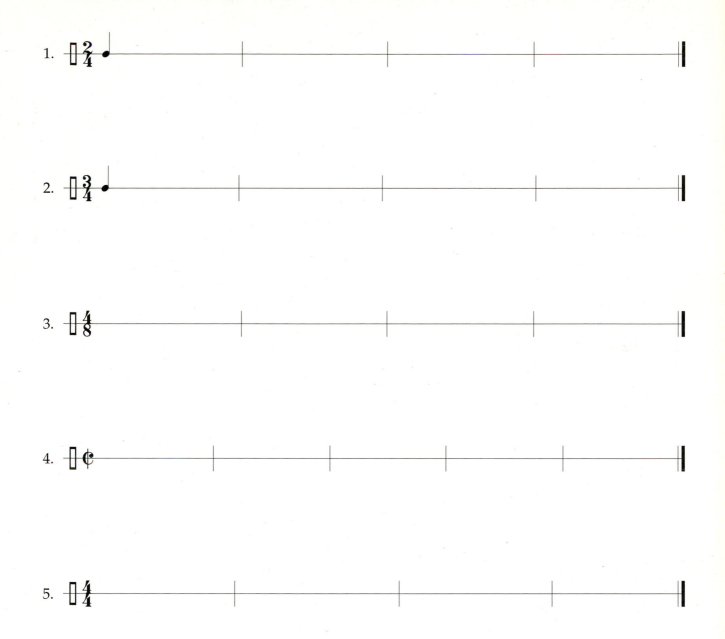

1. $\frac{2}{4}$

2. $\frac{3}{4}$

3. $\frac{4}{8}$

4. ¢

5. $\frac{4}{4}$

Rhythmic Dictation: QUIZ NO. 2

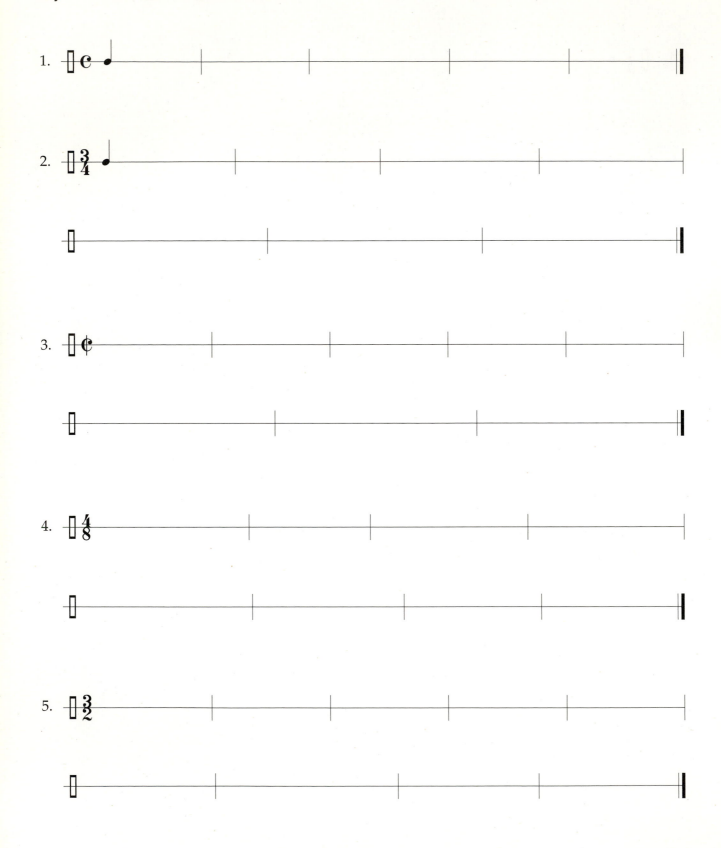

Name: _____

Rhythmic Dictation: QUIZ NO. 3

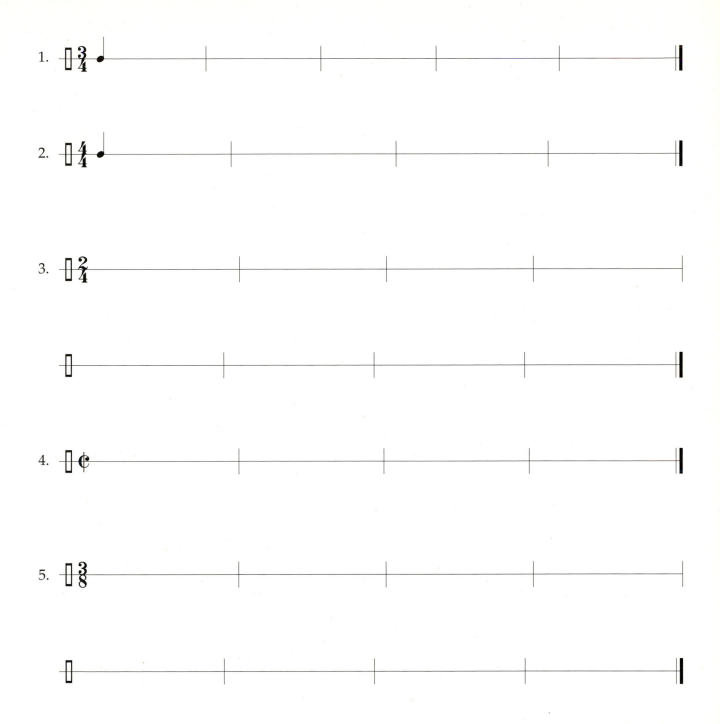

Melodic Dictation: The Tonic Triad and Dominant Seventh

Preliminary Exercises

7.

8.

9.

10.

Melodies

56-61
62-72
73-88

> These exercises introduce the dominant seventh chord. As before, first establish the key by singing the scale along with the arpeggiations of the I, V, and V7 chords. Then listen to the example. Where do skips occur? Are there consecutive skips outlining a chord? Which chord is it? What is the lowest note of the arpeggiation? The highest?

Allegretto

1.

yolo

Swing

Poco animato

2.

Allegro

3.

Semplice

4.

5. Moderato

6. Cantabile

7. Moderato

8. Maestoso

9. Grazioso

Andante

14.

Cantabile

15.

Allegro assai

16.

Melodic Dictation: QUIZ NO. 1

1. Moderato

2. Grazioso

3. With determination

4. Adagietto

5. Ländler

Melodic Dictation: QUIZ NO. 2

1. Semplice

2. Ben marcato

3. Cantabile

4. Giocoso

5. Allegro ma non troppo

Melodic Dictation: QUIZ NO. 3

Name: _____

Melodic Dictation: QUIZ NO. 4

Minuet

1.

Moderato

2.

Con brio

3.

Cantabile

4.

5.

Espressivo

Harmonic Dictation: The Tonic Triad and Dominant Seventh

Basic Progressions

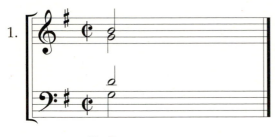

1.

G: I

2.

D: I

3.

B♭: I

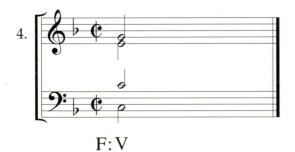

4.

F: V

5.

A: V

6.

A♭: V

7.

E♭: I

8.

D: I

9.

Bb: I

10.

D: I

11.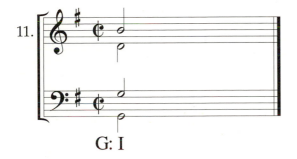

G: I

12.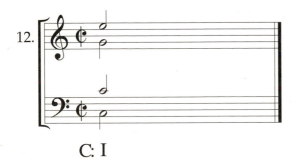

C: I

13.

F: V^7

14.

E: V^7

15.

E♭: V^7

16.
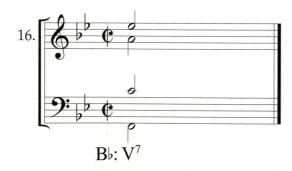

B♭: V^7

17.

G: V

18.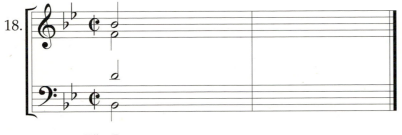

B♭: I

19.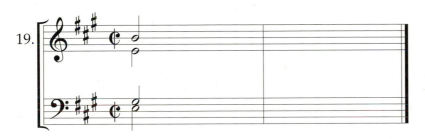

A: V

20.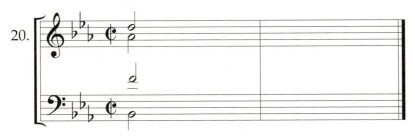

E♭: V⁷

21.

C: I

22.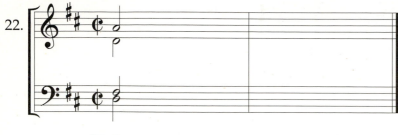

D: I

23.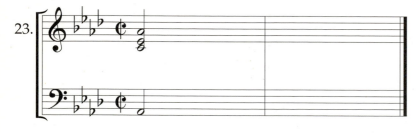

A♭: I

24.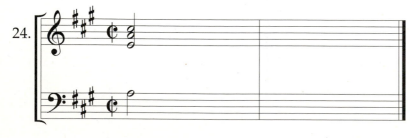

A: I

25.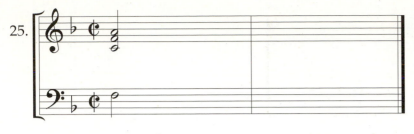

F: I

26.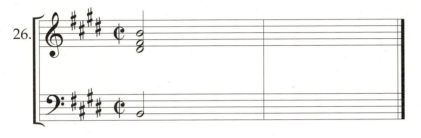

E: V

27.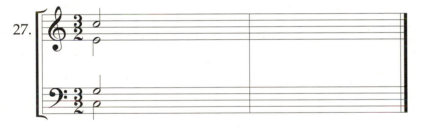

C: I

28.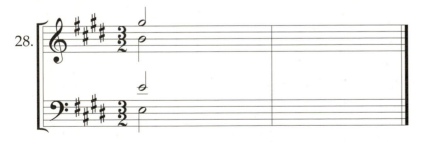

E: I

29.

F: V

30.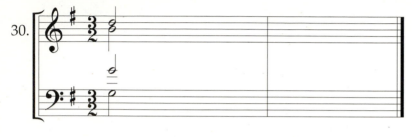

G: I

31.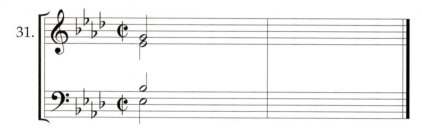

A♭: V

32.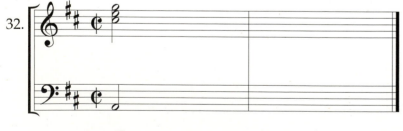

D: V⁷

33.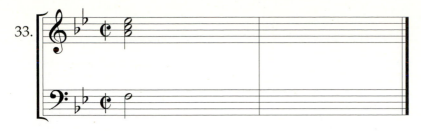

       B♭: V⁷

34.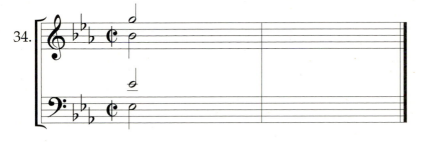

       E♭: I

35.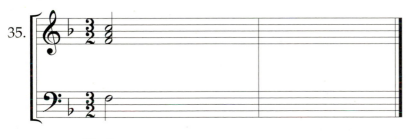

       F: I

36.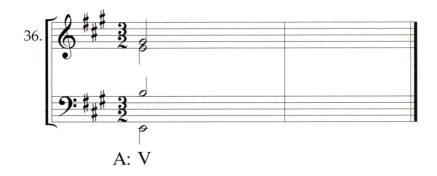

       A: V

Phrase-Length Exercises

These exercises present a variety of connections of tonic and dominant. Concentrate on chord pairs. (The basic progressions will provide you a secure point of reference and should be mastered first!) Is the second chord of the pair the same or different? If it is the same, apply the skills acquired in Unit 3. If different, concentrate on the outer voices. Does the bass skip up or down? Fill in the bass line. Does the soprano move in similar or contrary motion? By step or by skip? Fill in the soprano, then complete the inner voices, paying particular attention to the rules of voice leading. With phrase-length exercises, listen for the degree of closure. Does the phrase end on tonic (authentic cadence) or dominant (half cadence)? If the phrase ends with an authentic cadence, is it perfect or imperfect?

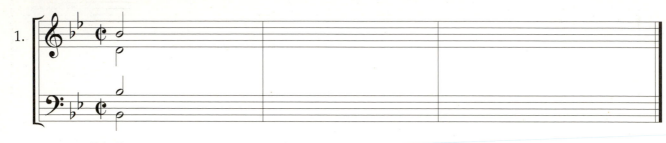

1. Bb: I

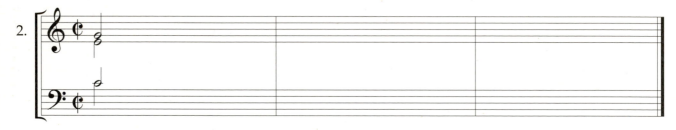

2. C: I

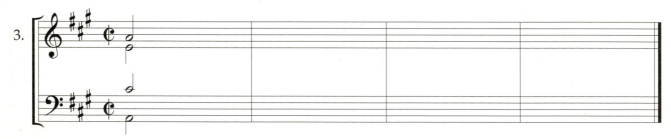

3. A: I

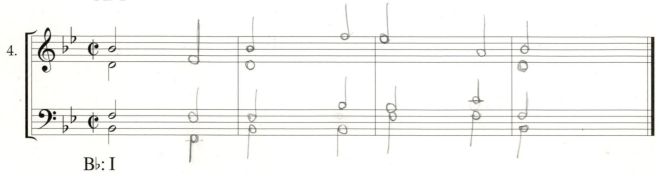

4. Bb: I

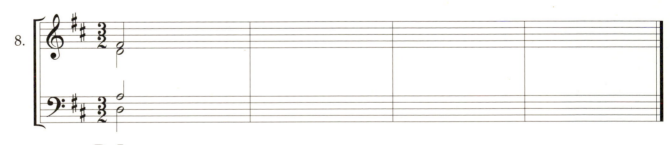

9.

10.

Class:

Professor:

Name: _____

Harmonic Dictation: QUIZ NO. 2

1.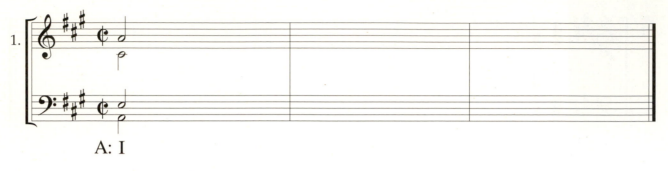

A: I

2.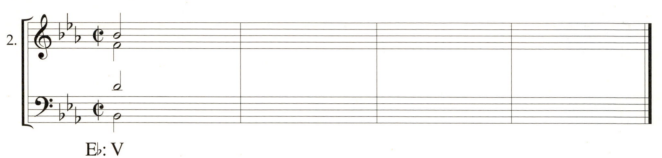

E♭: V

3.

D: I

4.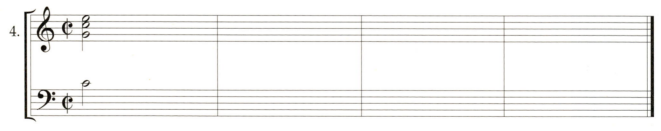

C: I

5.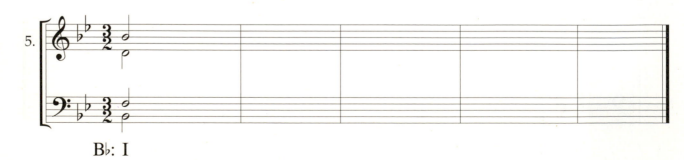

B♭: I

Class: _____   Name: _____

Professor: _____

Harmonic Dictation: QUIZ NO. 3

1.
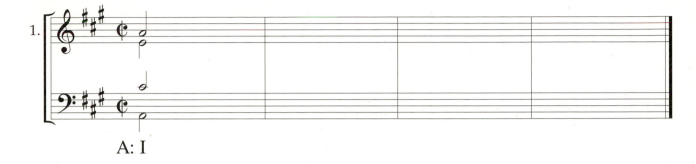

A: I

2.
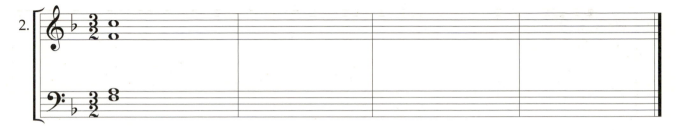

F: I

3.
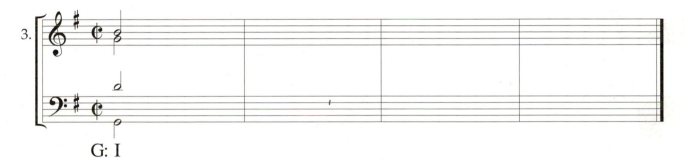

G: I

4.
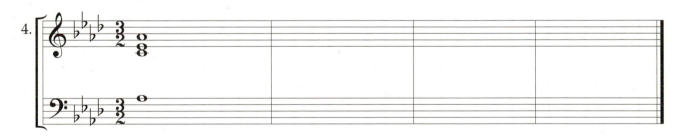

A♭: I

5.
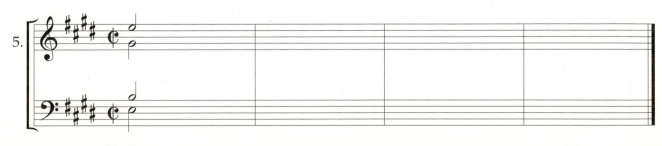

E: I

Harmonic Dictation: QUIZ NO. 4

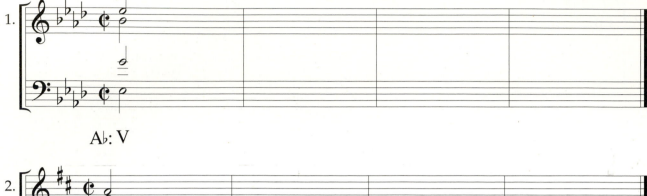

Ab: V

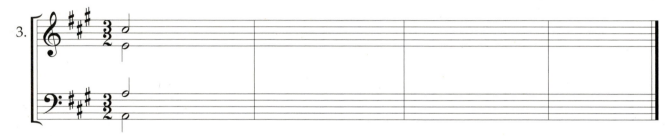

D: I

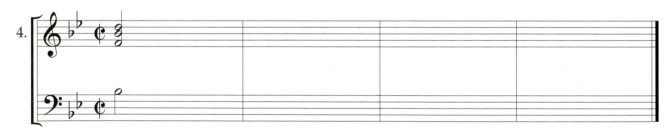

A: I

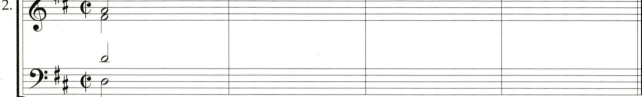

Bb: I

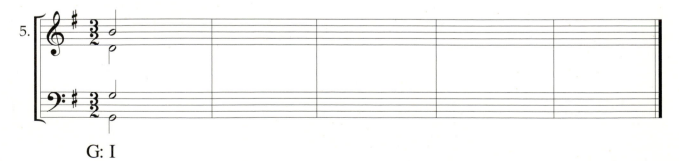

G: I

Unit 5

Rhythmic Dictation: 4:1 Subdivision of the Beat, Anacruses

These exercises introduce subdivisions of the beat. As before, listen to the example while counting or tapping the beat. Where do the subdivisions occur? How many notes are there within a beat? What pattern do you hear?

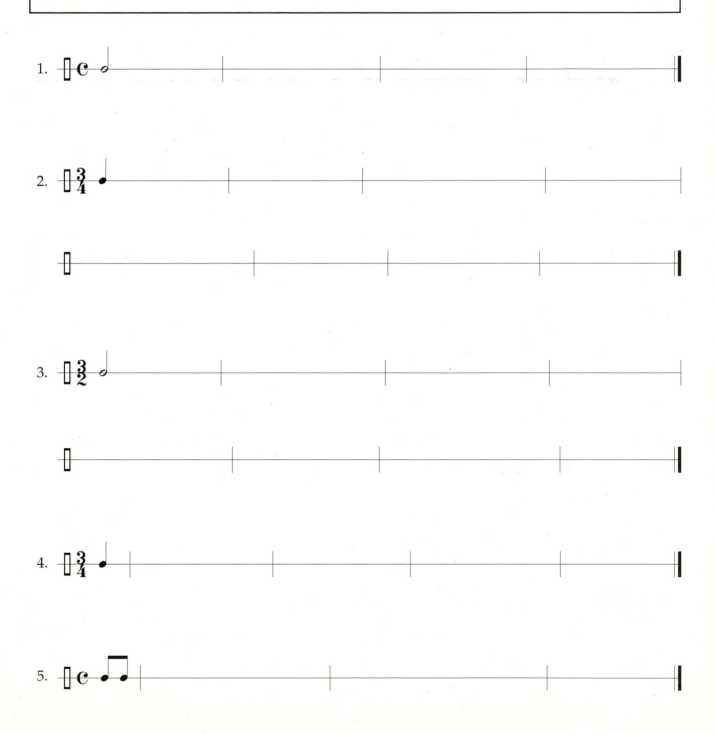

Name: _____

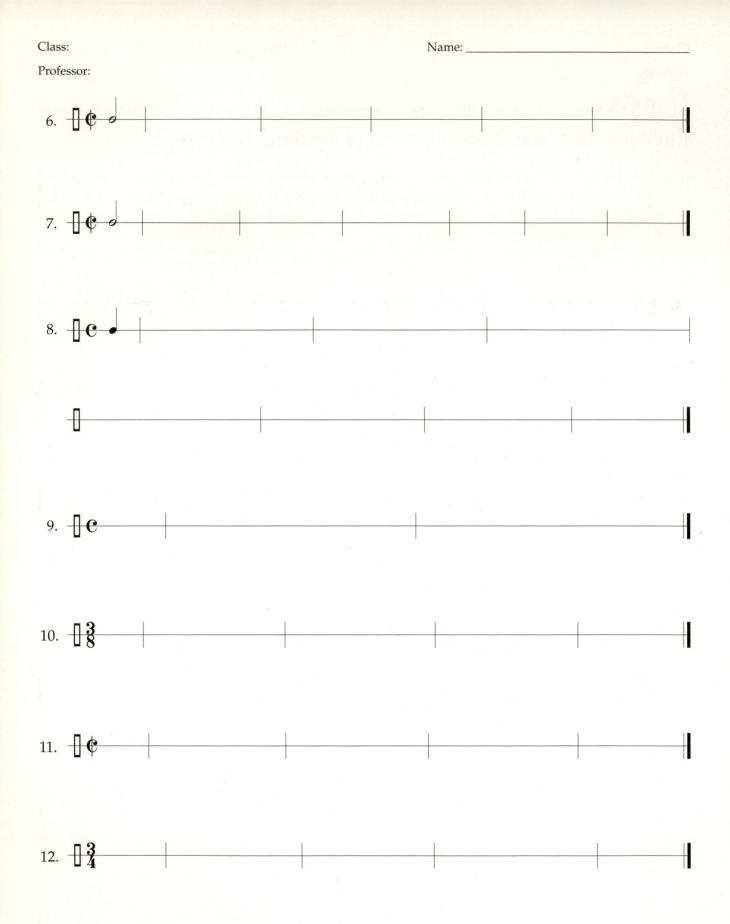

Rhythmic Dictation: QUIZ NO. 1

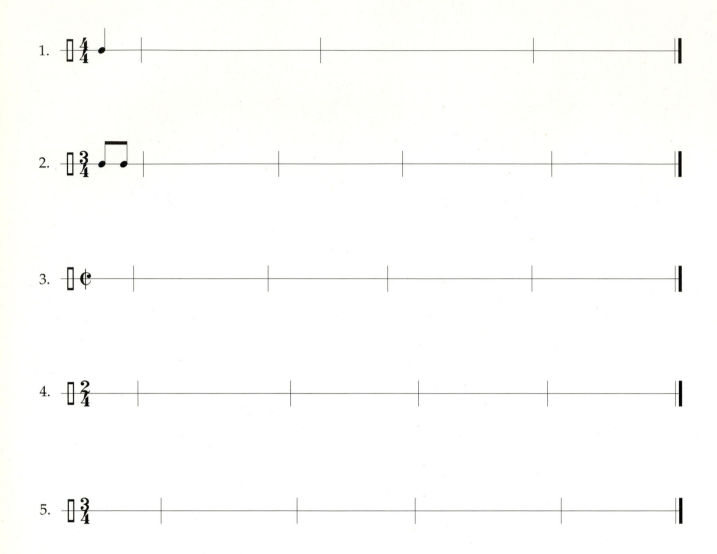

1.

2.

3.

4.

5.

Rhythmic Dictation: QUIZ NO. 2

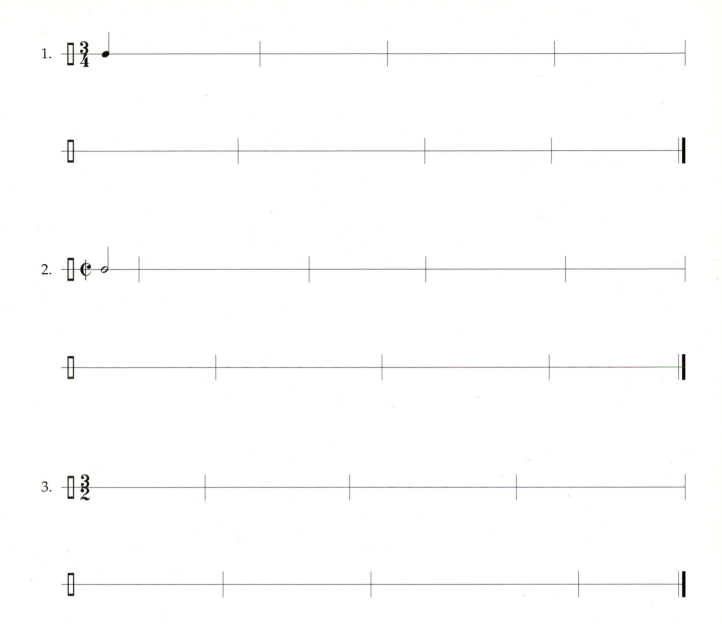

1.

2.

3.

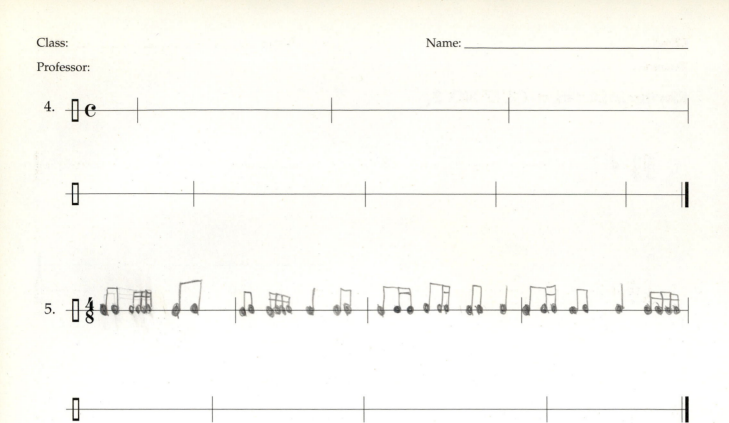

4.

5.

Rhythmic Dictation: QUIZ NO. 3

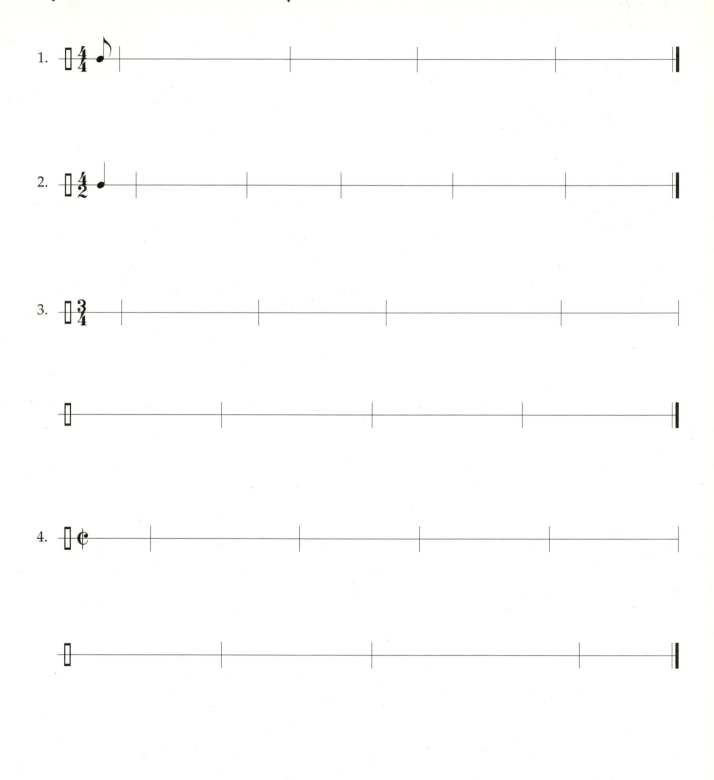

5.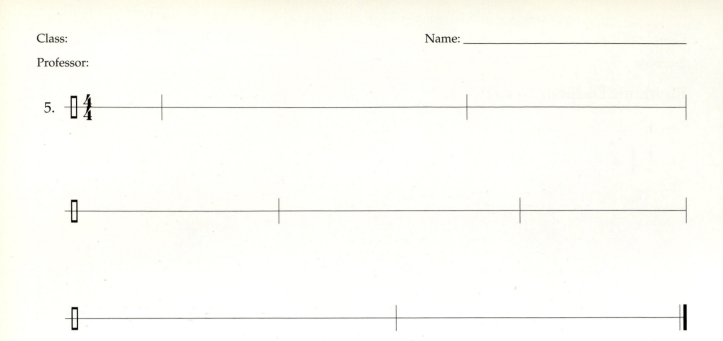

Melodic Dictation: Primary Triads and the Dominant Seventh

Preliminary Exercises

Melodies

These exercises contain patterns implying all the primary triads (I, IV, and V) and the dominant seventh. For each example, establish the key by singing the scale and the arpeggiations of each triad. As you listen, determine whether the line is moving by step or skip. If by step, what is the scale fragment? Focus on the framing pitches (lowest and highest of the scale fragment). If by skip, which triad is being arpeggiated? Again, concentrate on establishing the lowest and highest notes.

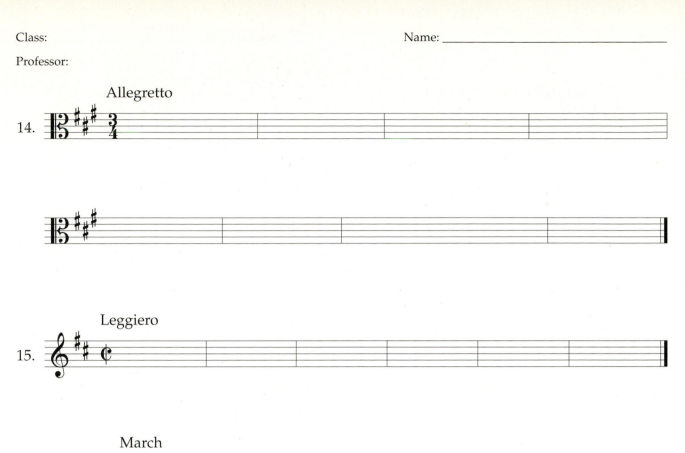

14. Allegretto

15. Leggiero

16. March

Melodic Dictation: QUIZ NO. 1

Spiritoso

1.

Grazioso

2.

Ländler

3.

Marziale

4.

Moderato

5.

Melodic Dictation: QUIZ NO. 2

Melodic Dictation: QUIZ NO. 3

Allegretto

1.

Tempo di valse

2.

Semplice

3.

Cantabile

4.

Allegro

5.

Melodic Dictation: QUIZ NO. 4

Harmonic Dictation: Primary Triads and the Dominant Seventh; Cadential Tonic Six-Four

Basic Progressions

Primary triads and the dominant seventh

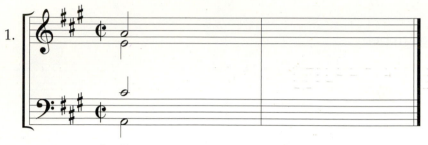

1.

A: I

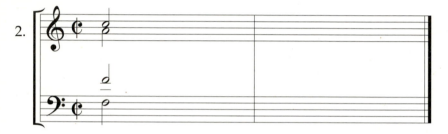

2.

C: IV

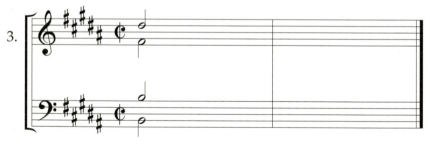

3.

B: I

4.

E: IV

5.
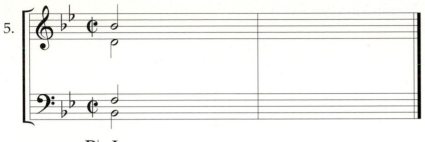

B♭: I

6.
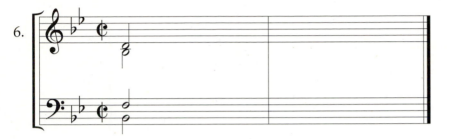

B♭: I

7.
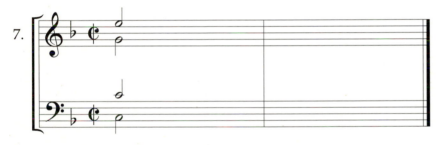

F: V

8.
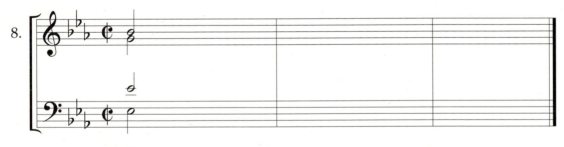

E♭: I

Name: _____

D: I

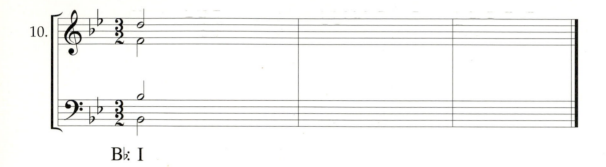

B♭: I

Cadential tonic six-four

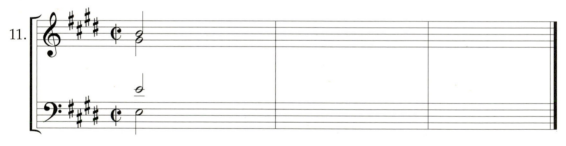

E: I

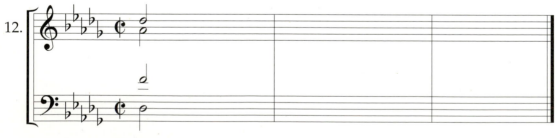

D♭: I

13.

C: I

14.

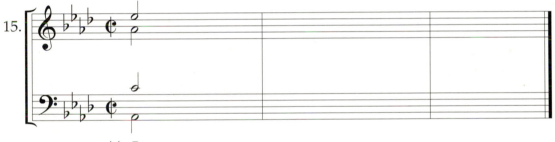

D: I

15.

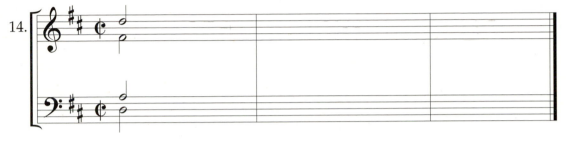

A♭: I

16.

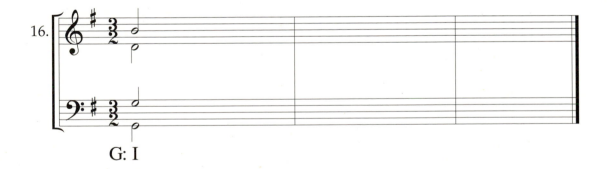

G: I

Phrase-Length Exercises

These exercises present all the primary triads and introduce the cadential six-four chord. As before, you should drill on the preliminary exercises. Then, listen to each phrase-length exercise, concentrating on the cadential progression. Do you hear an authentic cadence or a half cadence? Establish the goal chord and work backwards. What are the most likely chords to occur at the cadence? Is a dominant preparation (pre-dominant) chord used? A cadential six-four?

1.
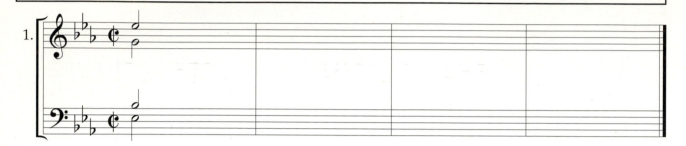

E♭: I

2.
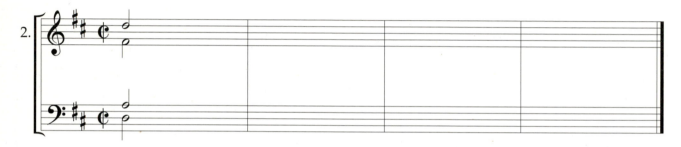

D: I

3.
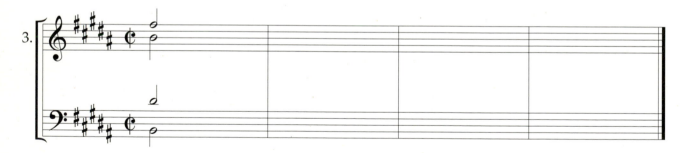

B: I

4.
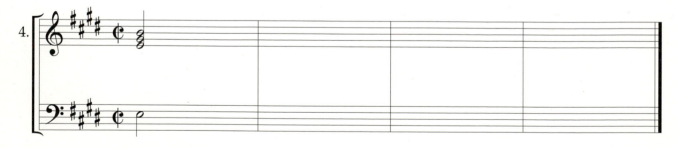

E: I

5.

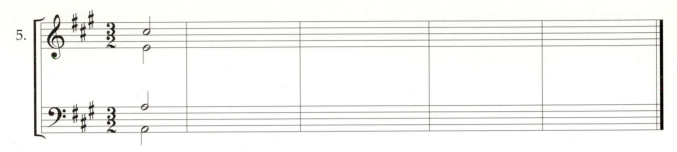

A: I

6.

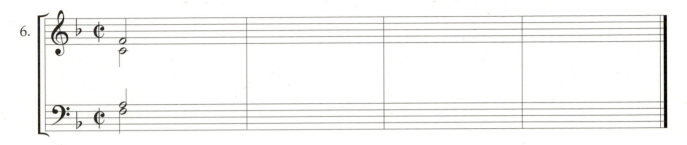

F: I

7.

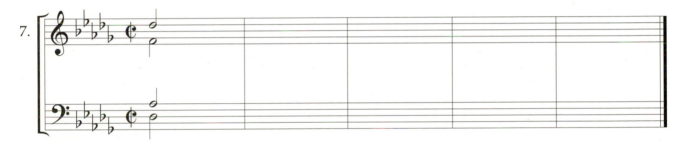

Db: I

8.

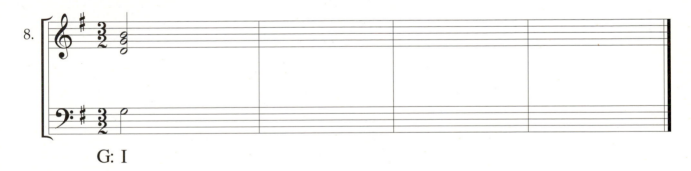

G: I

9.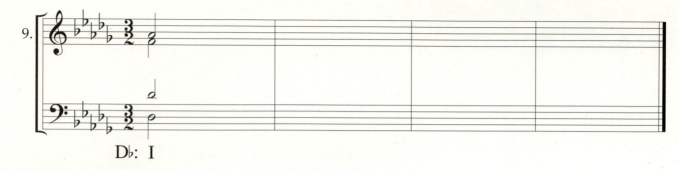

Db: I

10.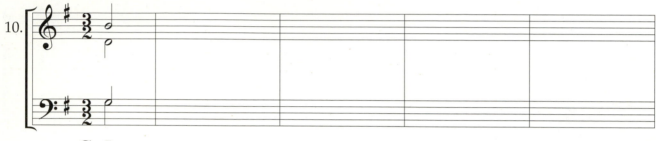

G: I

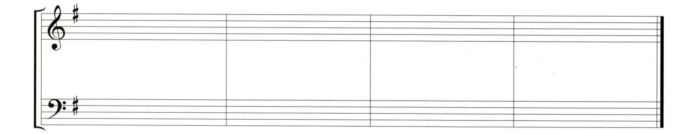

Harmonic Dictation: QUIZ NO. 1

1. E: I

2. F: I

3. D: I

4. A♭: I

5. G: I

Class: _____   Name: _____

Professor: _____

Harmonic Dictation: QUIZ NO. 2

1.

G: I

2.

B♭: I

3.
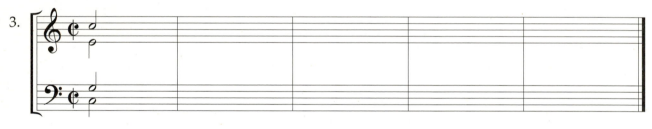

C: I

4.
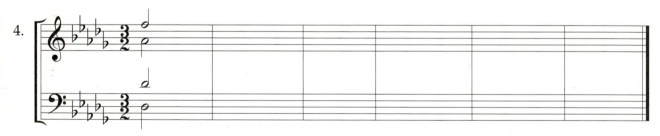

D♭: I

5.
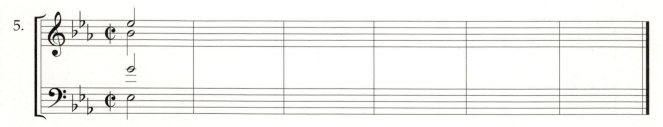

E♭: I

Harmonic Dictation: QUIZ NO. 3

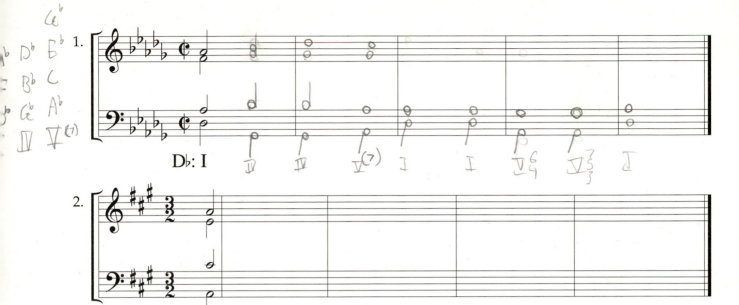

1. Db: I   IV   IV   V(7)   I   I   V$_4^6$ V$_3^5$ I

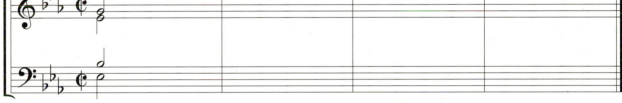

2. A: I

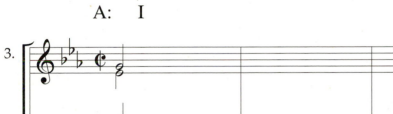

3. Eb: I

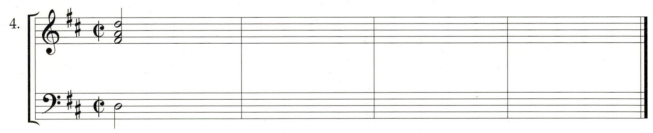

4. D: I

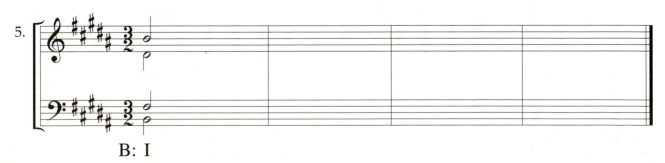

5. B: I

Class: _____   Name: _____

Professor: _____

Harmonic Dictation: QUIZ NO. 4

1.

E: I

2.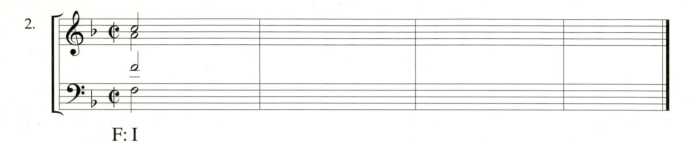

F: I

3.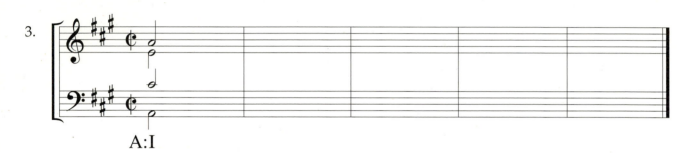

A: I

4.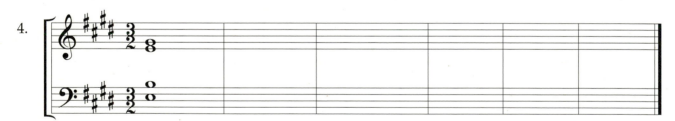

E: I

5.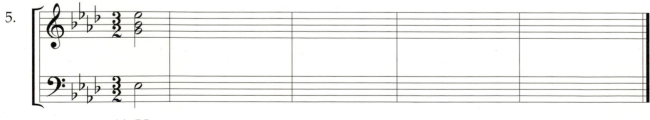

A♭: V

Unit 6

Rhythmic Dictation: Dots and Ties

Listen to each example while counting or tapping the beat. Focus on the division and subdivision of the beat. How many smaller values are contained within a given note? Listen for patterns of long and short note values. Will notes of longer duration require a dot or tie?

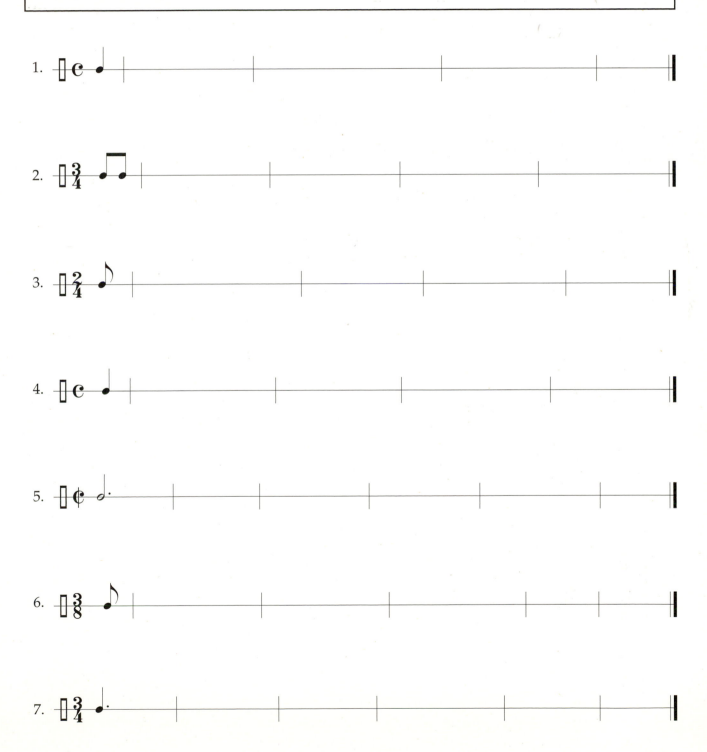

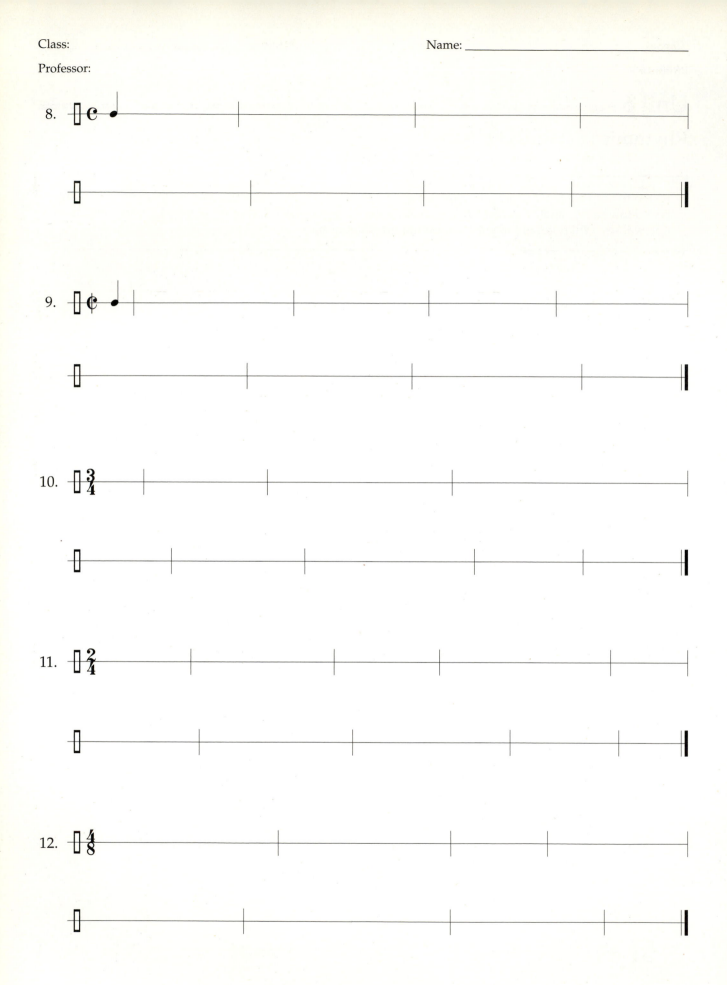

Rhythmic Dictation: QUIZ NO. 1

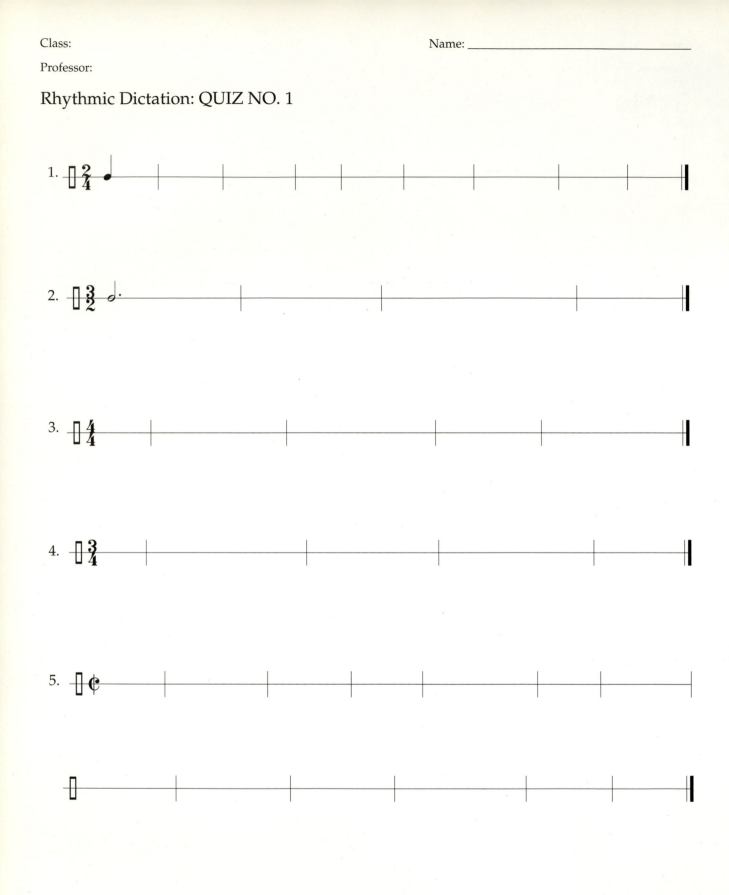

Rhythmic Dictation: QUIZ NO. 2

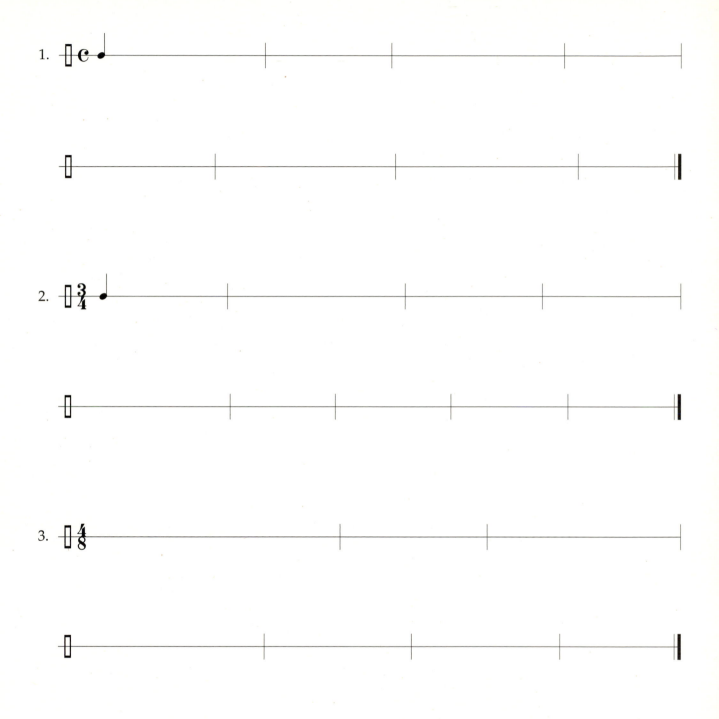

1.

2.

3.

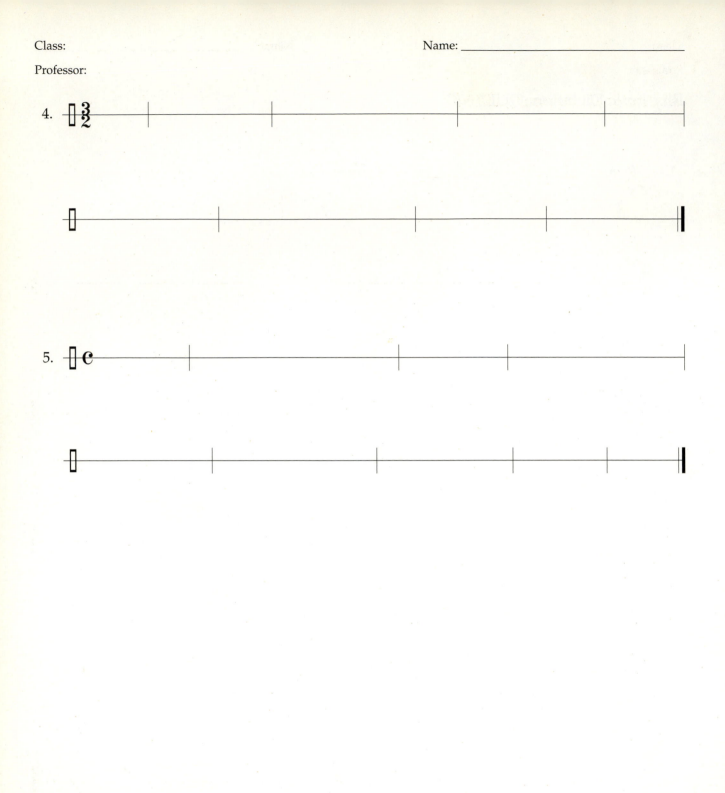

Rhythmic Dictation: QUIZ NO. 3

5.

Class:

Professor:

Name: _____

Melodic Dictation: Minor Mode

Preliminary Exercises

Melodies

First, drill on the preliminary exercises. Sing the three minor scale forms, using syllables. Which scale forms do you hear in each melody? Does the melody use only one form throughout or all three forms? What determines which form is used?

9. Cantabile

10. Dolce

11. Adagietto

12. Deciso

Melodic Dictation: QUIZ NO. 1

Melancholique

1.

Cantabile

2.

Buffo

3.

Adagietto

4.

Valse

5.

Melodic Dictation: QUIZ NO. 2

Melodic Dictation: QUIZ NO. 3

Gesangvoll

1.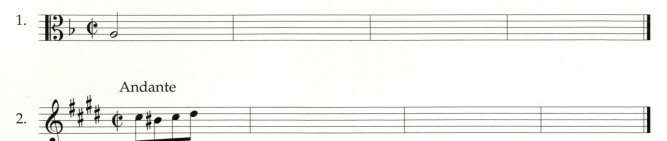

Andante

2.

Con forza

3.

Grazioso

4.

Geschwind

5.

Melodic Dictation: QUIZ NO. 4

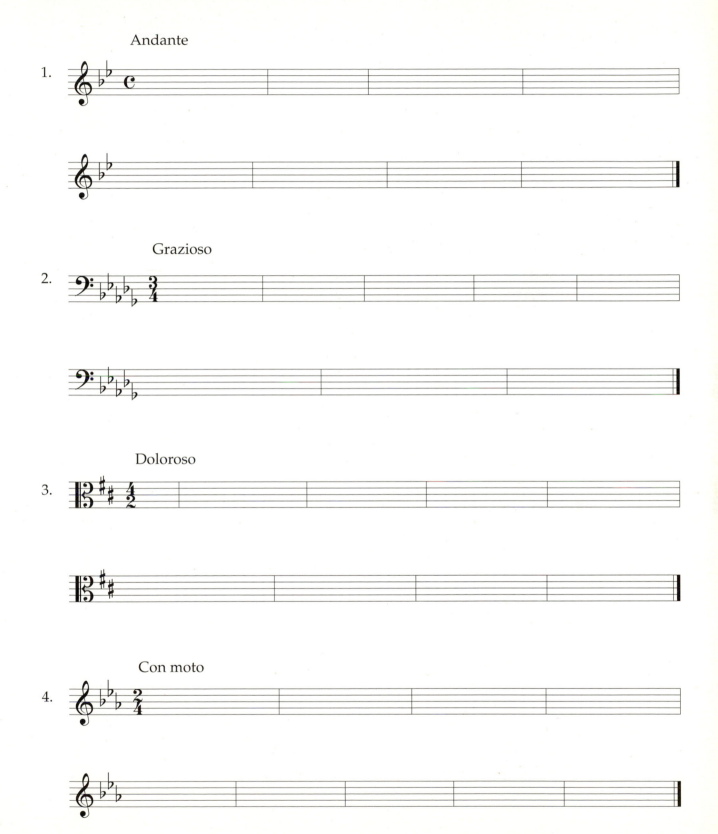

Andante

1.

Grazioso

2.

Doloroso

3.

Con moto

4.

Ben marcato

5.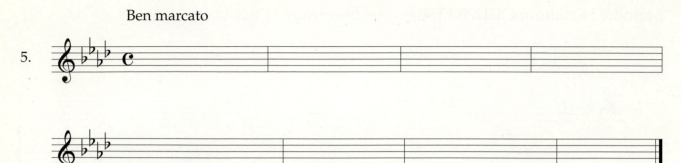

Harmonic Dictation: Minor Mode; First Inversion of Triads

Basic Progressions

Minor mode

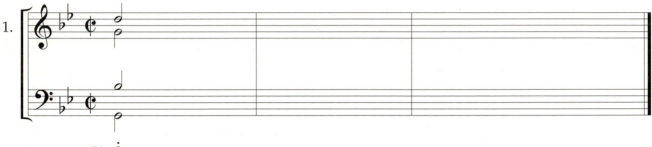

1. g: i

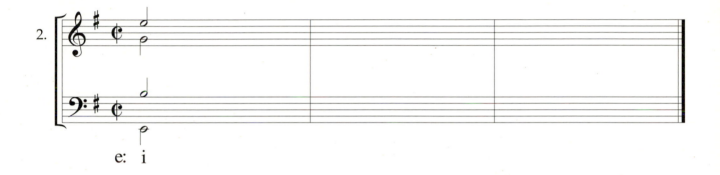

2. e: i

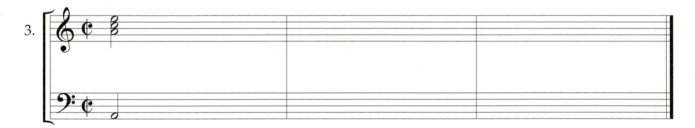

3. a: i

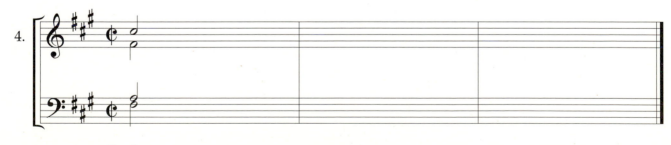

4. f#: i

5.

bb: i   iv

6.

b: i

First inversion of triads

7.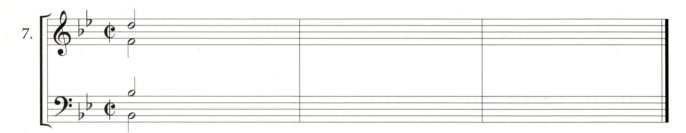

Bb: I

8.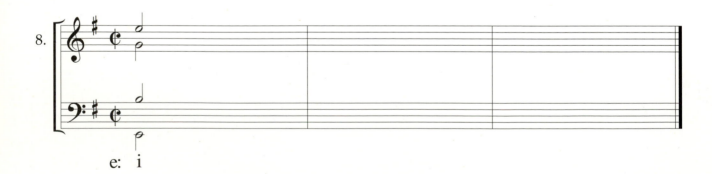

e: i

9.

d: V^6

10.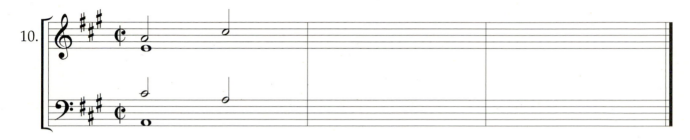

A: I

11.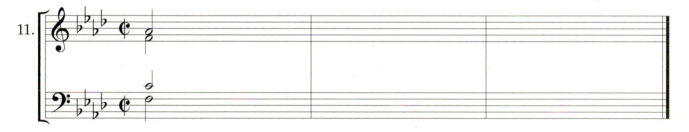

f: i

12.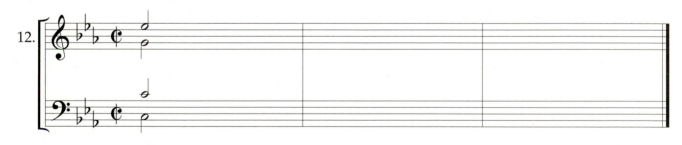

c: i

13.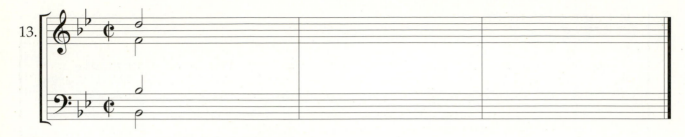

Bb: I

14.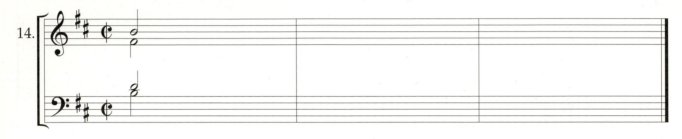

b: i

15.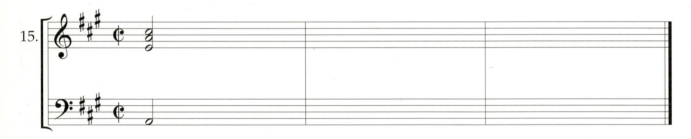

A: I

16.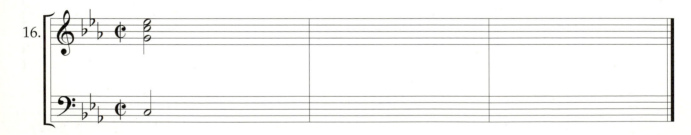

c: i

Phrase-Length Exercises

As before, drill first on the preliminary exercises. Concentrate on the outer voices. Does the bass move by step or skip? If by skip, is the leap large (fourth or fifth) or small (third)? Sketch in the bass line; this should tell you where inversions occur. After working out the soprano, fill in the inner voices, paying particular attention to the rules of good part-writing. If the exercise is in the minor mode, what is the quality of the dominant chord? Did you remember to raise the leading tone?

1.

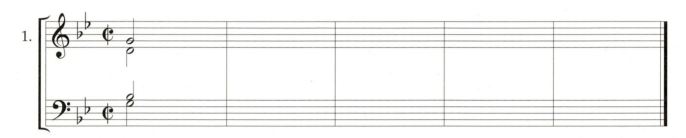

g: i

2.

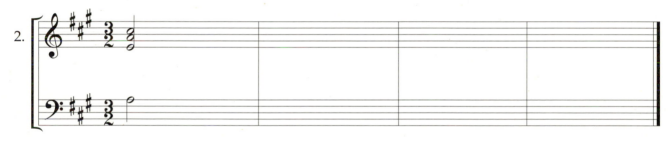

A: I

3.

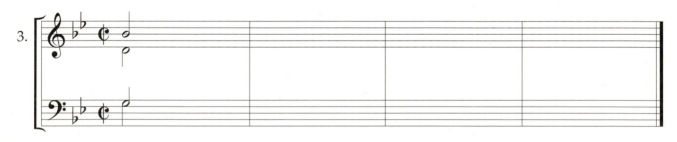

g: i

4.

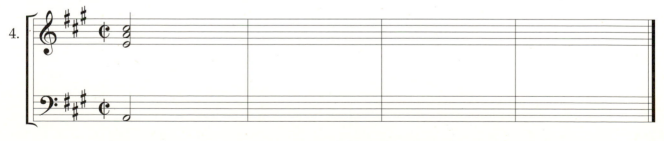

A: I

5.

b♭: i

6.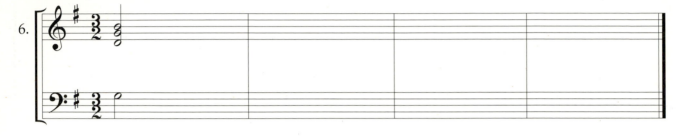

G: I

7.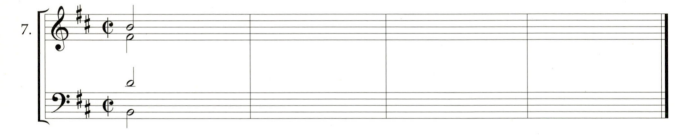

b: i

8.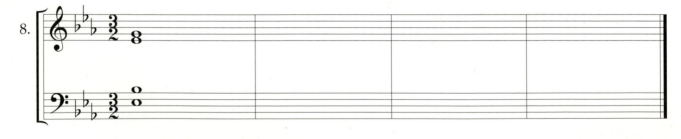

E♭: I

9.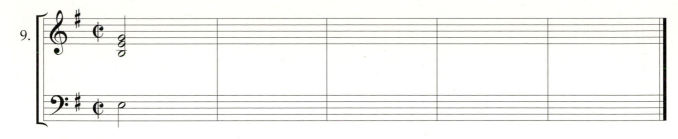

e: i

10.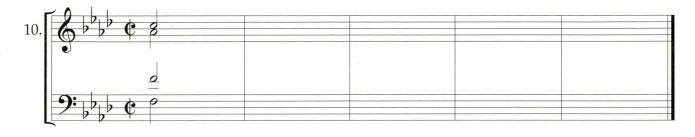

f: i

11.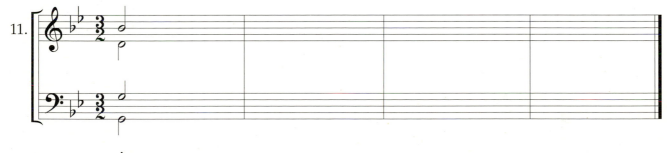

g: i

12.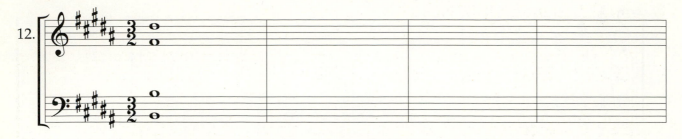

B: I

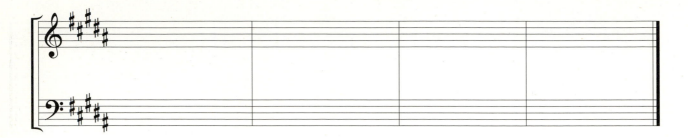

Class: _____   Name: _____

Professor: _____

Harmonic Dictation: QUIZ NO. 1

1.

f: i

2.
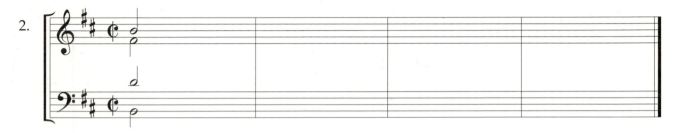

b: i

3.
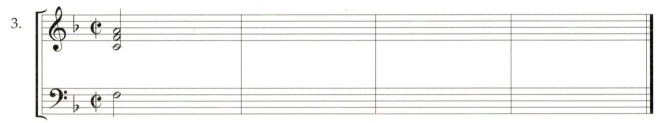

F: I

4.
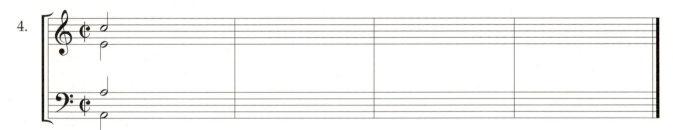

a: i

5.

B: I

Harmonic Dictation: QUIZ NO. 2

1.

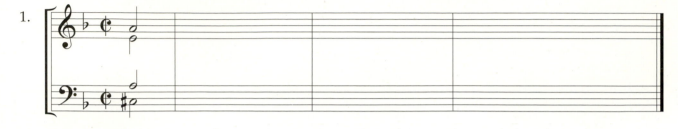

      d: V^6

2.
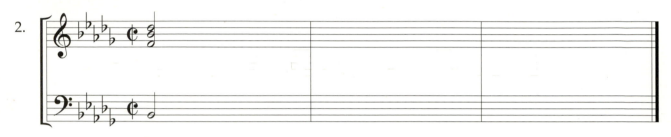

      b♭: i

3.

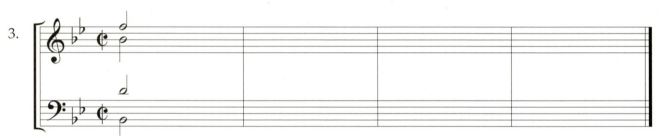

      B♭: I

4.

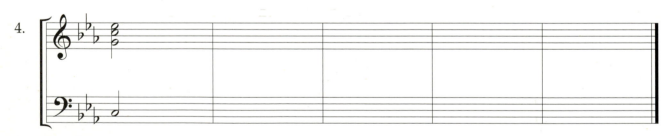

      c: i

5.

      D: I

Class:

Name: _____

Professor:

Harmonic Dictation: QUIZ NO. 3

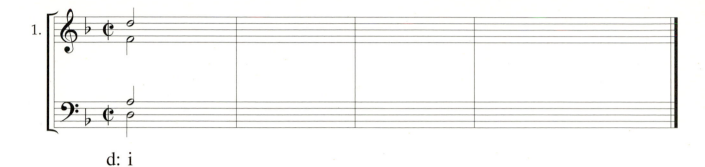

1.

d: i

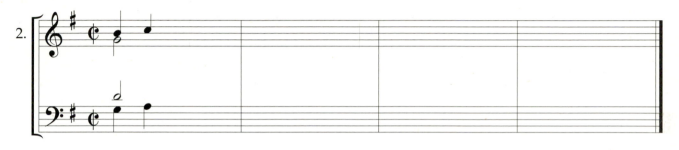

2.

G: I ___

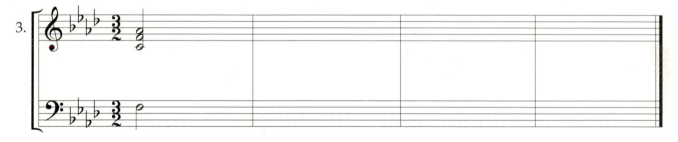

3.

f: i

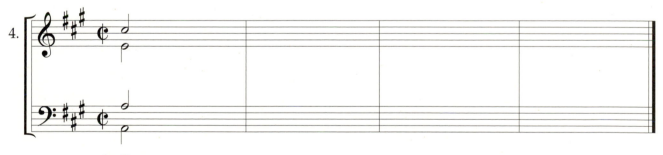

4.

A: I

5.

c: i

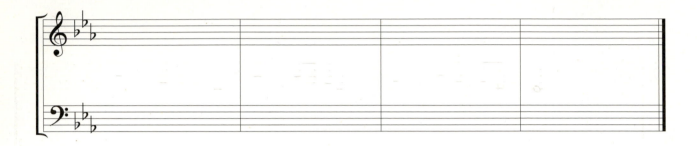

Class: _____   Name: _____

Professor: _____

Harmonic Dictation: QUIZ NO. 4

1.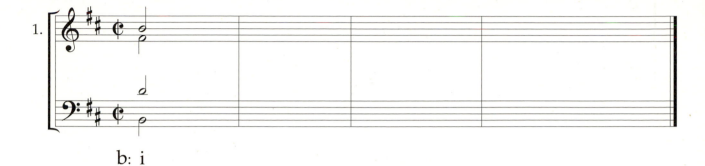

b: i

2.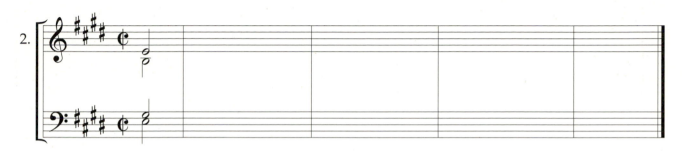

E: I

3.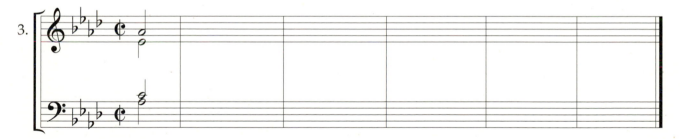

Ab: I

4.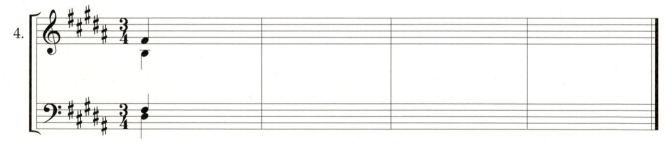

B: I⁶

c: i

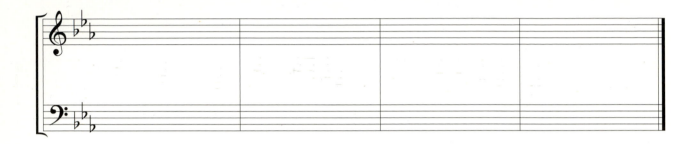

Unit 7

Melodic Dictation: The Supertonic Triad

Preliminary Exercises

Name: _____

Professor:

Melodies

Sing the supertonic triad in both modes, using syllables. What is its quality in each mode? Where will the supertonic triad most likely occur? Which chord is most likely to follow? How is the underlying progression expressed melodically?

Leggiero

5.

Lively

6.

Giocoso

7.

Lento

8.

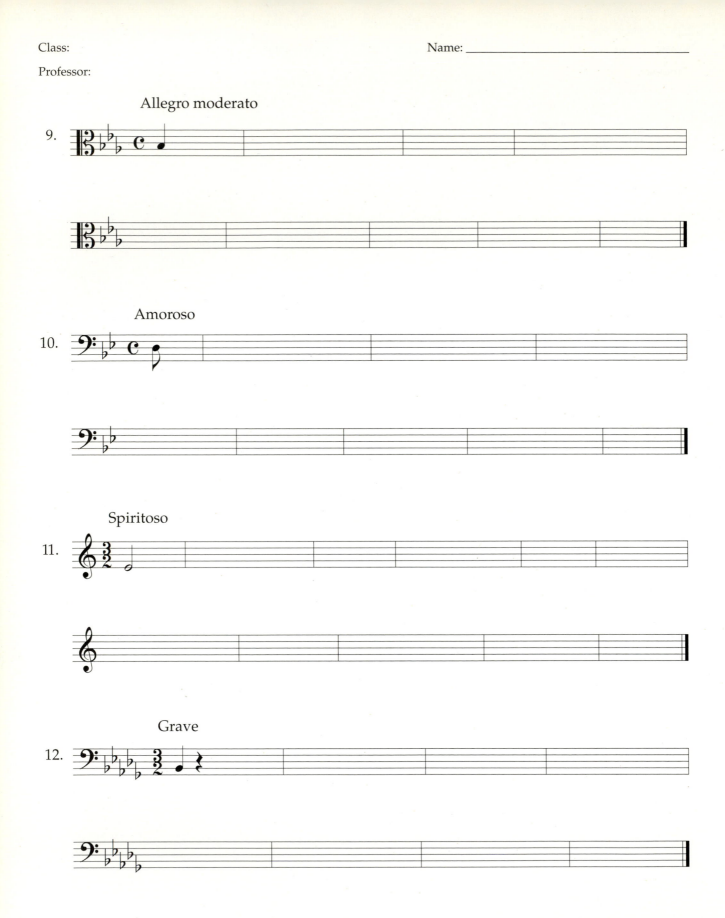

Allegro moderato

9.

Amoroso

10.

Spiritoso

11.

Grave

12.

Zart

13.

Allegretto

14.

Melodic Dictation: QUIZ NO. 1

Andantino

1.

Ländler

2.

Grazioso

3.

Allegro

4.

Andante

5.

Melodic Dictation: QUIZ NO. 2

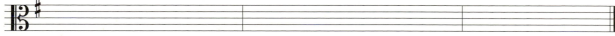

Melodic Dictation: QUIZ NO. 3

1. Animato

2. Comodo

3. Allegro

4. Cantabile

Allegro con brio

5.

Class: _____   Name: _____

Professor: _____

Melodic Dictation: QUIZ NO. 4

Passionato

5.

Harmonic Dictation: The Supertonic Triad; Inversions of V7

Basic Progressions

Supertonic triad

1.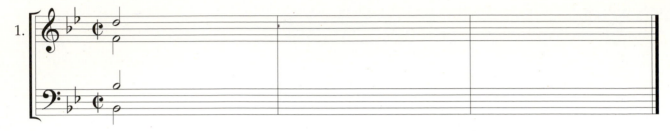

      Bb: I

2.

      b: i

3.

      C: I

4.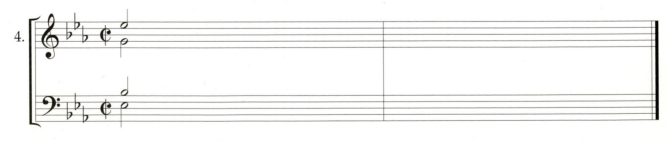

      Eb: I

5.
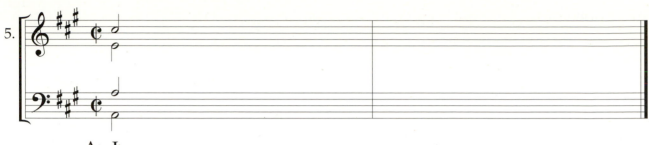

A: I

6.
e: i

iCEG   IIIEGB   VGBDF vii°
iiDFA   IVFAC   ViACE   IAC

7.

C–   c: i   iv6   ii°6   V7   7

8.
F: I

9.
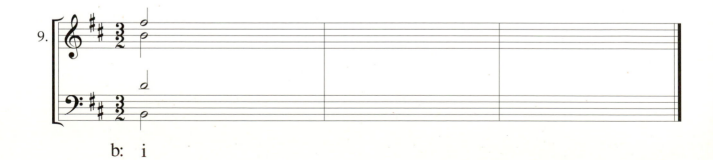

b: i

Inversions of V7

10. F: I

11. c: i

12. G: I   V$^4_3$ I^6 V$^4_3$ I

13. B♭: I

14.
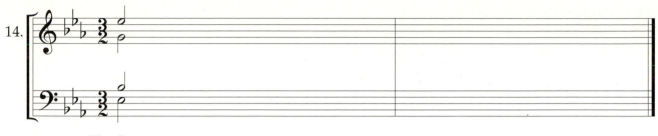

Eb: I

15.
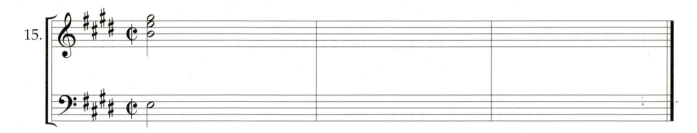

E: I

16.
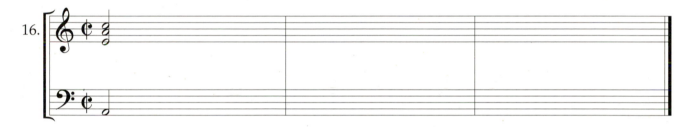

a: i

17.
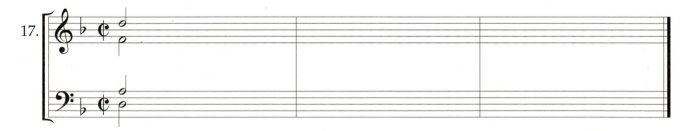

d: i

18.

Ab: I

Phrase-Length Exercises

These exercises introduce the supertonic triad and present inversions of the V7. As before, concentrate on the bass line. Does it move by step or skip? If by step, in which direction? What harmonic idioms using inversions of the V7 are suggested by the particular sequence of the scale degrees in the bass? As always, master the preliminary exercises before proceeding to the phrase-length exercises.

1.

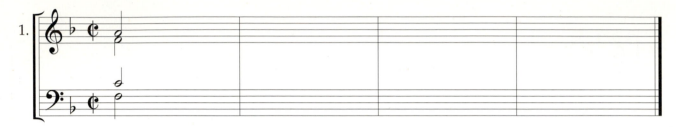

F: I

2.

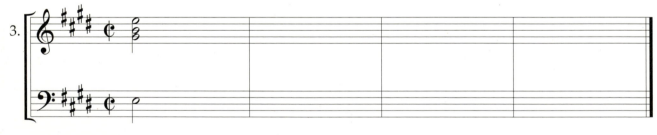

e: i

3.

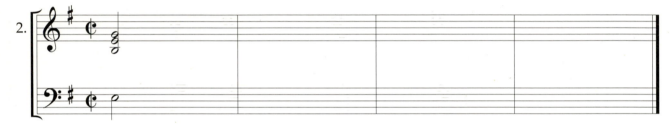

E: I

4.

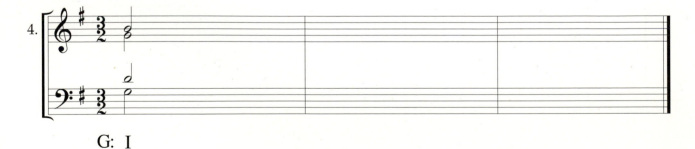

G: I

5.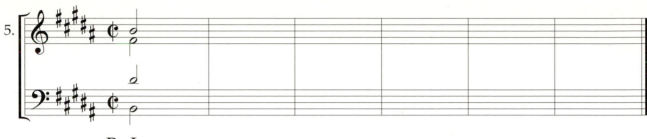

B: I

6.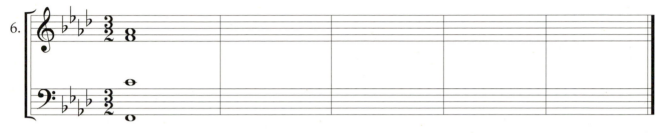

f: i

7.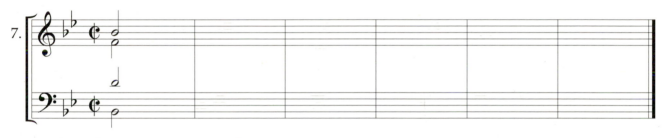

B♭: I

8.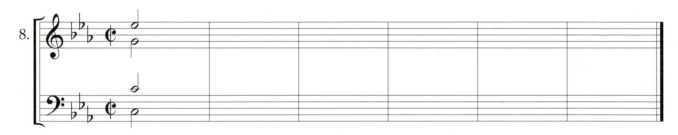

c: i

9.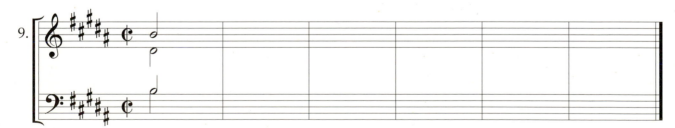

B: I

10.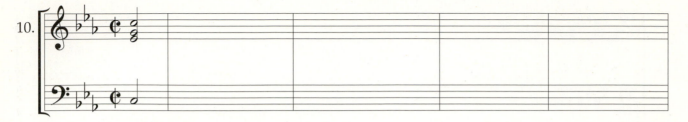

    c: i

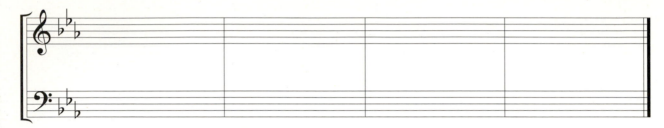

11.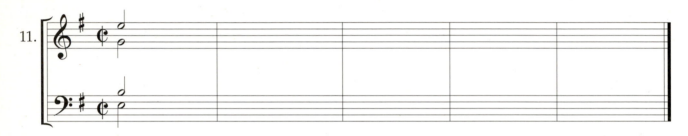

    e: i

12.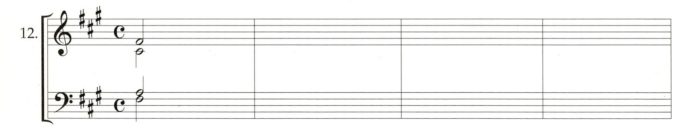

    f#: i

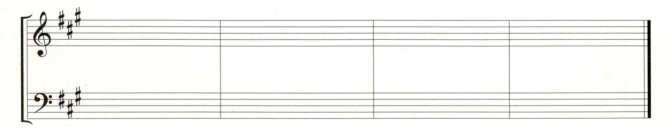

Harmonic Dictation: QUIZ NO. 1

1.

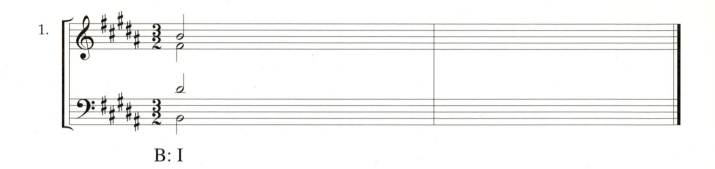

B: I

2.

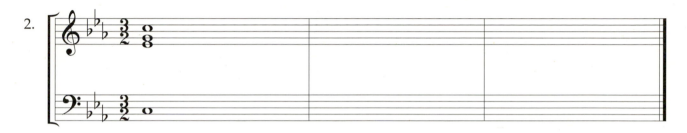

c: i

3.

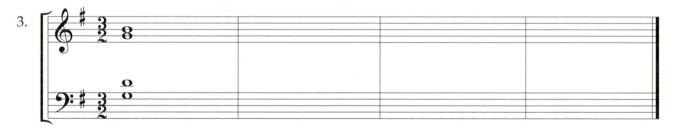

G: I

4.

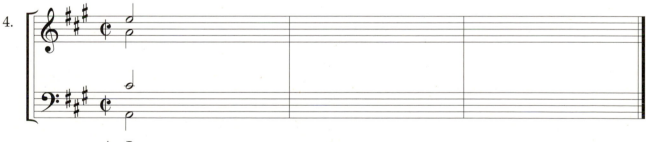

A: I

5.

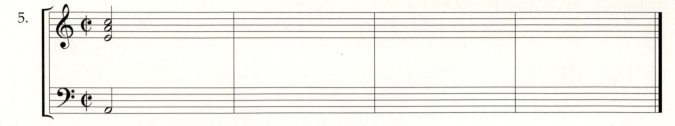

a: i

Name: _____

Harmonic Dictation: QUIZ NO. 2

1.
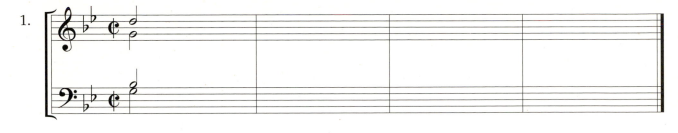

g: i

2.
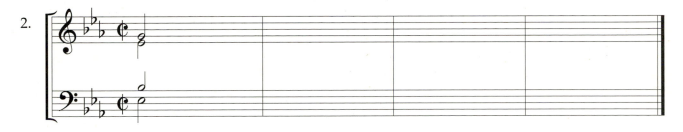

E♭: I

3.
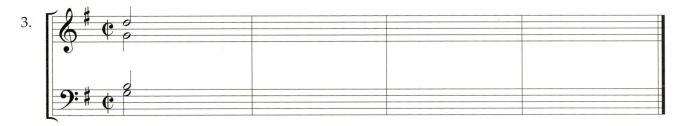

G: I

4.
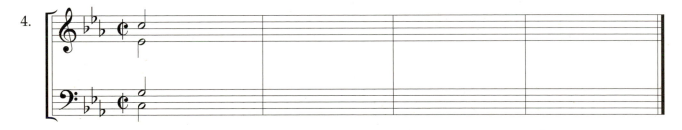

c: i

5.

E: I

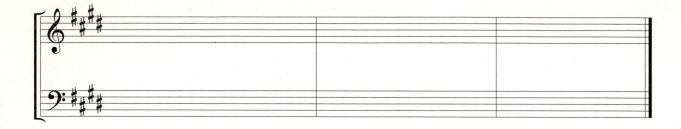

Class:

Professor:

Name: _____

Harmonic Dictation: QUIZ NO. 3

1.
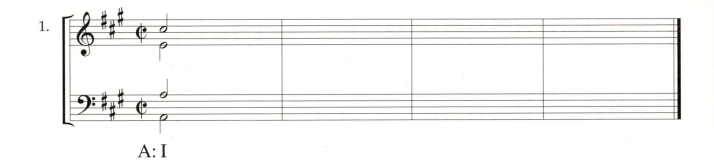

A: I

2.

d: i

3.
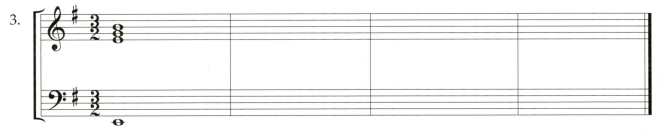

e: i

4.
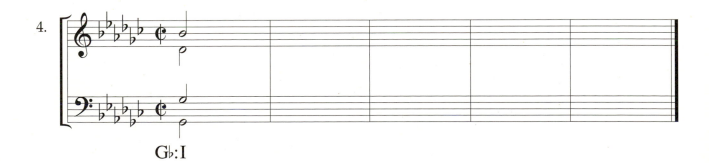

G♭: I

5.

g: i

Class: _____   Name: _____

Professor: _____

Harmonic Dictation: QUIZ NO. 4

1.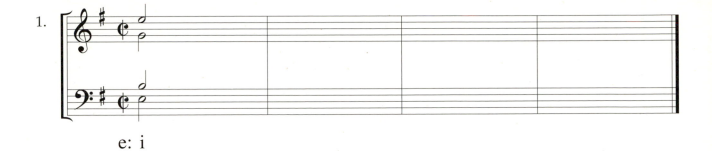

   e: i

2.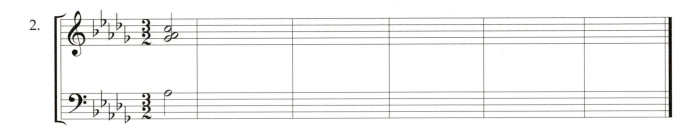

   D♭:   V

3.

   f♯: i

4.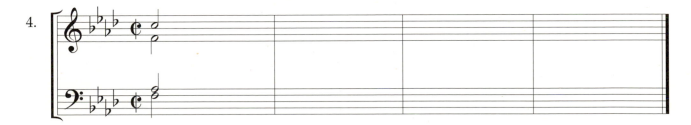

   f: i

5.

b: i

Unit 8

Rhythmic Dictation: Compound Meter

This unit introduces compound meter. Listen to each exercise while counting or tapping the beat. Do you feel the triple division of the beat? Within each beat, are there three equal values or long-short? Are notes within the beat themselves divided? Review the common patterns found in compound meter.

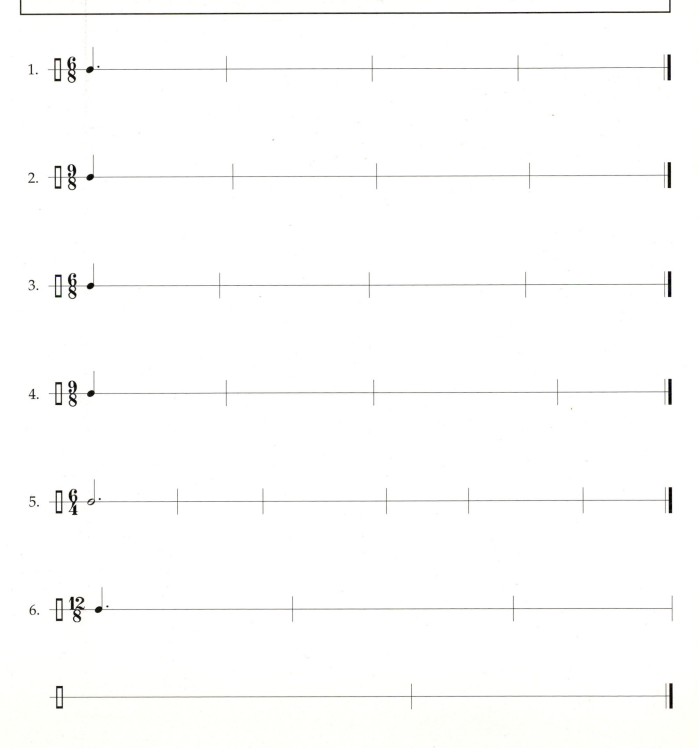

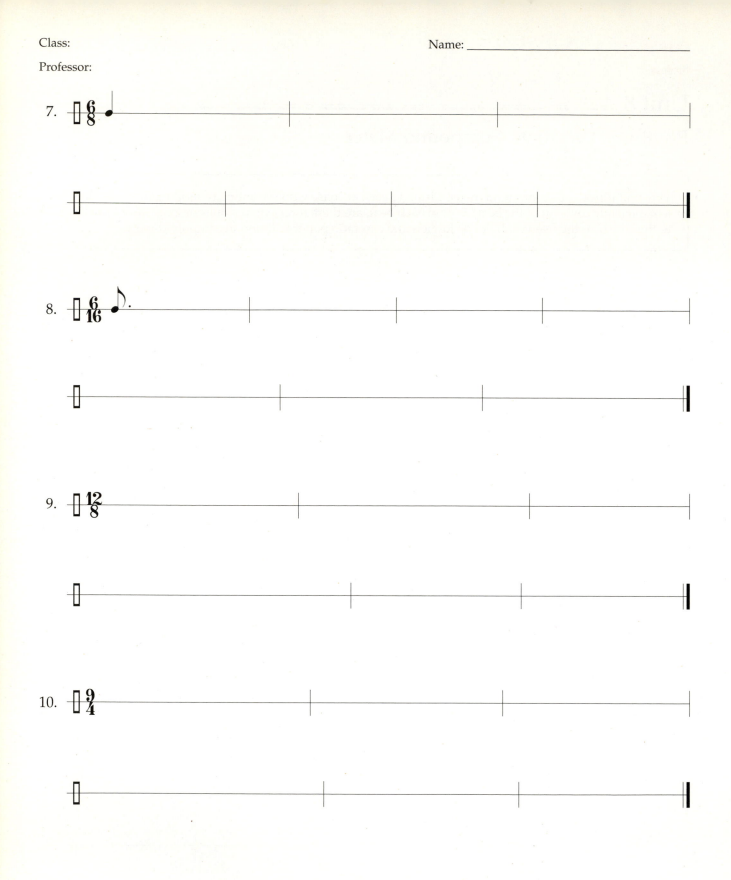

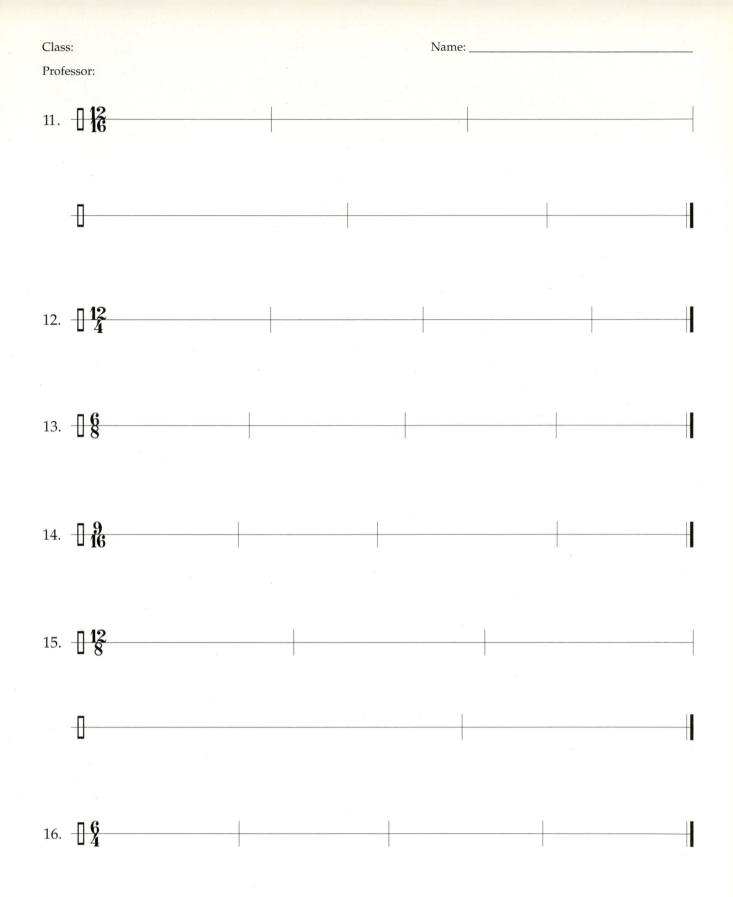

Class:

Name: _____

Professor:

Rhythmic Dictation: QUIZ NO. 1

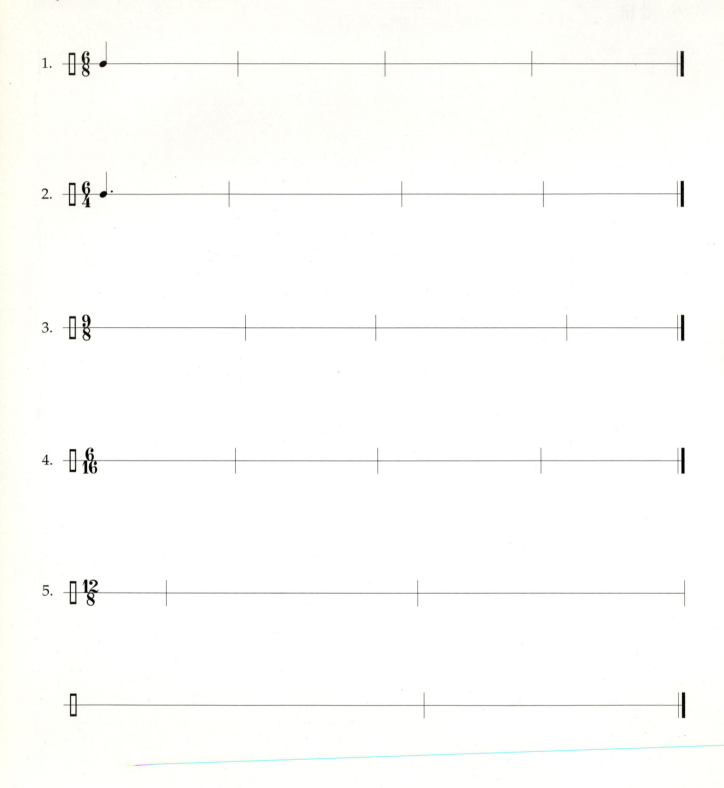

Rhythmic Dictation: QUIZ NO. 2

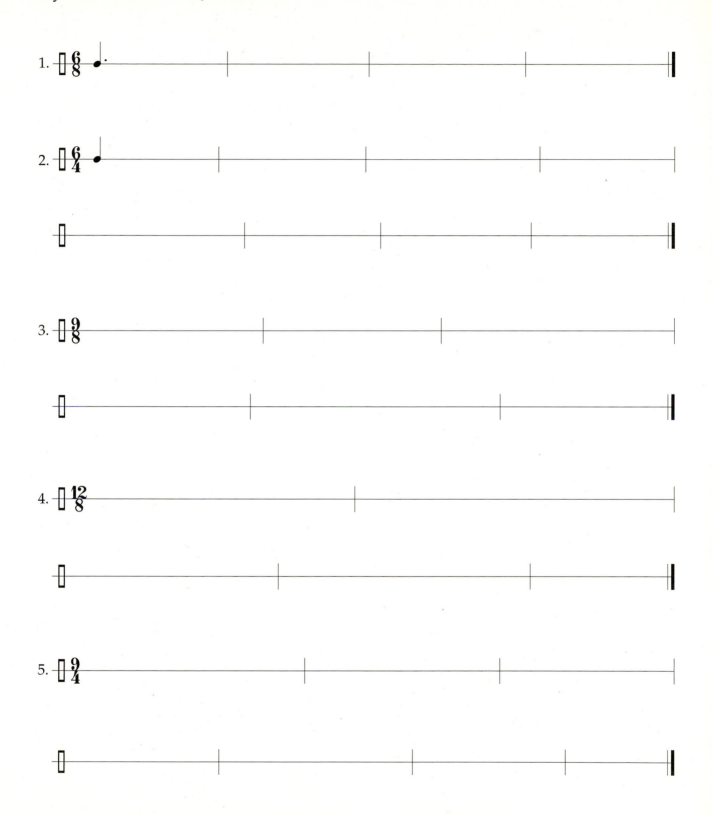

1. $\frac{6}{8}$

2. $\frac{6}{4}$

3. $\frac{9}{8}$

4. $\frac{12}{8}$

5. $\frac{9}{4}$

Class: _____   Name: _____

Professor: _____

Rhythmic Dictation: QUIZ NO. 3

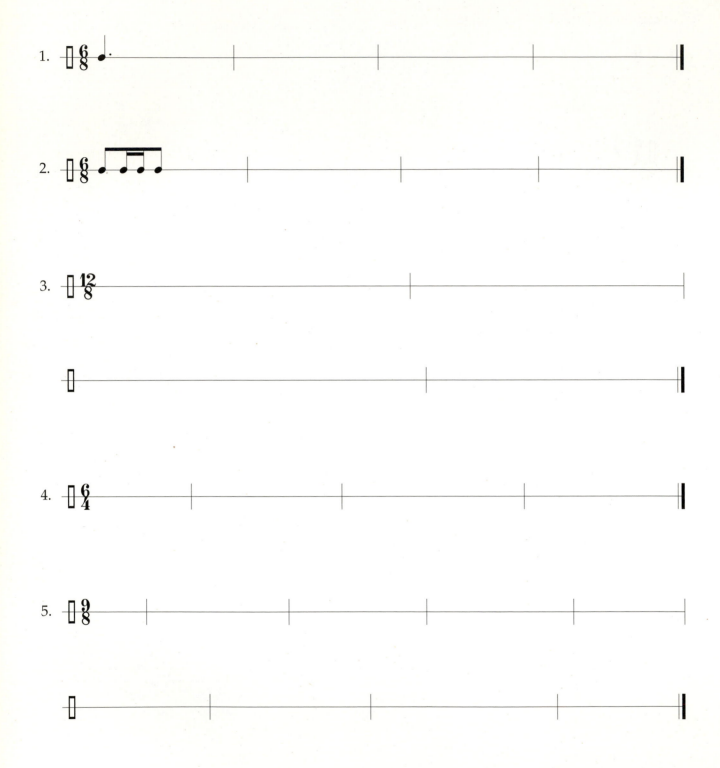

Class: _____

Name: _____

Professor: _____

Melodic Dictation: All Diatonic Triads

Preliminary Exercises

Melodies

These melodies contain implications of all the diatonic triads. Review the most common progressions which use the vi (or VI) and iii (or III) chords. Does the melody outline a chord? What are the framing pitches? The pattern of intervals?

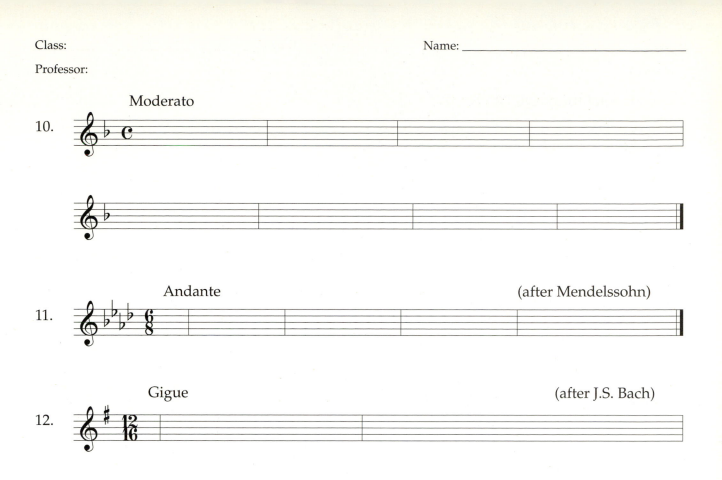

Moderato

10.

Andante   (after Mendelssohn)

11.

Gigue   (after J.S. Bach)

12.

Melodic Dictation: QUIZ NO. 1

1. Tempo di valse

2. Allegretto

3. Moderato

4. Allegro, ma non troppo

5. Lento

Melodic Dictation: QUIZ NO. 2

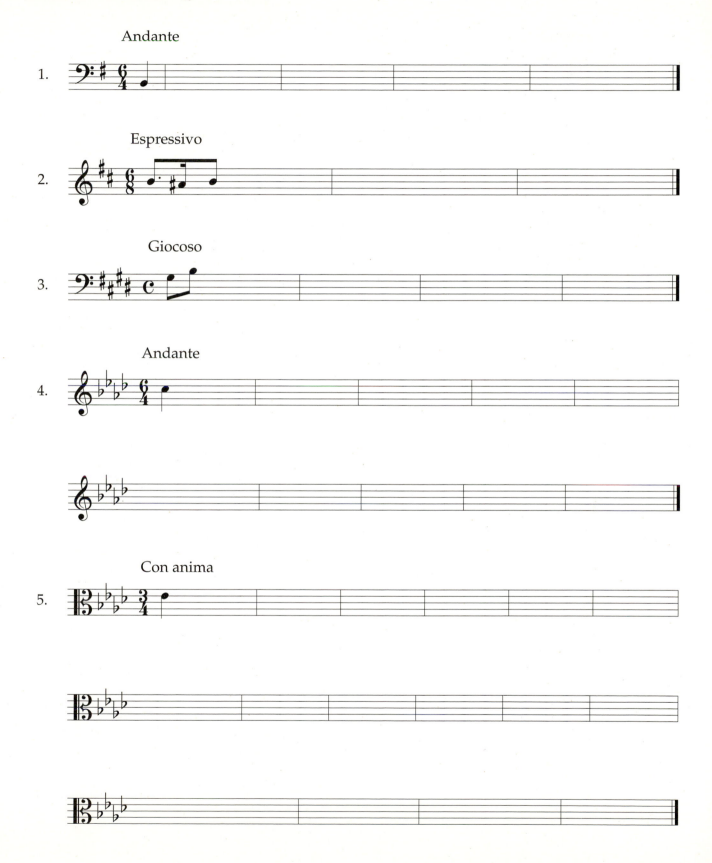

Melodic Dictation: QUIZ NO. 3

Moderato

1.

Giocoso

2.

Menuetto

3.

Melodic Dictation: QUIZ NO. 4

Brightly

1.

Adagio

2.

Moderato

3.

Cantabile

4.

Tempo di Valse

5.

Harmonic Dictation: All Diatonic Triads

Basic Progressions

1.

G: I

2.
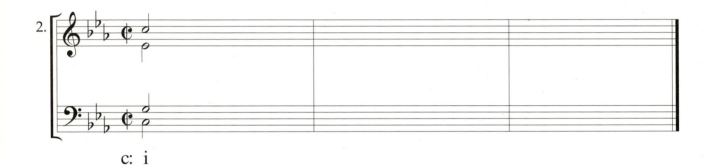
c: i

3.
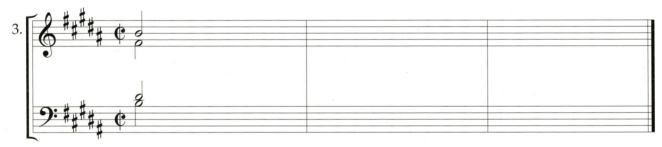
B: I

4.

e♭: i

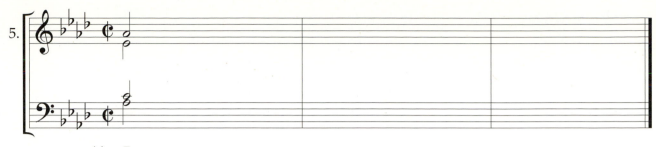

5. Ab: I

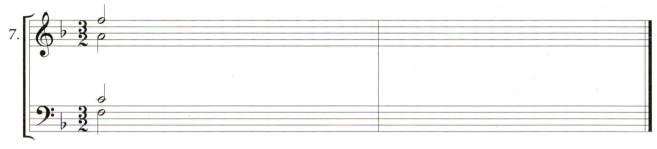

6. b: i

7. F: I

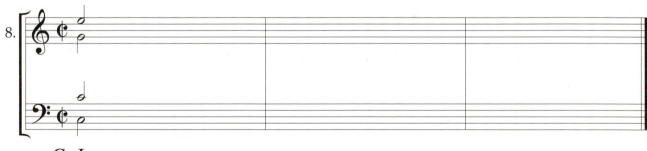

8. C: I

9.

Bb: I

10.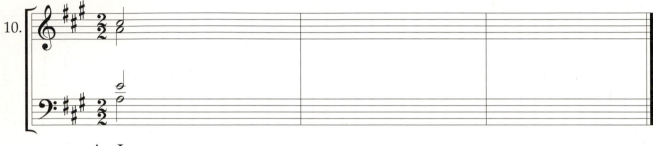

A: I

11.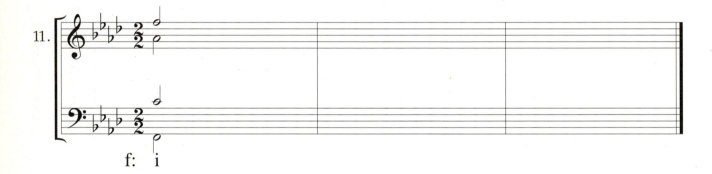

f: i

12.

C: I

A: I

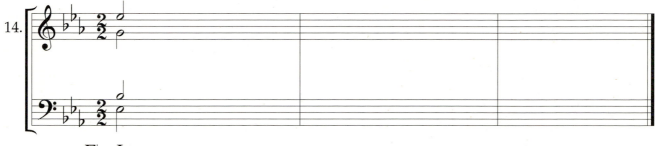

E♭: I

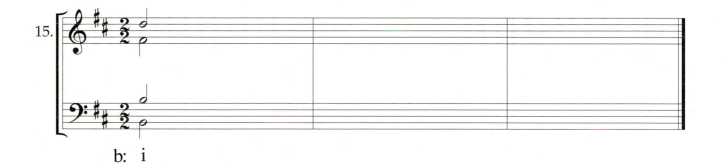

b: i

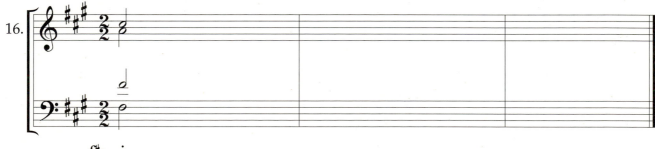

f♯: i

Class:

Professor:

Name: _____

13.

14.

15.

16.

17.

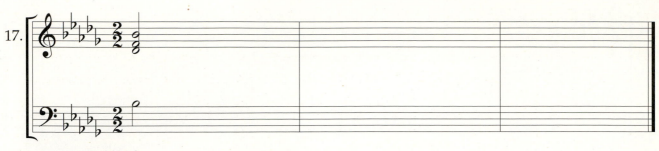

b♭: i

18.

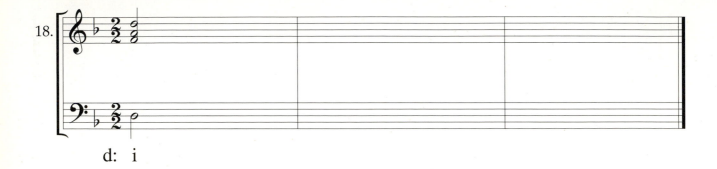

d: i

Phrase-Length Exercises

These exercises present progressions using all the diatonic triads. Review the most common progressions containing the vi (or VI) and iii (or III) chords.

1.
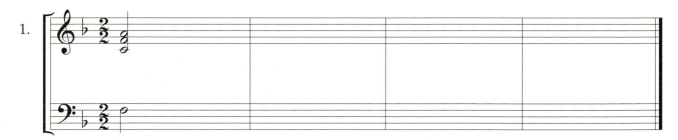

F: I

2.
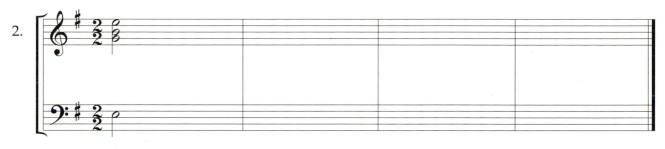

e: i

3.
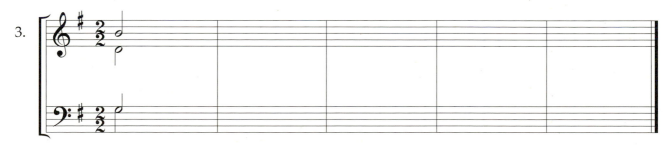

G: I

4.
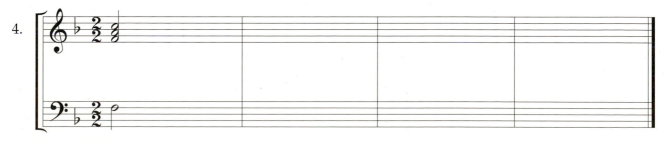

F: I

5.

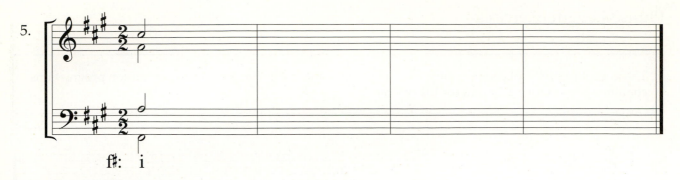

f#: i

6.

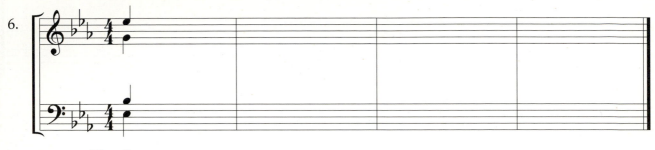

E♭: I

7.

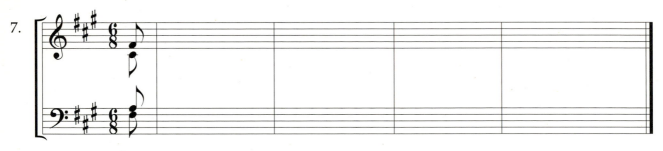

f#: i

8.

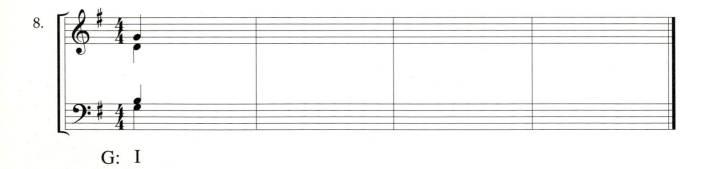

G: I

9.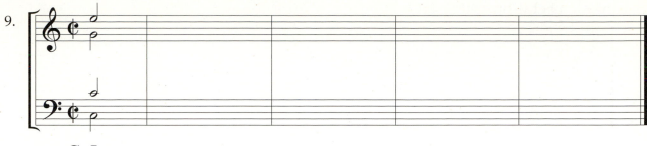

C: I

10.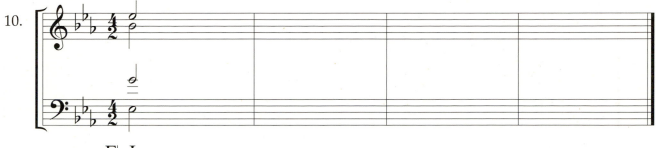

E♭: I

Harmonic Dictation: QUIZ NO. 1

1.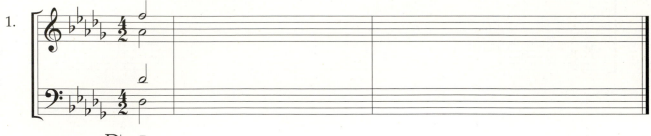

     D♭: I

2.

     A: I

3.

     e: i

4.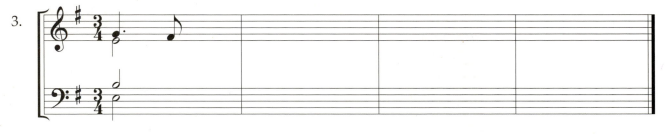

     c♯: i

5.

     B♭: I

Class:

Professor:

Name: _____

Harmonic Dictation: QUIZ NO. 2

1.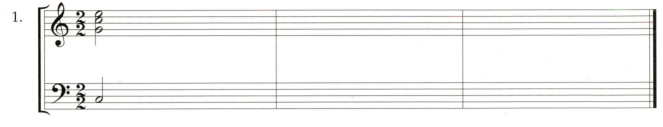

C: I

2.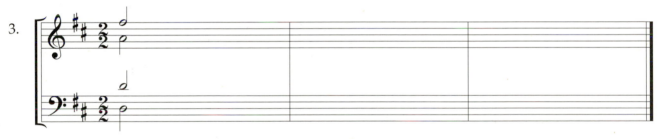

f: i

3.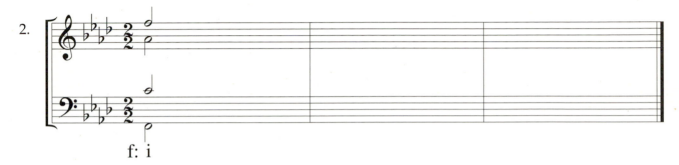

D: I

4.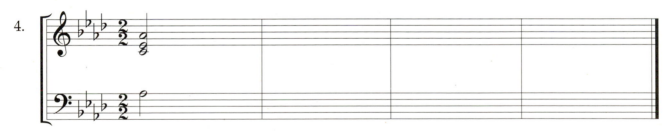

A♭ : I

5.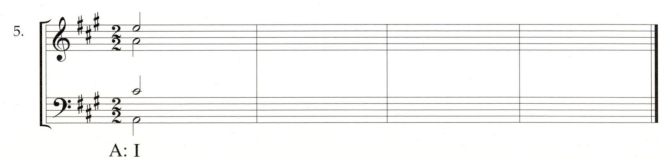

A: I

Harmonic Dictation: QUIZ NO. 3

1.

E: I

2.
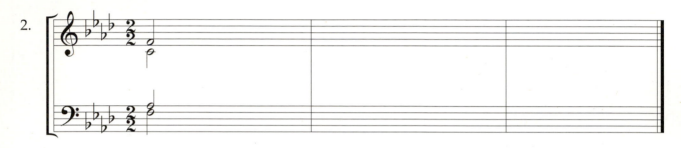

f: i

3.
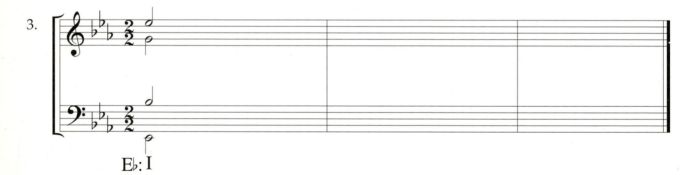

E♭: I

4.
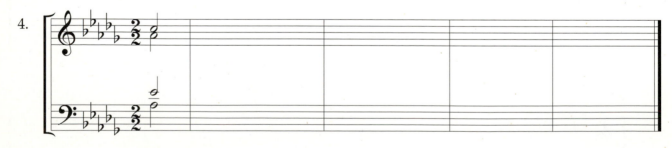

D♭: V

5.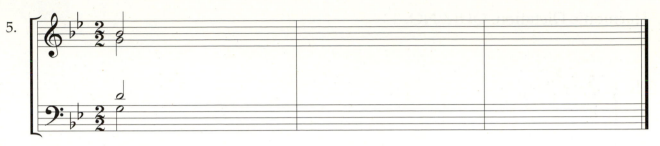

g: i

Harmonic Dictation: QUIZ NO. 4

1.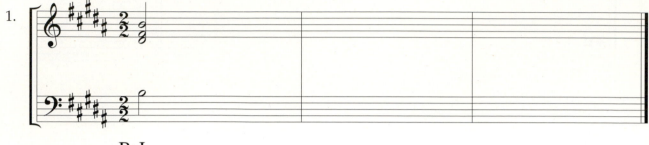

B: I

2.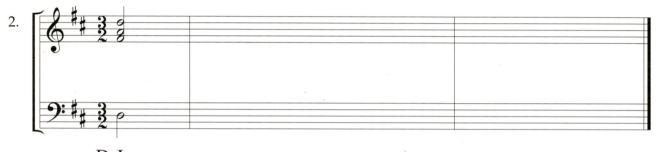

D: I

3.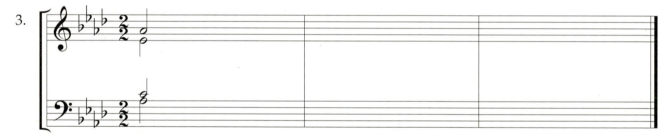

A♭: I

4.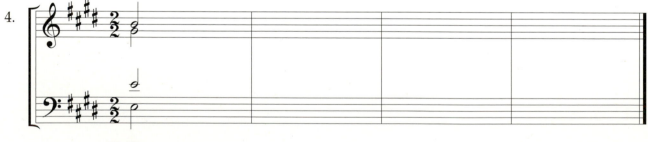

E: I

5.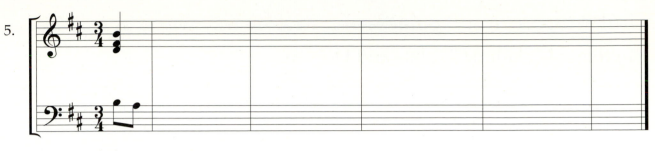

b:i

Unit 9

Rhythmic Dictation: Triplets and Duplets

This unit introduces triplets (in simple meters) and duplets (in compound meters). Listen to each exercise while counting or tapping the beat. Concentrate on those beats where divisions occur. Do you hear two or three notes of even value? Are the beats subdivided? Do you hear even groupings of fours or sixes? Or, do you hear a long-short group? Mentally count the values within the beat. The quarter-eighth note figure and the dotted eighth-sixteenth note figure are frequently confused or mistakenly transcribed. Listen carefully!

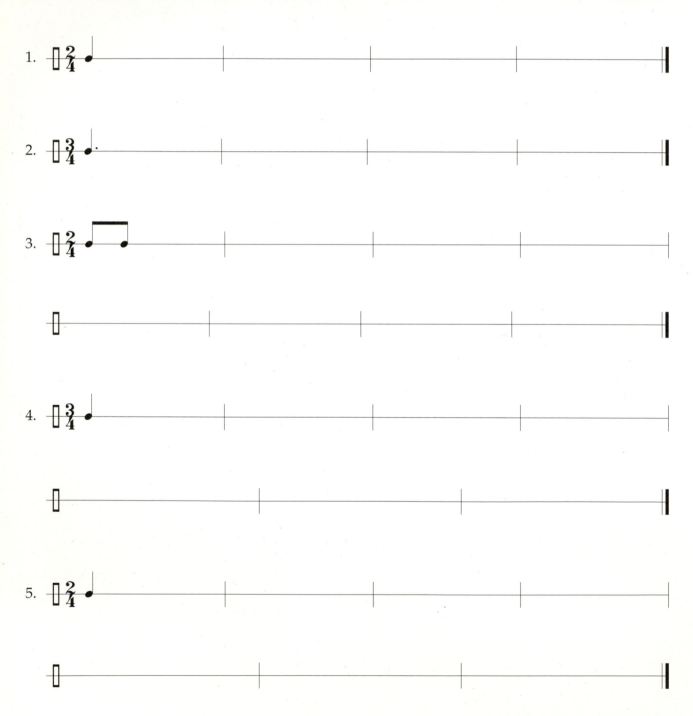

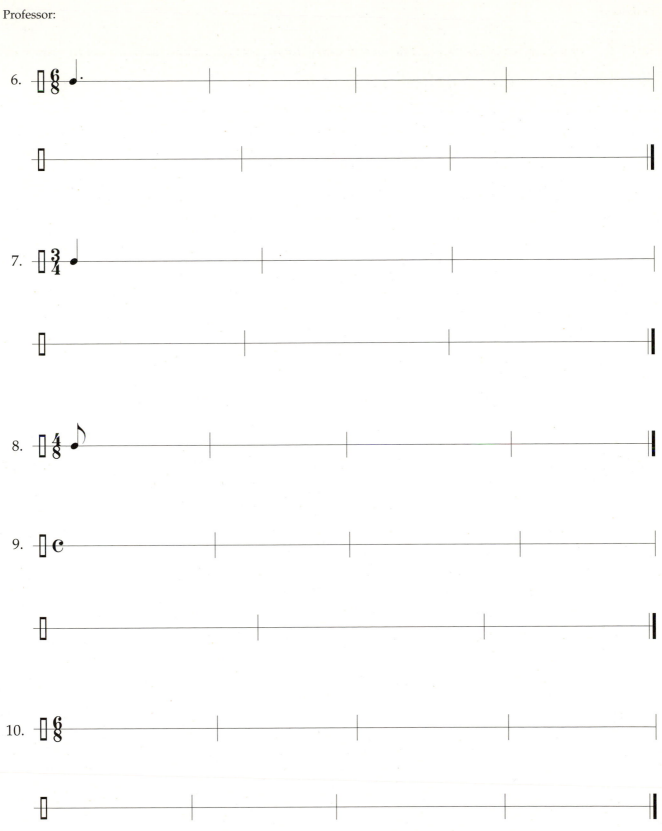

11.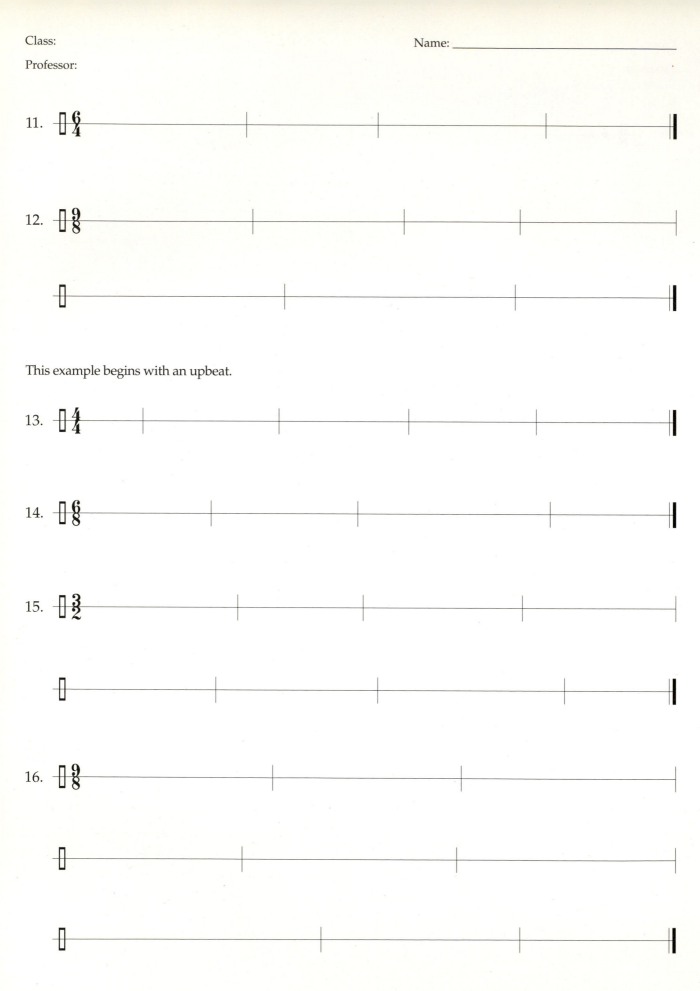

12.

This example begins with an upbeat.

13.

14.

15.

16.

Rhythmic Dictation: QUIZ NO. 1

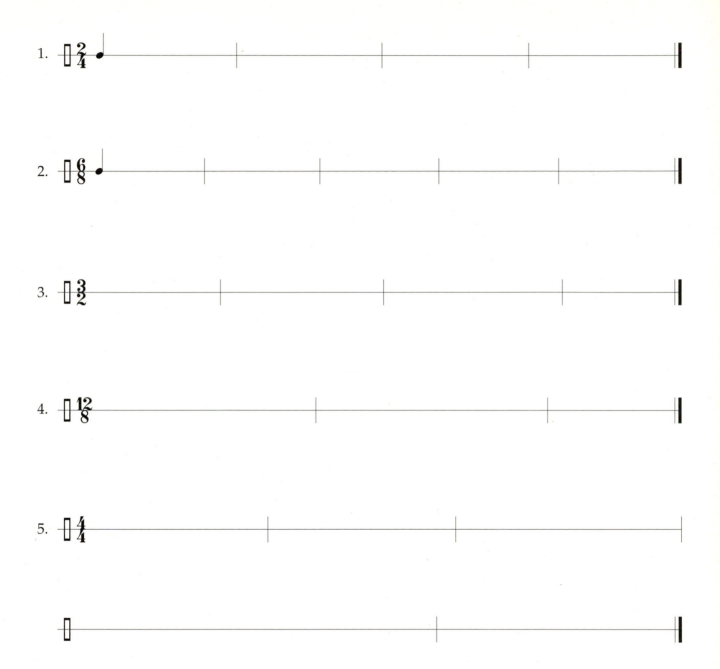

1. $\frac{2}{4}$

2. $\frac{6}{8}$

3. $\frac{3}{2}$

4. $\frac{12}{8}$

5. $\frac{4}{4}$

Rhythmic Dictation: QUIZ NO. 2

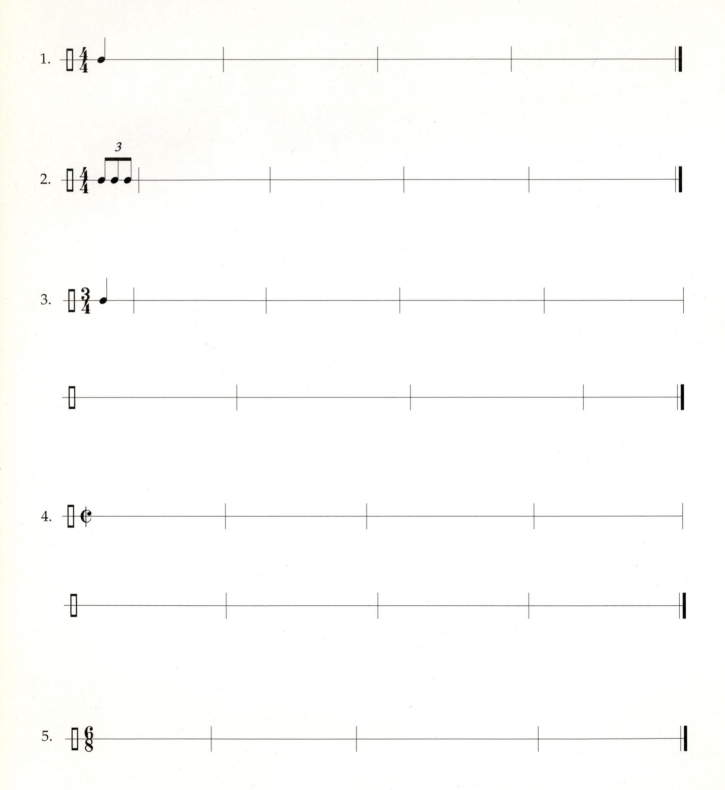

Rhythmic Dictation: QUIZ NO. 3

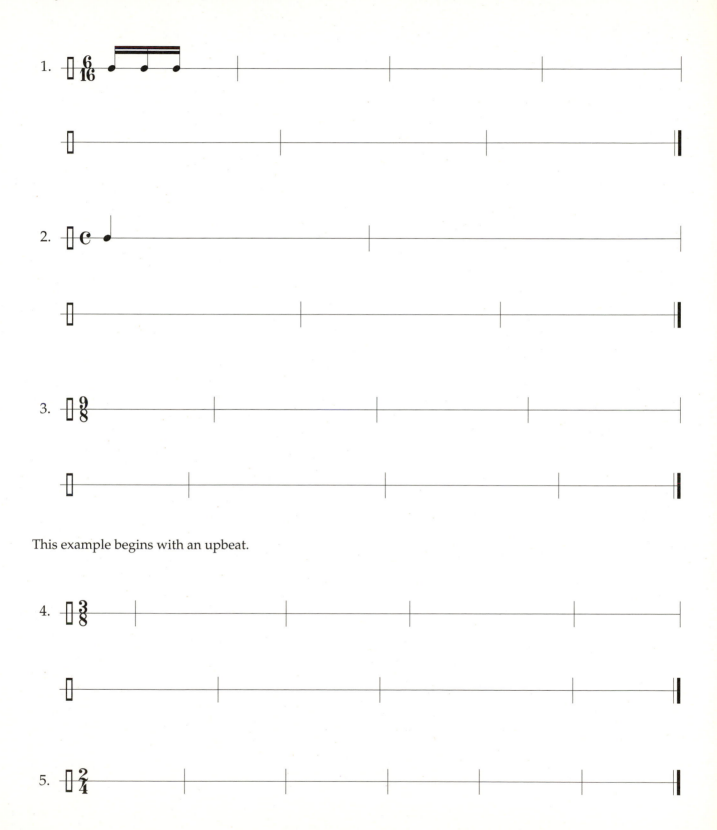

This example begins with an upbeat.

Melodic Dictation: Supertonic and Leading Tone Sevenths

Preliminary Exercises

Melodies

These melodies contain implications of ii7 (ii⌀7) and vii°7 (vii⌀7). As before, listen for arpeggiations. Do chord sevenths resolve as expected?

Teneramente

5.

Lento

6.

Cantabile

7.

Moderato

8.

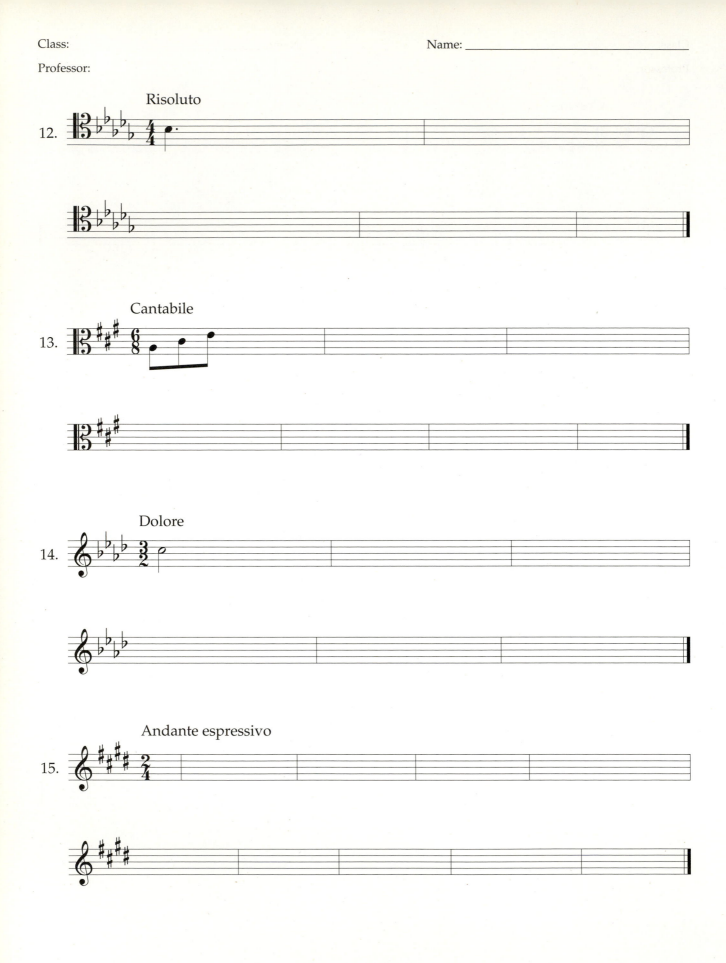

12. Risoluto

13. Cantabile

14. Dolore

15. Andante espressivo

16. Spiritoso

Melodic Dictation: QUIZ NO. 1

Gesangvoll

1.

Triumphantly

2.

Tempo di Siciliana

3.

Andante

4.

Andante espressivo

5.

Class: _____   Name: _____

Professor: _____

Melodic Dictation: QUIZ NO. 2

Maestoso

1.

Cantabile

2.

Allegretto

3.

Andantino

4.

Moderato

5.

Melodic Dictation: QUIZ NO. 3

Moderato

1.

Lively

2.

Con moto

3.

Cantabile

4.

Allegro piacevole

5.

Melodic Dictation: QUIZ NO. 4

1. Marziale

2. Moderato

3. Allegro non troppo

4. Comodo

Amoroso

5.

Class: _____

Name: _____

Professor: _____

Harmonic Dictation: Supertonic and Leading Tone Sevenths

Basic Progressions

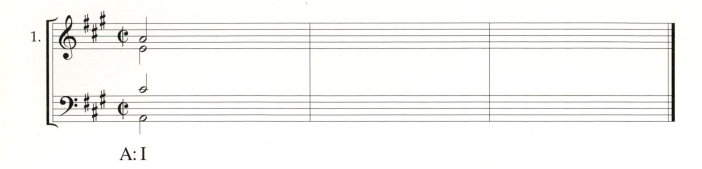

1.

A: I

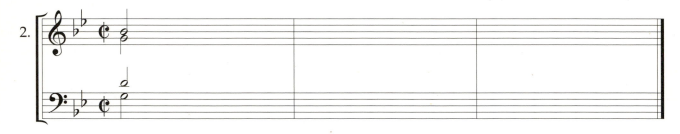

2.

g: i

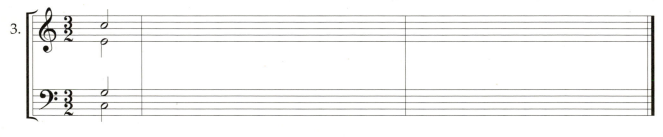

3.

C: I

4.

g♯: i

5.

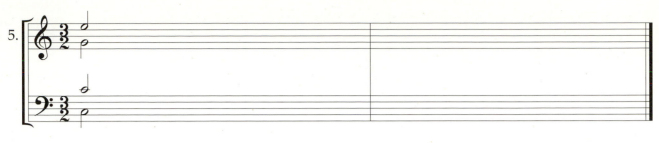

C: I

6.

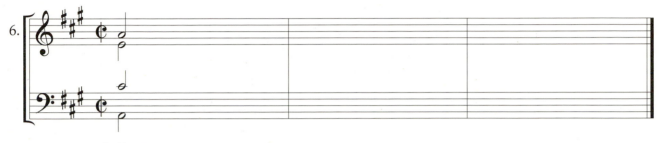

A: I

7.

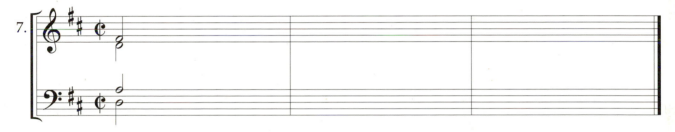

D: I

8.

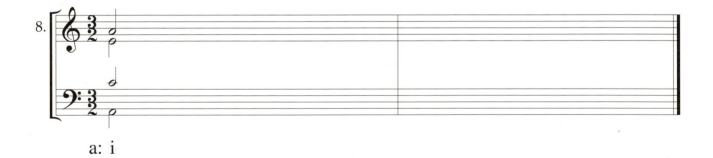

a: i

9.

c: i

10.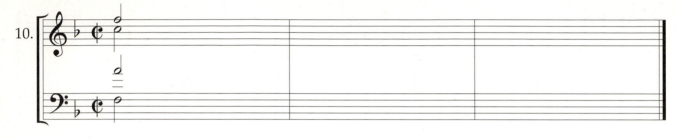

F: I

11.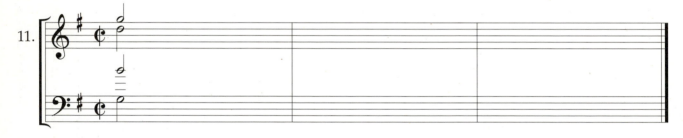

G: I

12.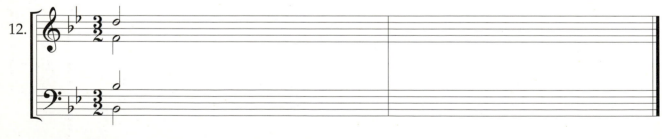

B♭: I

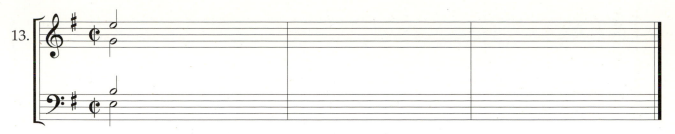

13. e: i

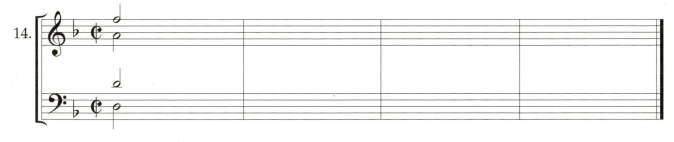

14. d: i

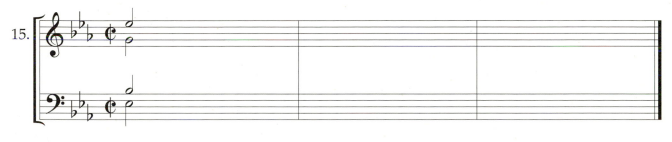

15. E♭: I

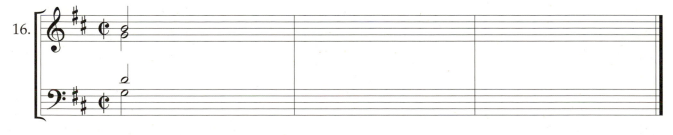

16. D: IV

17.

d: i

18.

c#: i

19.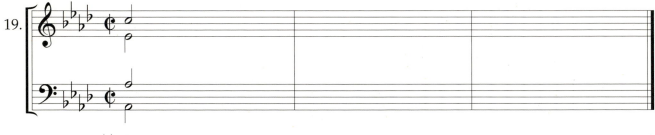

A♭: I

20.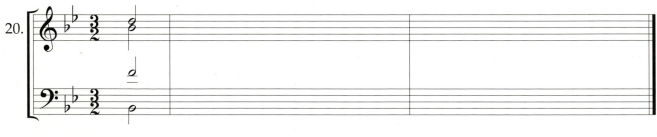

B♭: I

Phrase-Length Exercises

These exercises contain progressions using ii7 (ii⌀7) and vii°7 (vii⌀7). As before, listen for the type of cadence. Establish the cadential chords and work backwards. Review the most common progressions involving these chords.

1.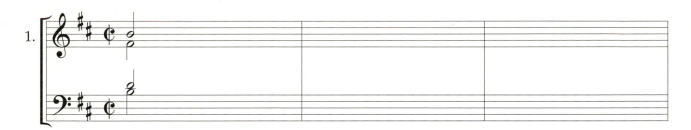

  b: i

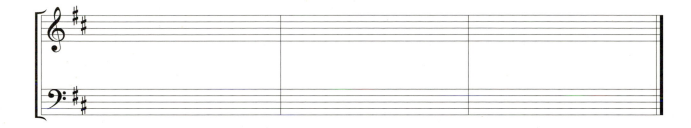

2.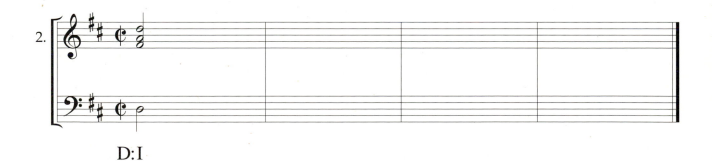

  D: I

3.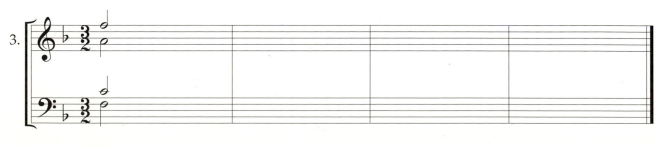

  F: I

4.

A: I

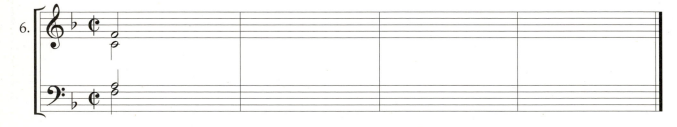

5.

b♭: i

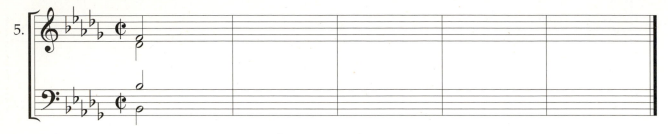

6.

F: I

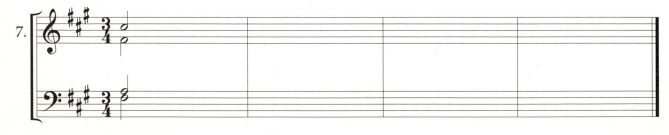

7.

f♯: i

8.

C: I

9.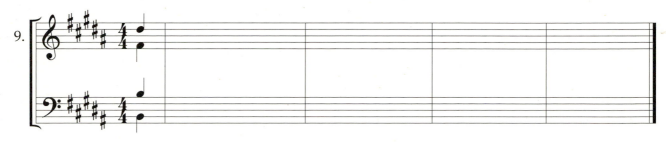

B: I

10.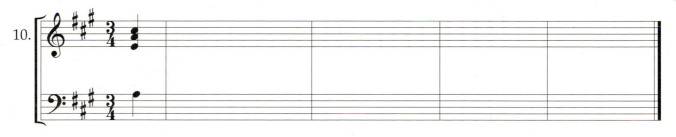

A: I

11.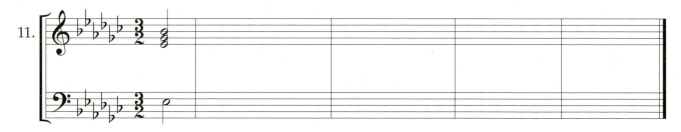

e♭: i

12.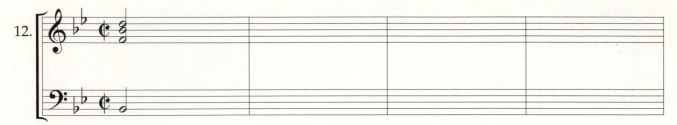

       B♭: I

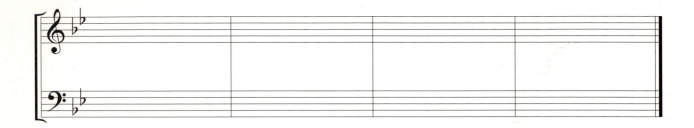

Class: _____

Name: _____

Professor: _____

Harmonic Dictation: QUIZ NO. 1

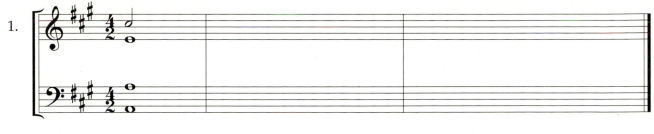

A: I

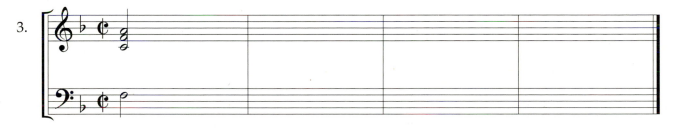

d: i

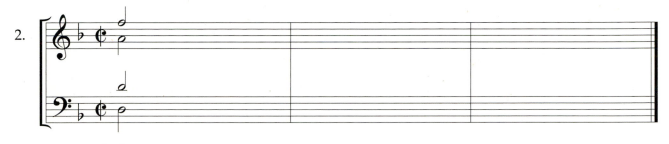

F: I

f: i

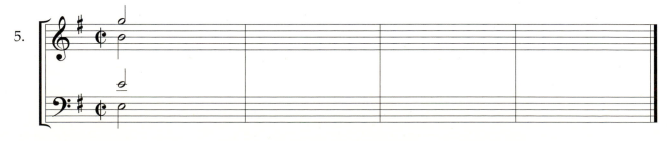

e: i

Harmonic Dictation: QUIZ NO. 2

1.

b: i

2.

B♭: I

3.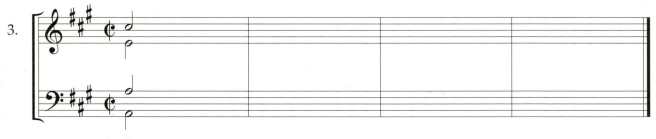

A: I

4.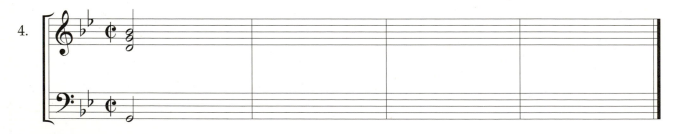

g: i

5.

E: I

Harmonic Dictation: QUIZ NO. 3

1.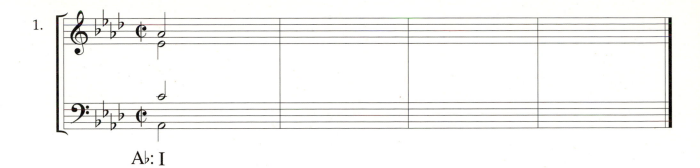

Ab: I

2.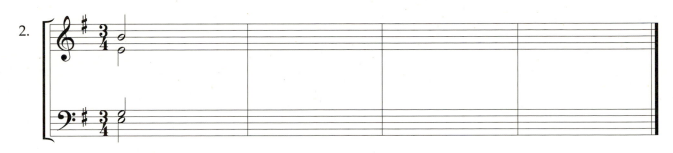

e: i

3.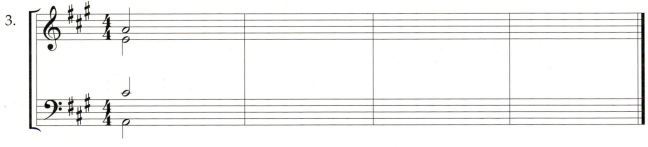

A: I

4.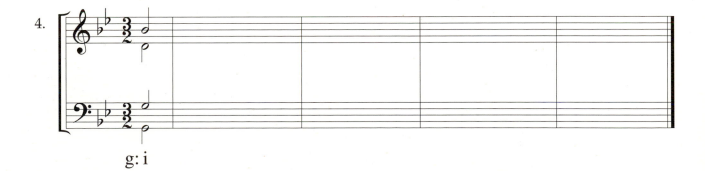

g: i

5.

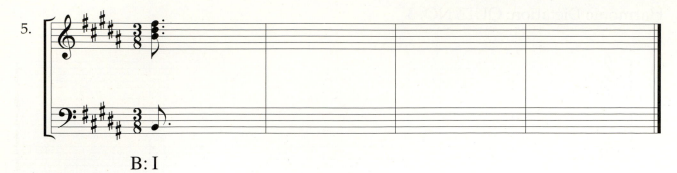

B: I

Harmonic Dictation: QUIZ NO. 4

1.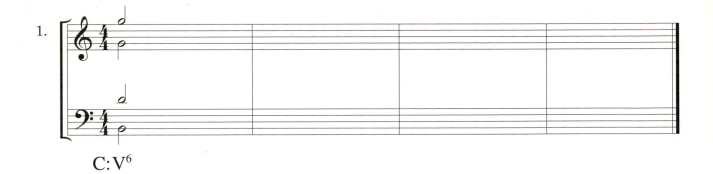

C: V^6

2.

c: vii°^{7}

3.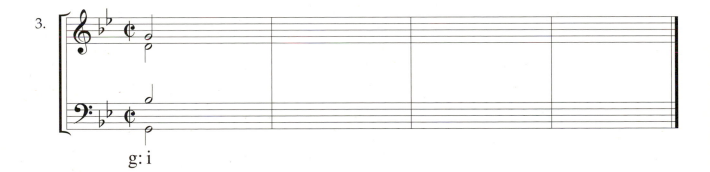

g: i

4.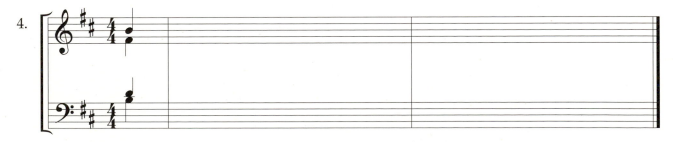

b: i

5.

G: I⁶

Unit 10

Examples from Music Literature

These exercises present actual musical examples for you to transcribe. At this point, you should be able to transcribe each excerpt completely. Listen to the example first. What is the texture? What kinds of cadences do you hear? Concentrate on individual lines and then listen harmonically. Isolate any unusual rhythmic patterns.

1. Johann Sebastian Bach. Minuet in G

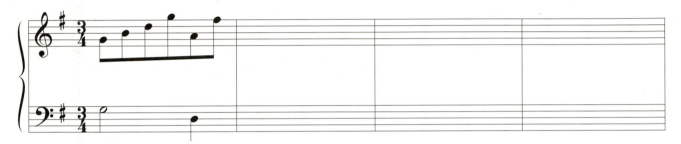

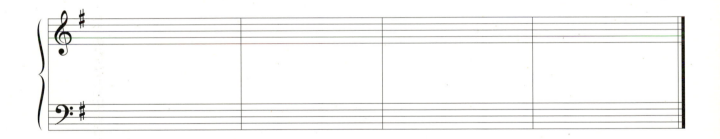

2. Johann Sebastian Bach. *Aus meines Herzens Grunde* (chorale)

3. Johann Sebastian Bach. *Wir glauben all' an einen Gott* (chorale)

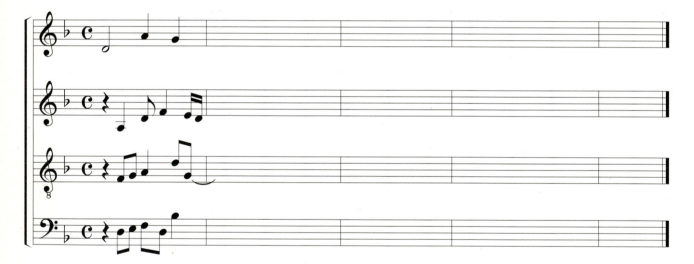

4. Ludwig van Beethoven. Six Variations on *Nel cor più non mi sento*

5. Friedrich Kuhlau. Sonatina Op. 88, No. 3, Mvt. III

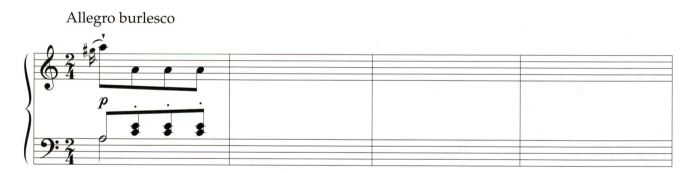

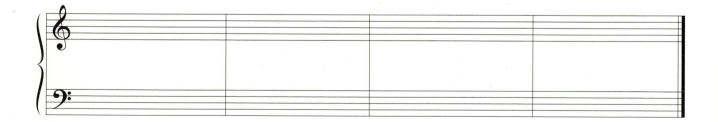

6. Wolfgang Amadeus Mozart. String Quintet, K. 581 Mvt. IV

Class:

Professor:

Name: _____

QUIZ NO. 1

Joseph Haydn. Sonata in D Major, Hob. XVI:33, Menuetto con Variazioni

Tempo di Menuetto

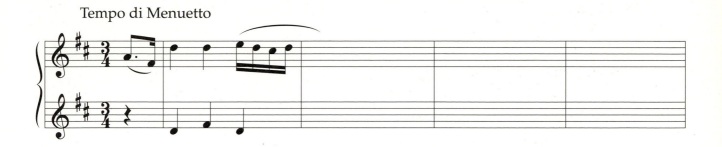

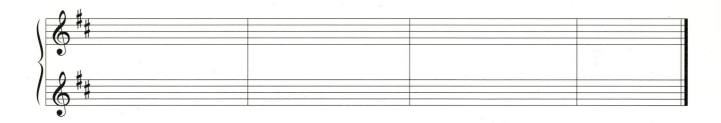

Name: _____

QUIZ NO. 2

John Farmer. *Fair Phyllis* (chorale)

Name: _____

QUIZ NO. 3

Wolfgang Amadeus Mozart. String Quartet, K. 80, Mvt. III, Trio

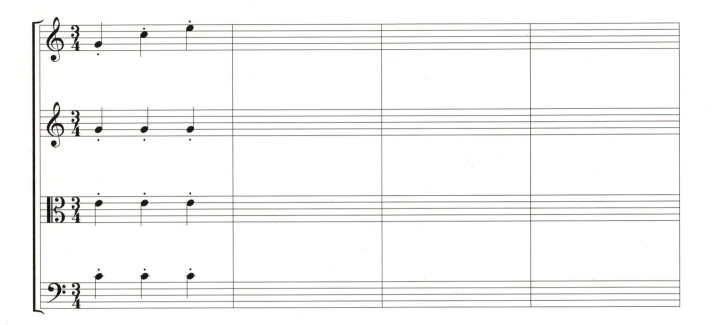

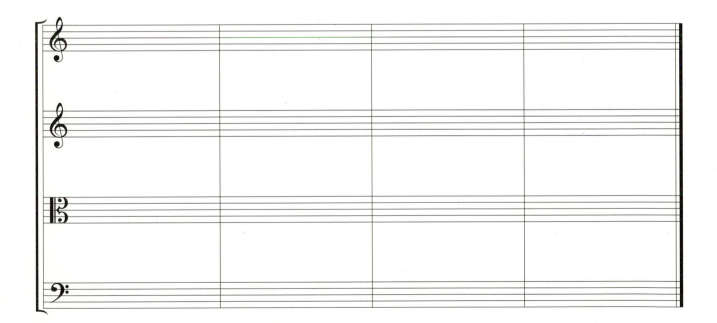

Unit 11

Rhythmic Dictation: Syncopation

This unit introduces syncopation, the displacement of the accent through the occurrence of longer notes on normally weak beats or parts of beats. As always, first listen to each exercise while counting or tapping the beat. Isolate those places where longer values fall off the beat or occur on weak beats. Does the syncopation occur at the beat level or at the division (or subdivision) level? After writing out your solution, check your work by singing along to spot any errors you may have made.

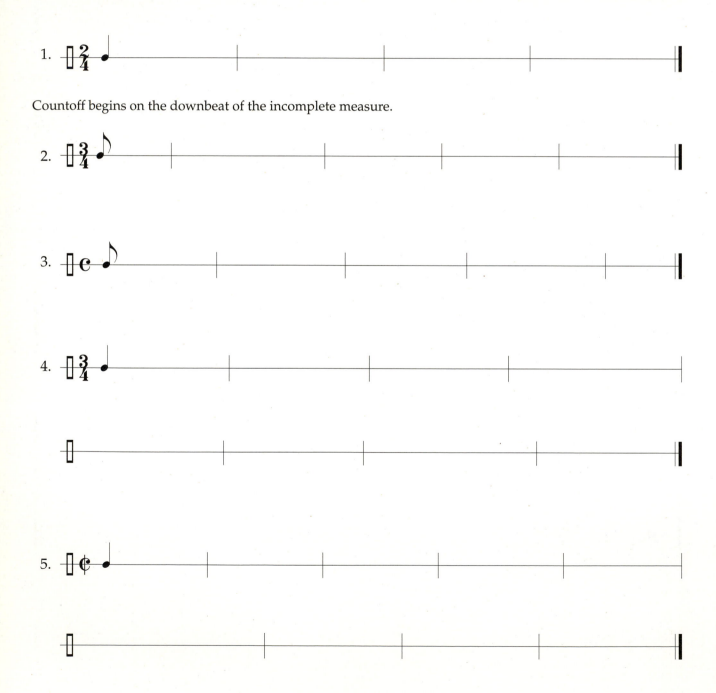

1.

Countoff begins on the downbeat of the incomplete measure.

2.

3.

4.

5.

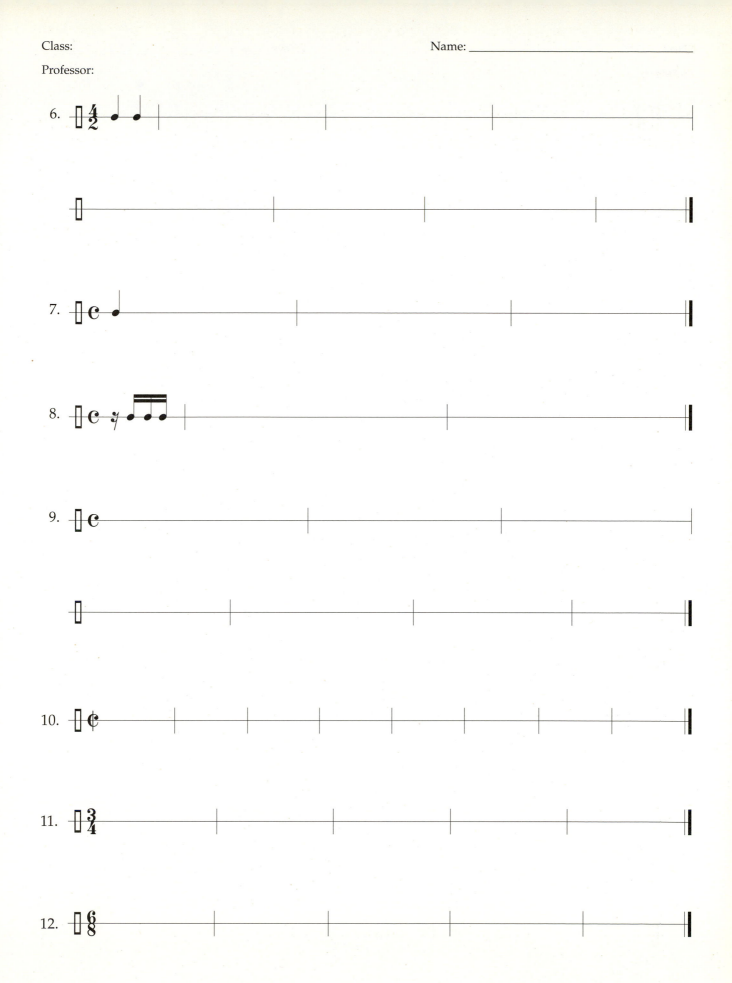

13.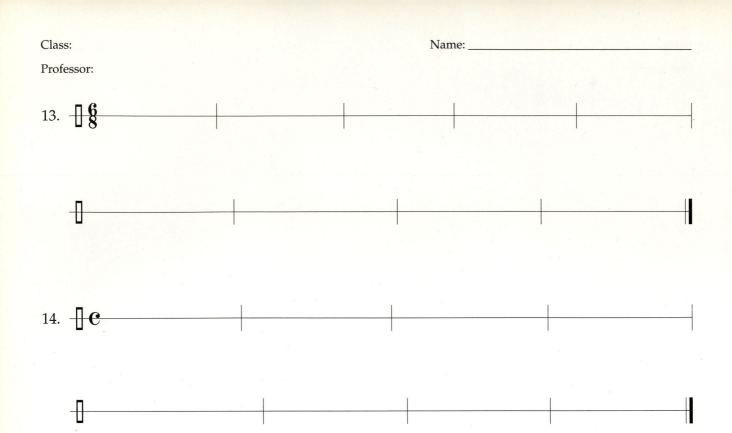

14.

Rhythmic Dictation: QUIZ NO. 1

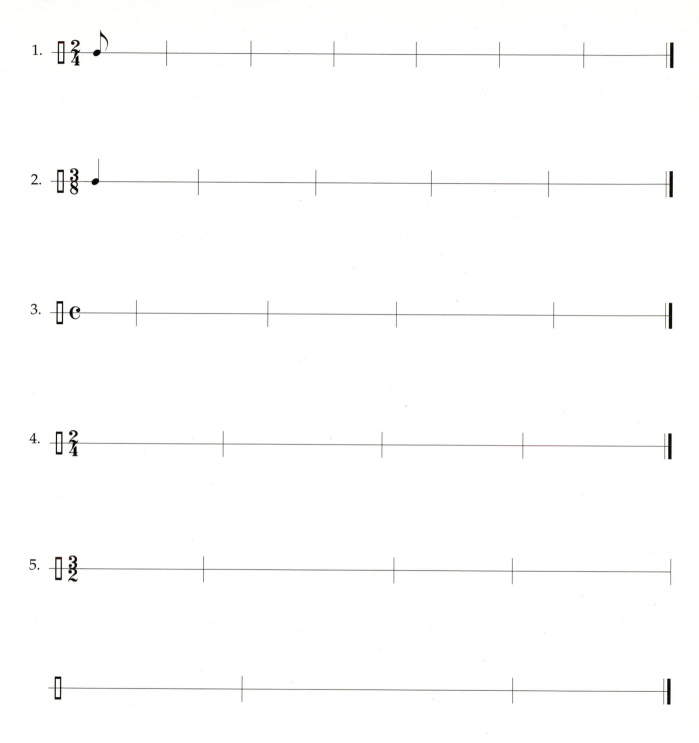

Rhythmic Dictation: QUIZ NO. 2

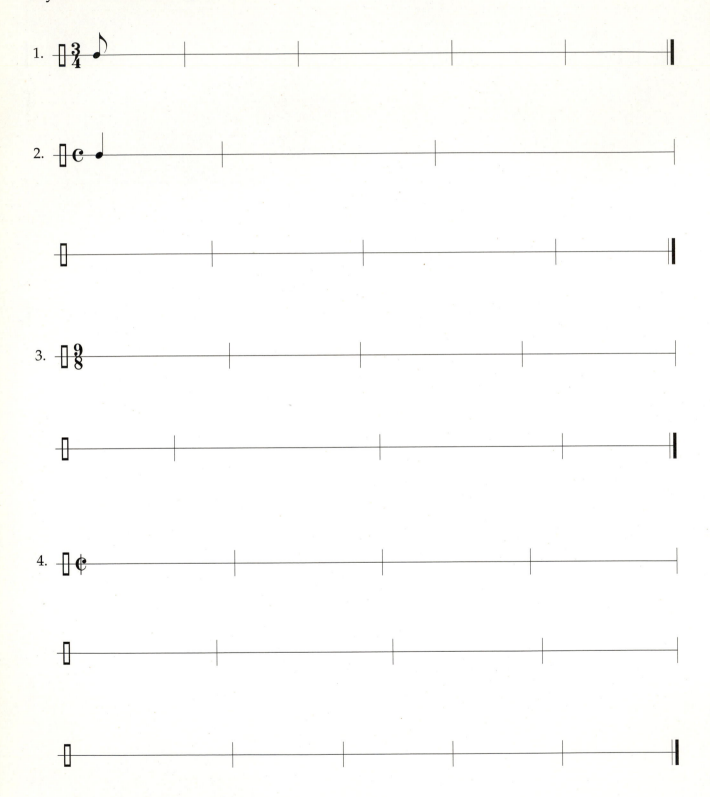

5.

Rhythmic Dictation: QUIZ NO. 3

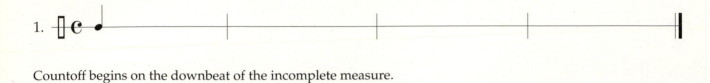

1.

Countoff begins on the downbeat of the incomplete measure.

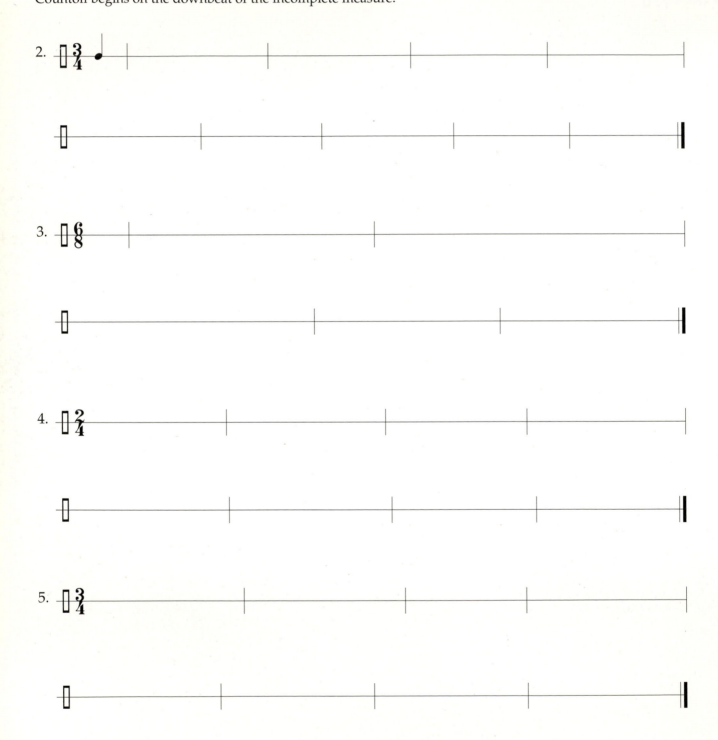

2.

3.

4.

5.

Melodic Dictation: Non-Dominant Seventh Chords

Preliminary Exercises

Melodies

After drilling on the preliminary exercises, listen for the implications of non-dominant seventh chords in these melodies. Where do arpeggiations of these seventh chords occur? Do you hear the resolution of the seventh? Sketch out the structural line formed by the chord seventh moving to the note of resolution. Do you hear sequence? What is the underlying progression? Try adding Roman numeral analysis.

Marziale

5.

Cantabile

6.

Grazioso

7.

Con brio

8.

Melodic Dictation: QUIZ NO. 1

1. Raggy

2. Sospirando

3. Grazioso

4. Andantino

5. Moderato

Melodic Dictation: QUIZ NO. 2

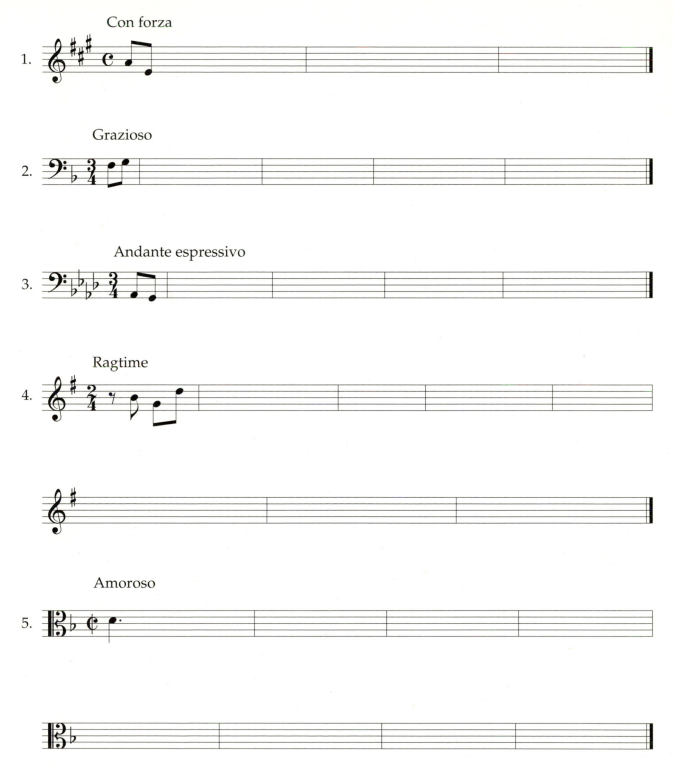

Melodic Dictation: QUIZ NO. 3

1. Cantabile

2. Sea Shanty

3. Energico

4. Largo

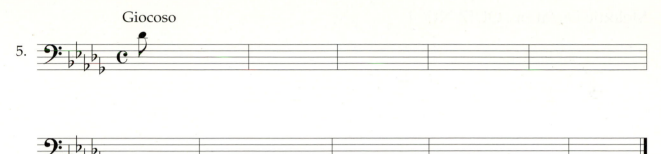

Melodic Dictation: QUIZ NO. 4

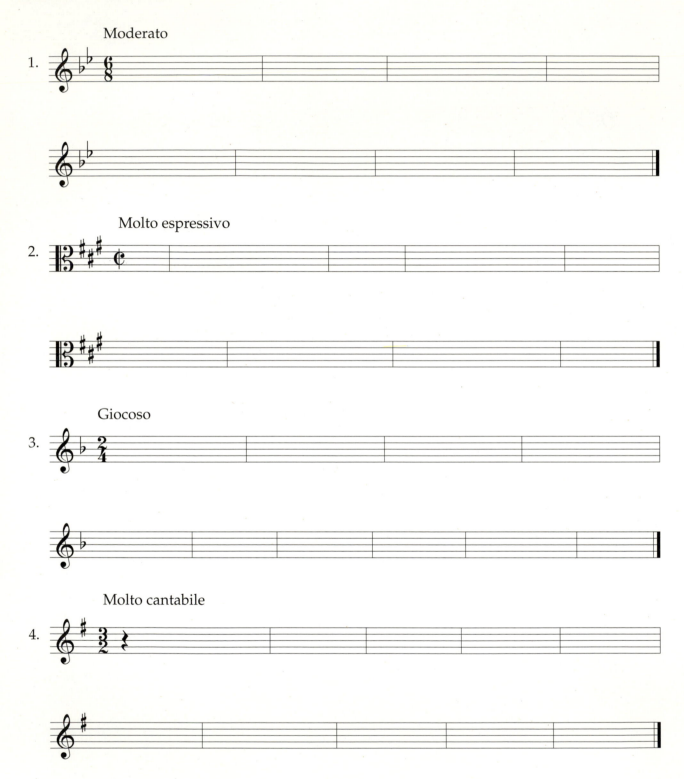

Moderato

1.

Molto espressivo

2.

Giocoso

3.

Molto cantabile

4.

Habanera

5.

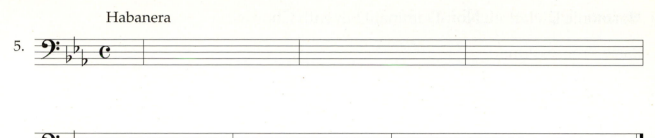

Harmonic Dictation: Non-Dominant Seventh Chords

Basic Progressions

1.

  E♭: I

2.
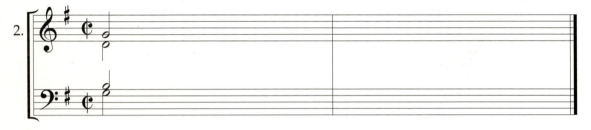

  G: I

3.

  a: i

4.

  f: i

5.

B: I

6.

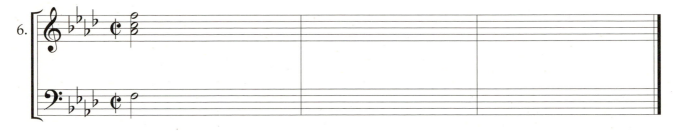

f: i

7.

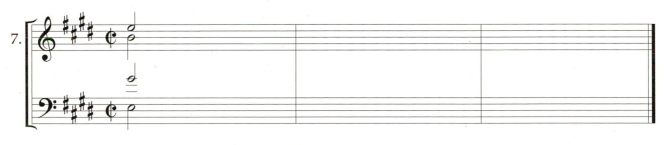

E: I

8.

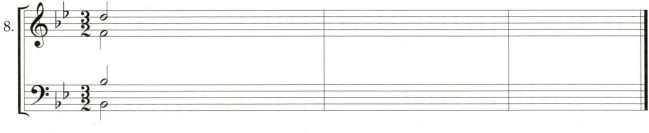

B♭: I

9.

D: I

10.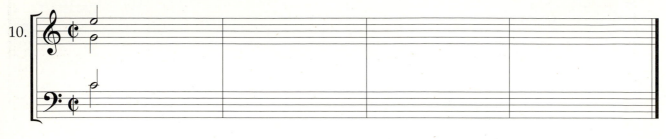

C: I

Phrase-Length Exercises

> Focus on the occurrence of seventh chords. In which voice is the seventh? Does it resolve normally? Concentrate as always on the outer voices.

1.

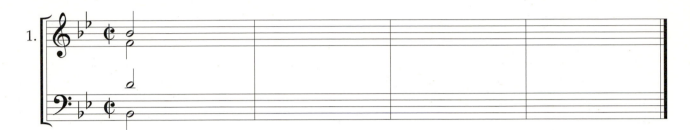

Bb: I

2.

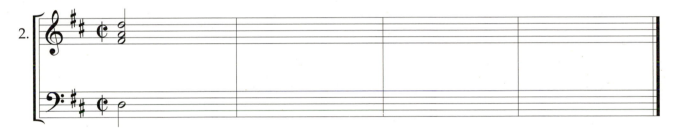

D: I

3.

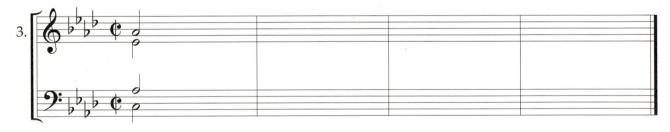

Ab: I⁶

4.

A: I

5.

b: i

6.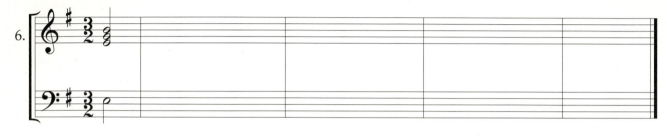

e: i

7.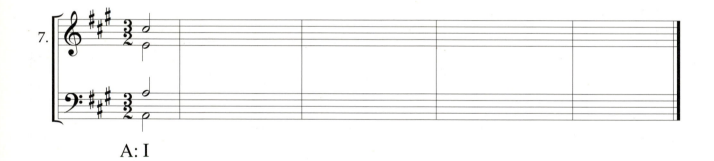

A: I

8.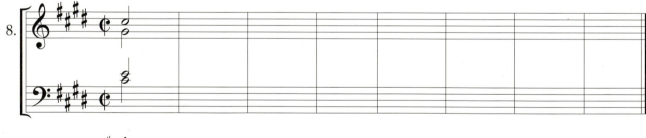

c#: i

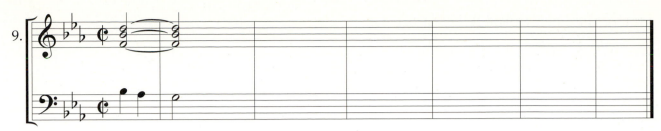

9.

Eb: V   iii⁷

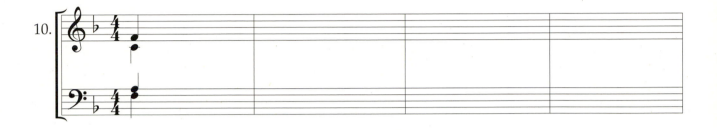

10.

F: I

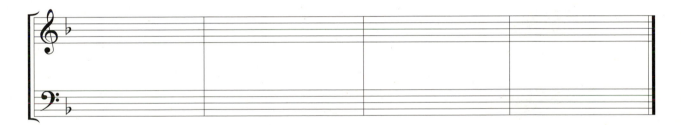

Harmonic Dictation: QUIZ NO. 1

1.

     B: I

2.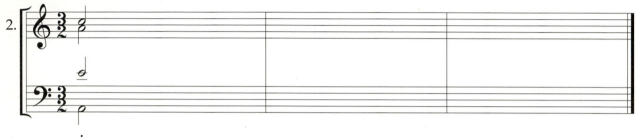

     a: i

3.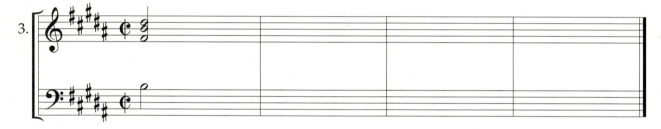

     B: I

4.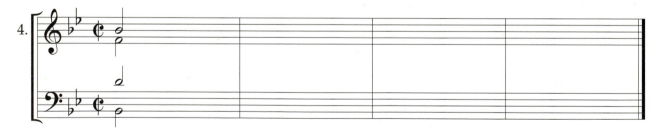

     B♭: I

5.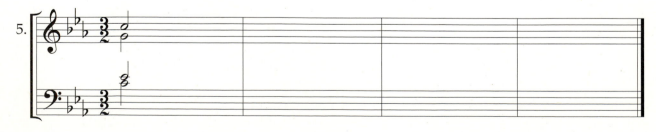

     c: i

Harmonic Dictation: QUIZ NO. 2

1.
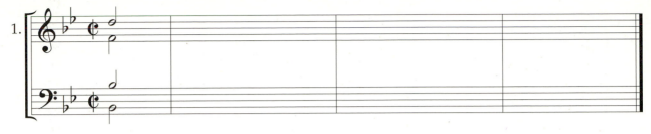

B♭: I

2.
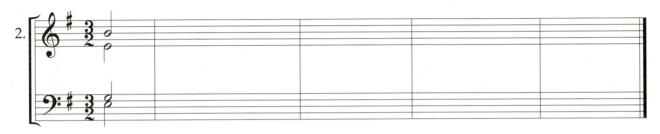

e: i

3.
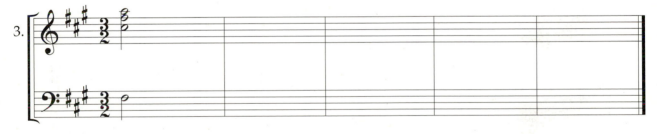

f♯: i

4.
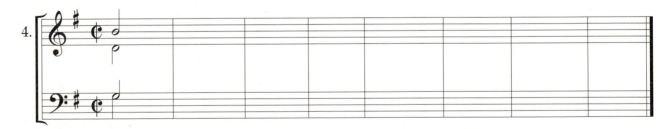

G: I

5.
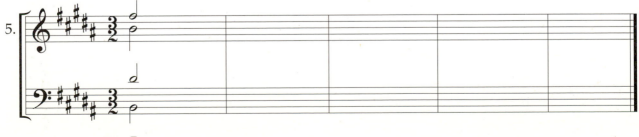

B: I

Name: _____

Harmonic Dictation: QUIZ NO. 3

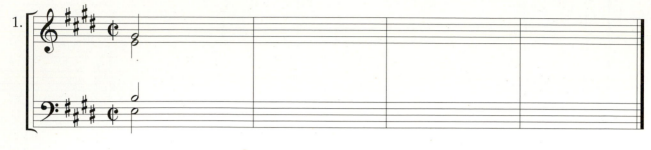

1.

E: I

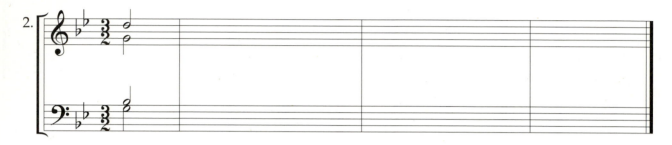

2.

g: i

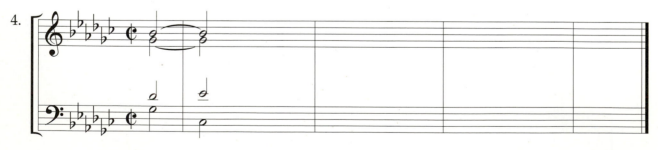

3.

e: V^7 VI^7

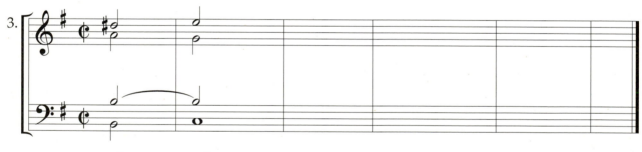

4.

G♭: I   IV^7

5.

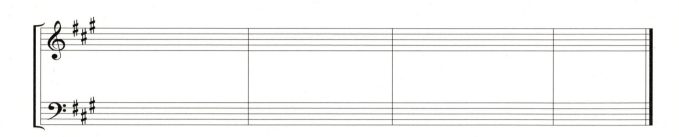

A: I

Harmonic Dictation: QUIZ NO. 4

1.

g: i⁶

2.

A: I

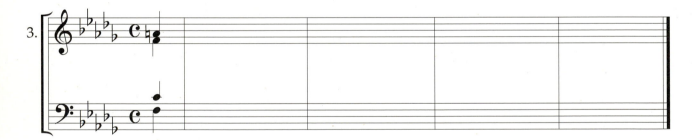

3.

b♭: V♮

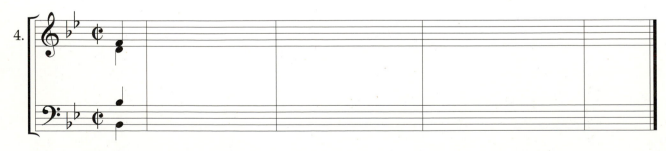

4.

B♭: I

5.

c#: i

Unit 12

Melodic Dictation: Scalar Variants, Modal Borrowing, Decorative Chromaticism

This unit introduces chromatic pitches. *Scalar variants* derive from alterations to the sixth and seventh scale degrees found in the melodic minor scale. *Modal borrowing* involves mixtures of major and minor modal inflection. *Decorative chromaticism* occurs in melodies ornamented with chromatic neighbor or passing tones. After first practicing the Preliminary Exercises, proceed to the melodies. What is the mode? Does the mode change? Where do you hear altered scale degrees or notes not found in the diatonic scale? Sing the scale first to establish a point of reference. Listen for the shape and direction of the line. Do chromatic pitches occur as neighbors or as passing tones?

Preliminary Exercises

Scalar variants

6.

7.

8.

Modal borrowing

9.

10.

11.

12.

13.

14.

15.

16.

Decorative chromaticism

17.

18.

24.

25.

26.

Class:

Professor:

Name: _____

Melodies

Cantabile

1.

Andante

2.

Doloroso

3.

Amoroso

4.

Grazioso

5.

Andantino

6.

Deliberamente

7.

Con moto

8.

Gioviale

9.

Moderato

10.

Professor:

16. Espressivo

17. Andantino

18. A la marcia

19. Andante moderato

20. Allegretto

Class:

Name: _____

Professor:

Melodic Dictation: QUIZ NO. 1

Melodic Dictation: QUIZ NO. 2

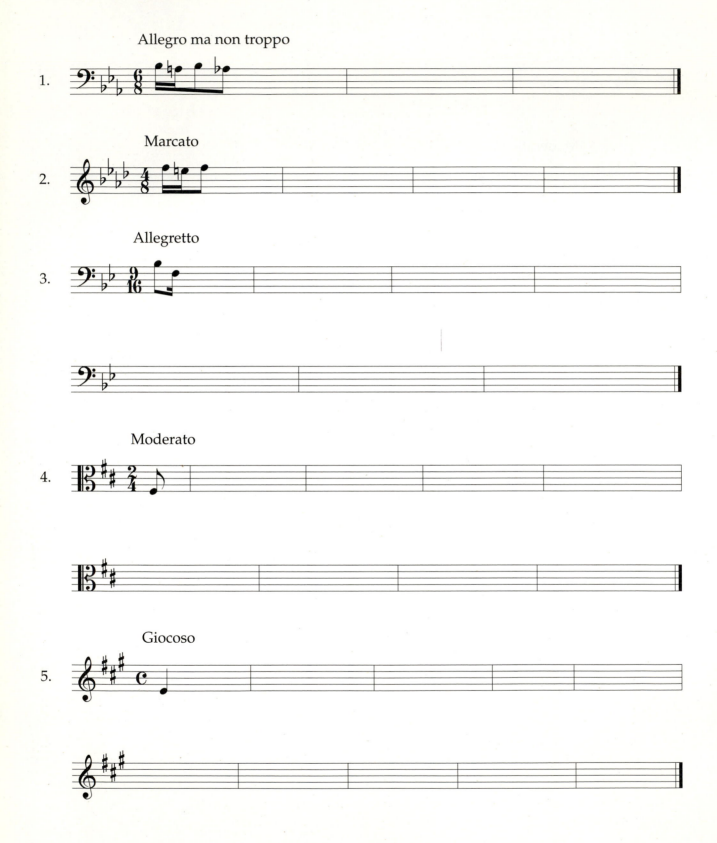

Melodic Dictation: QUIZ NO. 3

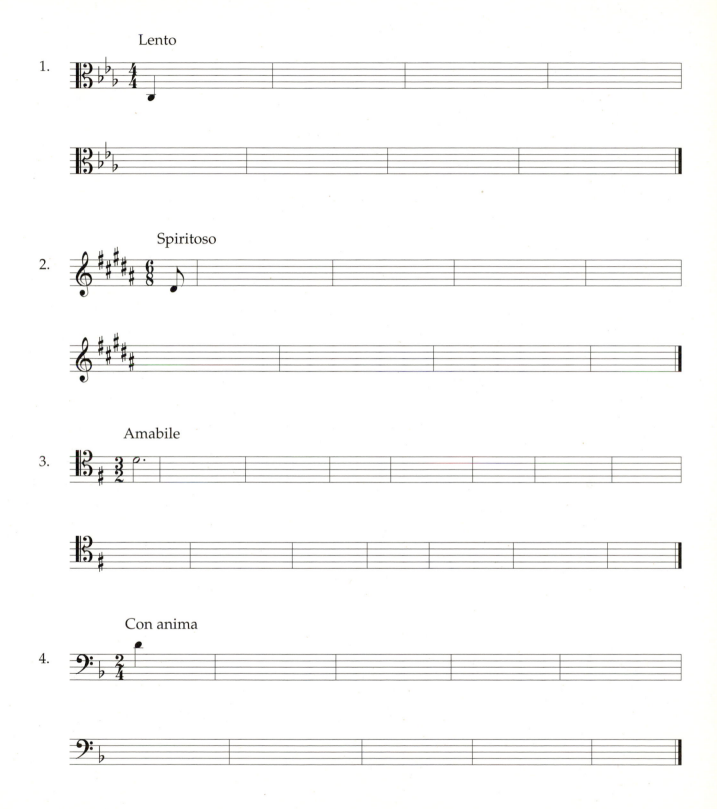

1. Lento

2. Spiritoso

3. Amabile

4. Con anima

Con amore

5.

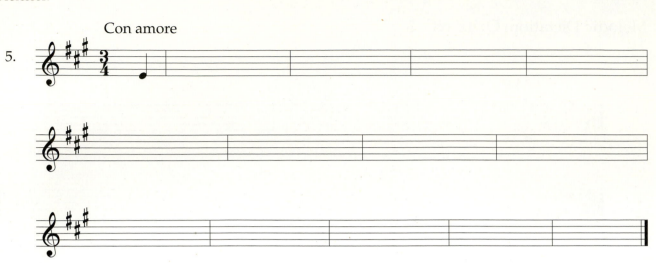

Melodic Dictation: QUIZ NO. 4

1. Allegretto

2. Pesante

3. Flowing

4. Marziale

5. Amabile

Harmonic Dictation: Scalar Variants, Modal Borrowing

The harmonic possibilities that arise through altered scale degrees in the minor mode (scalar variants) and borrowed inflections of the minor mode while in a major key (modal borrowing) are explored here. Once you feel confident with the basic progressions found in the Preliminary Exercises, proceed to the Phrase-length Exercises. Where do you hear altered chords? To which chord do they resolve? How do the tendency tones resolve? What kind of cadence do you hear? Establish the cadential chords and work backwards. As always, focus on the outer voices and then fill in the inner voices.

Basic Progressions

Scalar variants

d: i

f♯: i

f: i

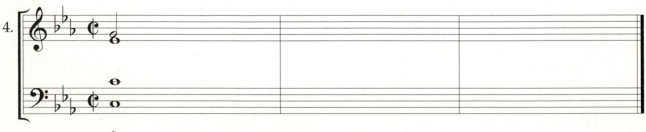

c: i

5.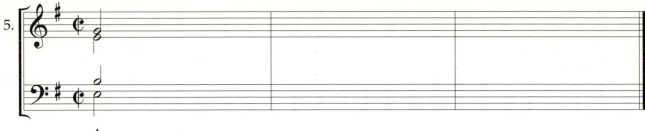

e: i

6.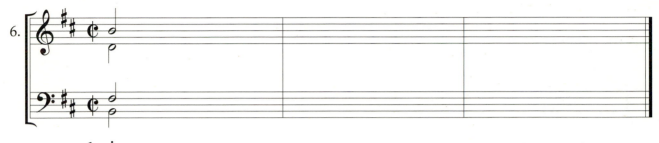

b: i

7.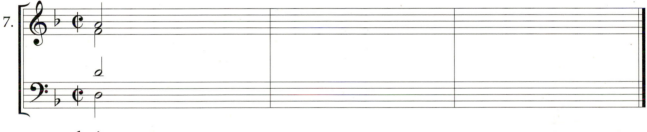

d: i

8.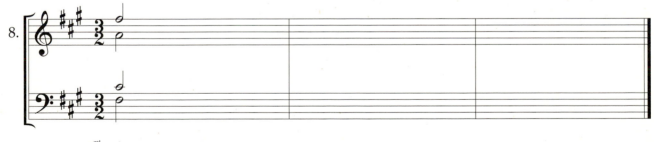

f♯: i

9.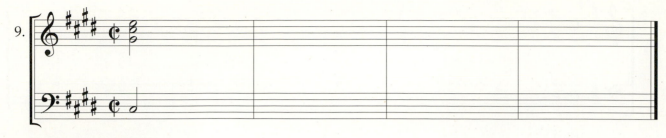

    c#: i

10.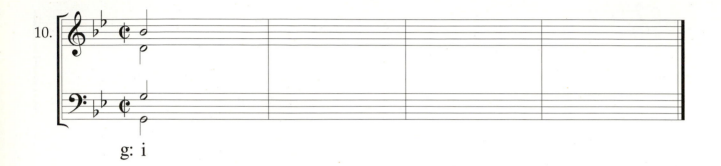

    g: i

Modal borrowing

11.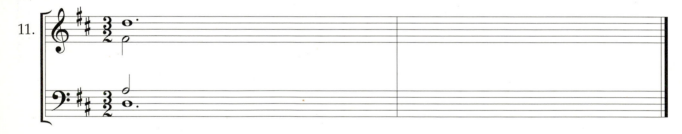

    D: I

12.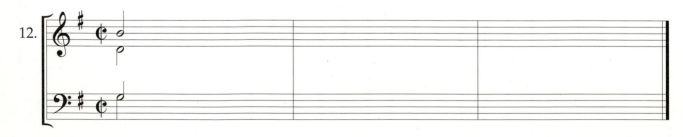

    G: I

13.
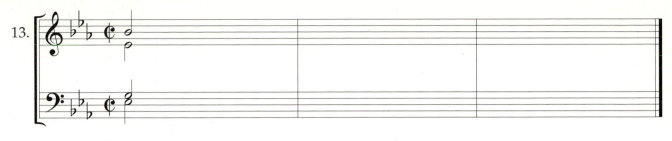

E♭: I

14.
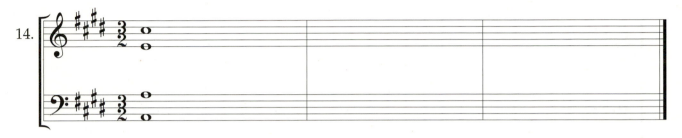

E: IV

15.
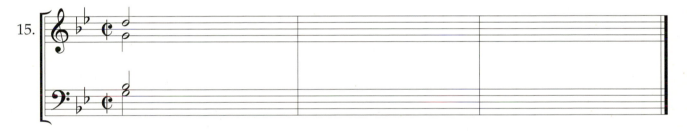

g: i

16.
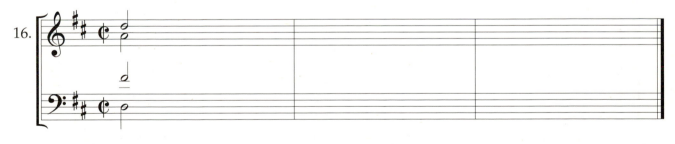

D: I

17.

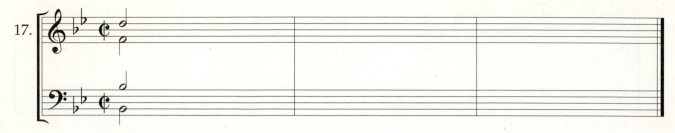

B♭: I

18.

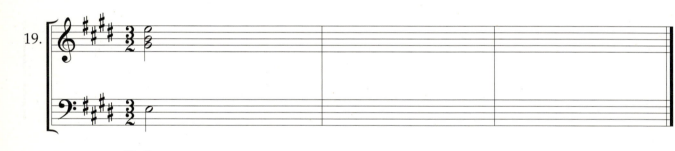

A: I

19.

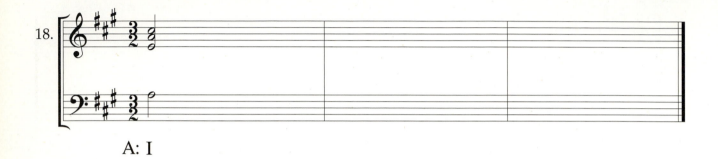

E: I

20.

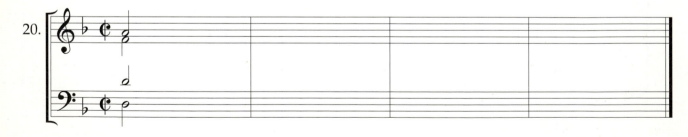

d: i

Phrase-Length Exercises

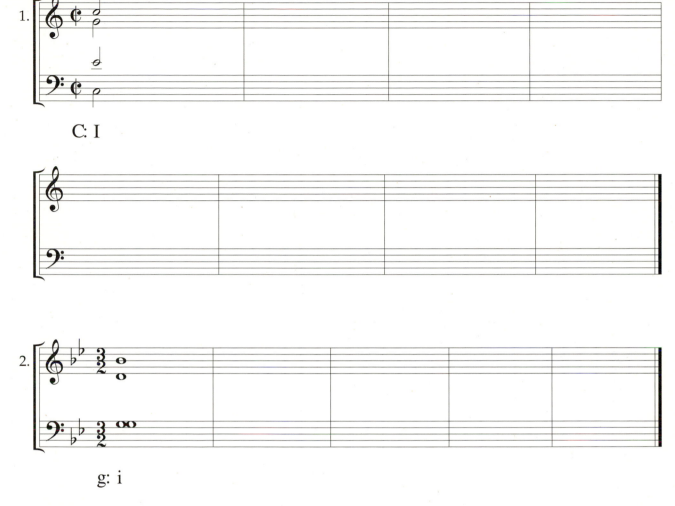

1.

C: I

2.

g: i

3.

D: I

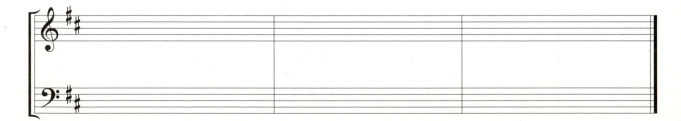

Class: _____

Name: _____

Professor: _____

d: V#

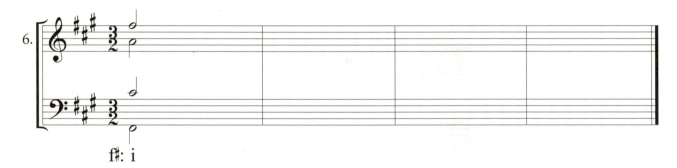

G: I

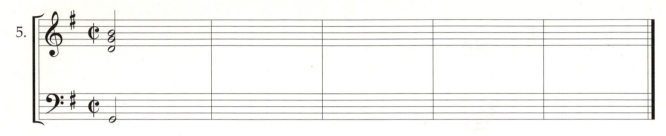

f#: i

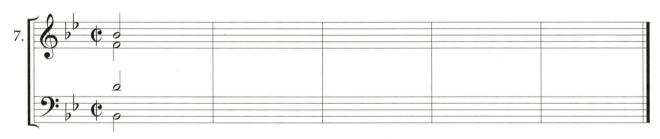

Bb: I

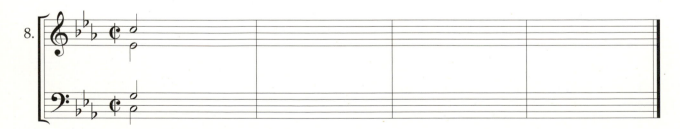

c: i

9.

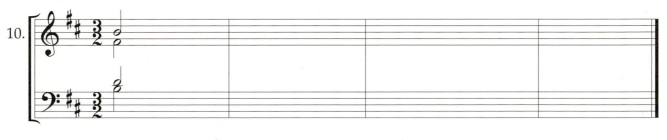

F: I

10.

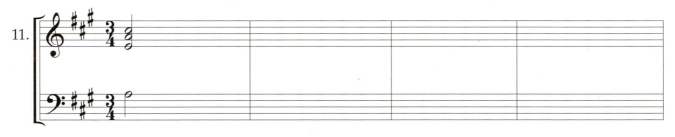

b: i

11.

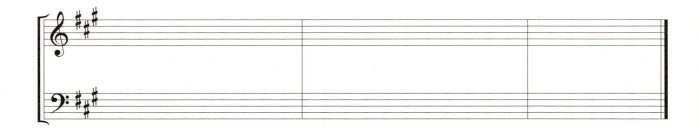

A: I

12.

    E: I

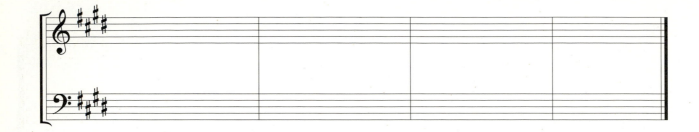

13.

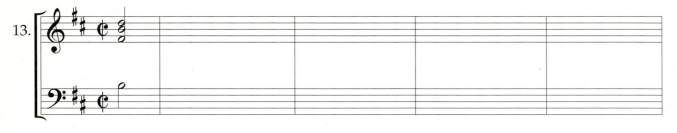

    b: i

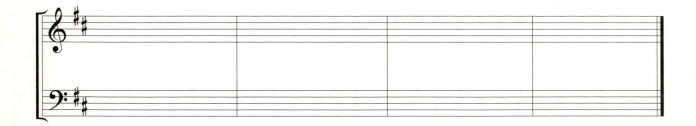

Name: _____

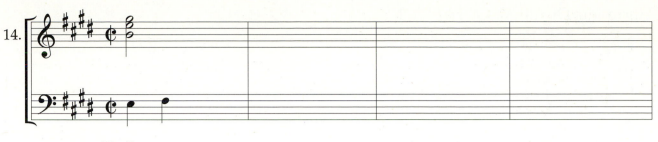

14.

E: I

Class: _____

Name: _____

Professor: _____

Harmonic Dictation: QUIZ NO. 1

1.

       E♭: I

2.

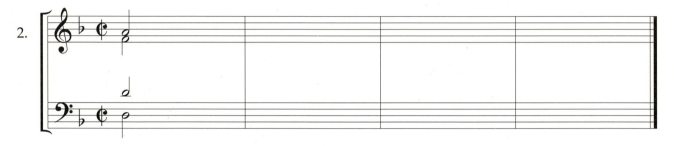

       d: i

3.

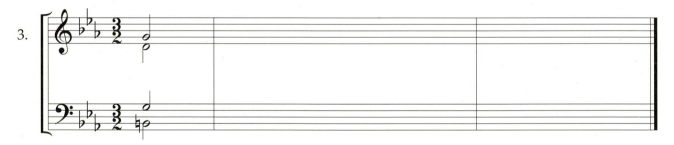

       c: V⁶

4.

       e: i ___

5.

A: I

Harmonic Dictation: QUIZ NO. 2

1.

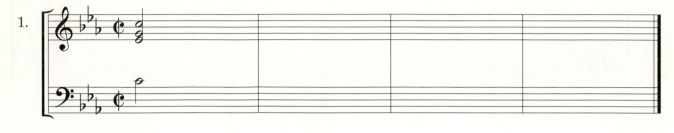

c: i

2.

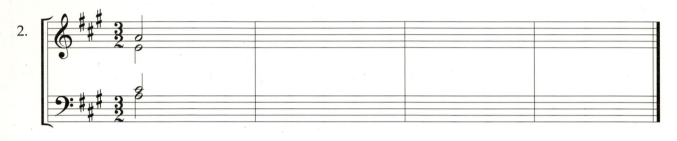

A: I

3.

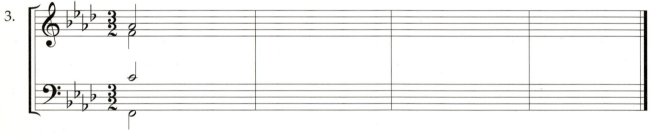

f: i

4.

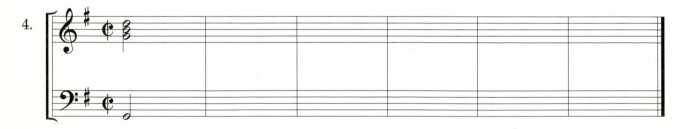

G: I

5.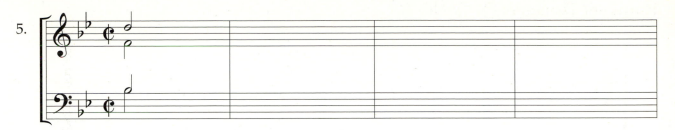

B♭: I

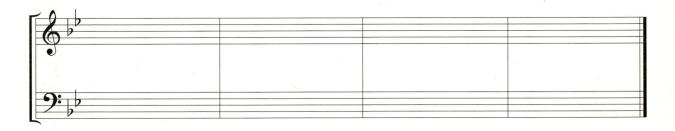

Class: _____ Name: _____

Professor: _____

Harmonic Dictation: QUIZ NO. 3

1.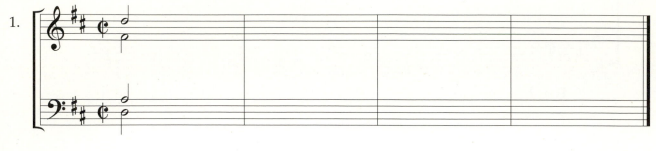

D: I

2.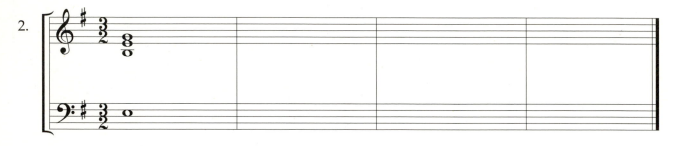

e: i

3.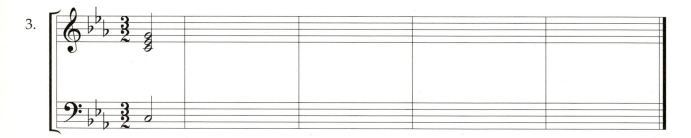

c: i

4.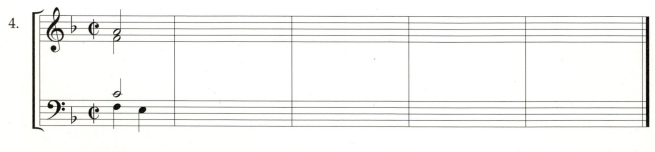

F: I

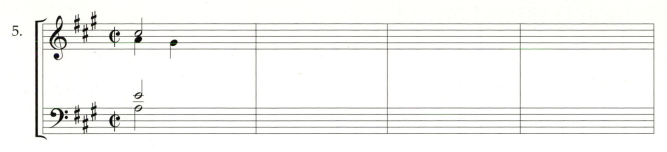

A:I

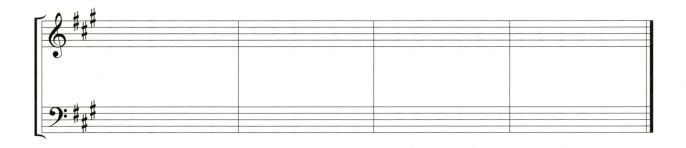

Harmonic Dictation: QUIZ NO. 4

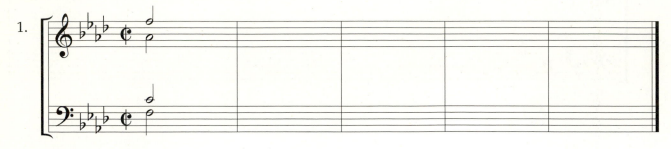

f: i

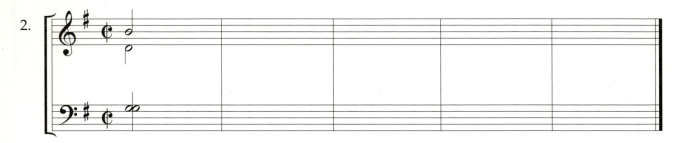

G:I

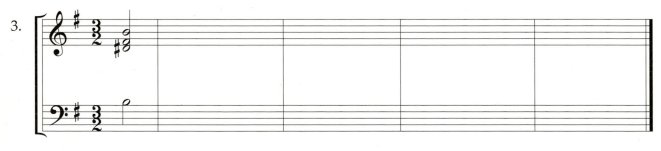

e: V♯

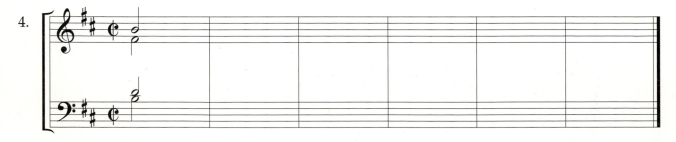

b: i

5.

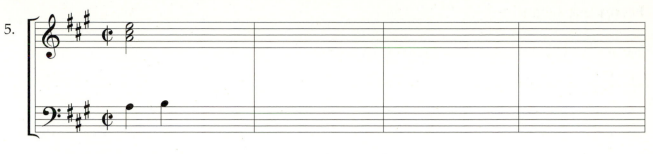

A: I

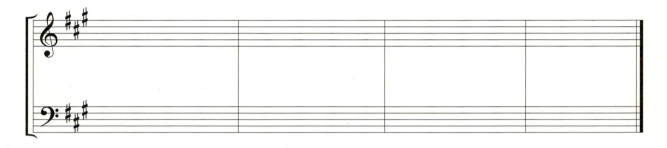

Unit 13

Melodic Dictation: Secondary Dominants

For examples of secondary dominant chords in pieces by Bach, Haydn, Chopin, and others, see Unit 14.

Preliminary Exercises

8.

9.

10.

Melodies

This unit requires an understanding of secondary dominant chords. Any major or minor triad may be preceded by its own dominant. Drill on the Preliminary Exercises first to familiarize yourself with the most common progressions. Then, listen to each melody, concentrating on occurrences of chromaticism. Listen for those altered pitches that sound like leading tones. Which scale degrees are being altered? Listen for the partial chromatic scales formed by the structural pitches. You will find it helpful to do a preliminary Roman numeral analysis.

9. Andantino

10. Allegro ma non troppo

11. Gigue

12. Siciliano

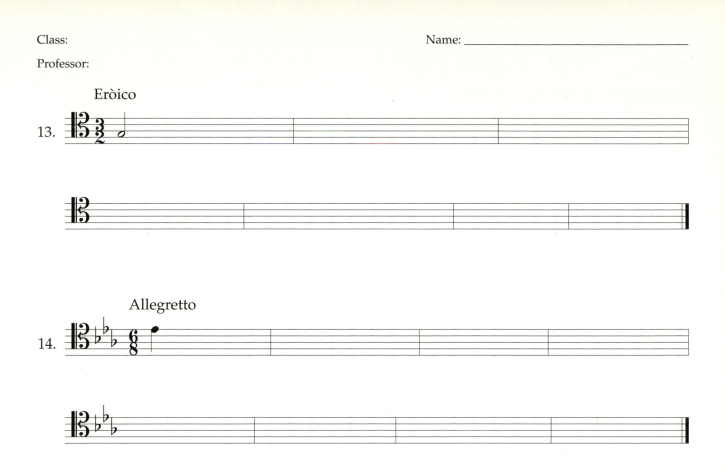

Melodic Dictation: QUIZ NO. 1

Class:

Name: _____

Professor:

Melodic Dictation: QUIZ NO. 2

1. Comodo

2. Deliberamente

3. Cantabile

4. Adagietto

Moderato

Name: _____

Melodic Dictation: QUIZ NO. 3

Giocoso

5.

Class: _____

Name: _____

Professor: _____

Harmonic Dictation: Secondary Dominants

Basic Progressions

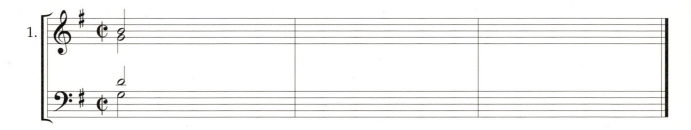

G: I

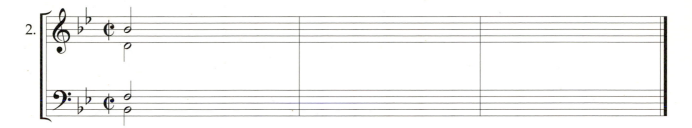

B♭: I

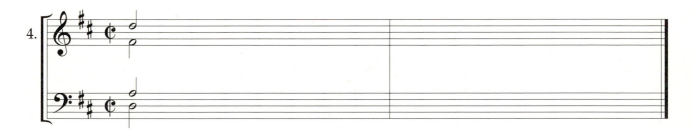

c: i

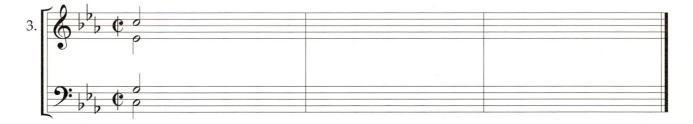

D: I

5.

f: i

6.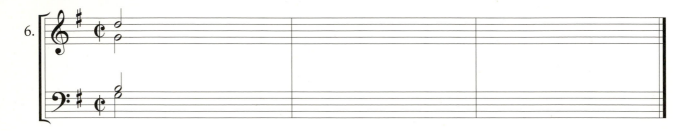

G: I

7.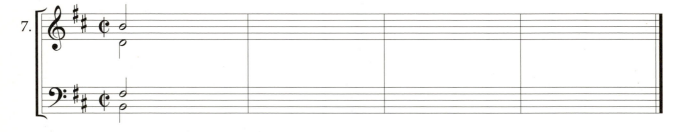

b: i

8.

E♭: I

9.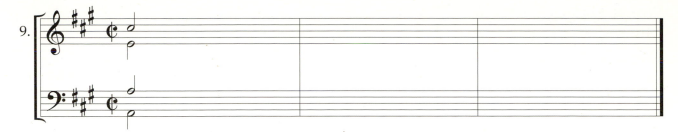

A: I

10.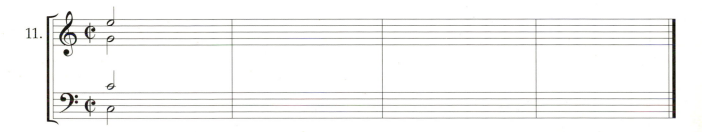

F: I

11.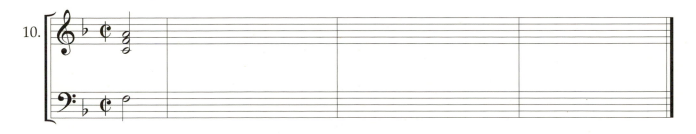

C: I

12.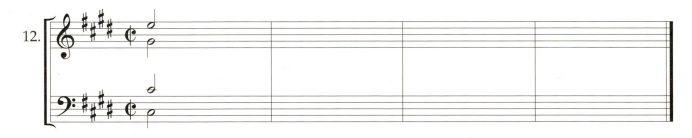

c#: i

Phrase-Length Exercises

After you familiarize yourself with the most common secondary dominant progressions in the Preliminary Exercises, listen to each phrase-length exercise. Where do you hear secondary dominants? To which chord do they resolve? Do you hear a chromatic line in one of the voices? Do secondary dominants occur in sequence? As always, concentrate on the outer voices and then fill in the inner voices. For examples of secondary dominant chords in pieces by Bach, Haydn, Chopin, and others, see Unit 14.

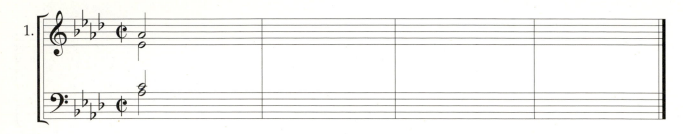

A♭: I

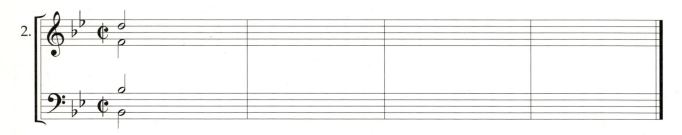

B♭: I

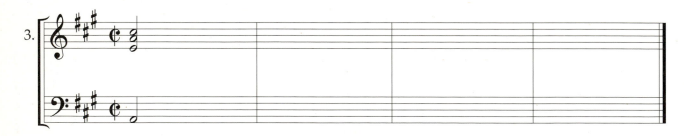

A: I

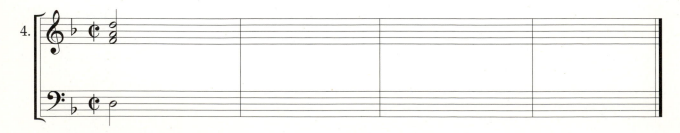

d: i

5.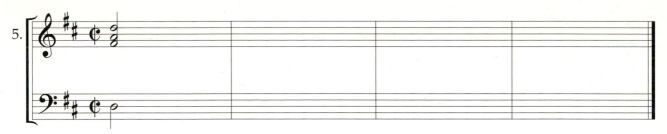

D: I

6.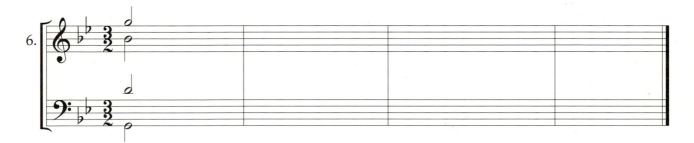

g: i

7.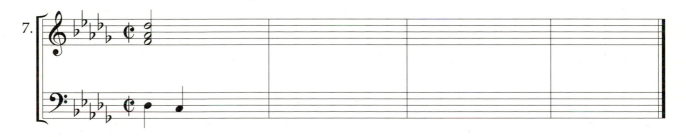

Db: I

8.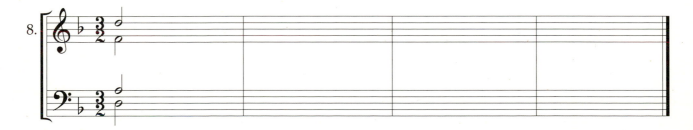

d: i

9.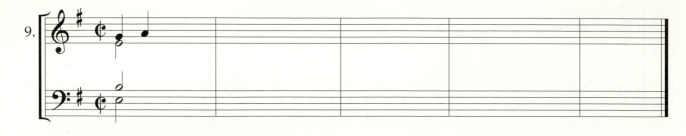

e: i

10.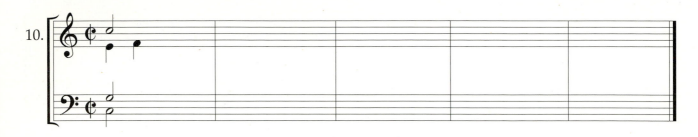

C: I

11.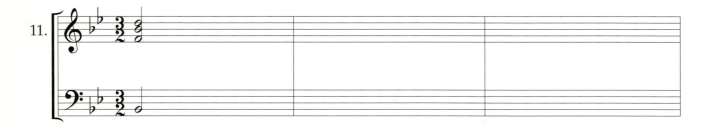

B♭: I

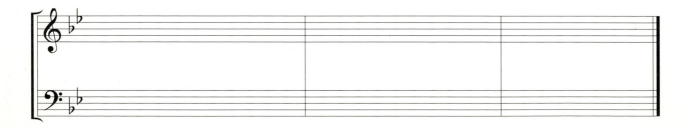

12.

e: i

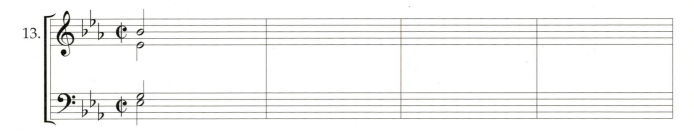

13.

E♭: I

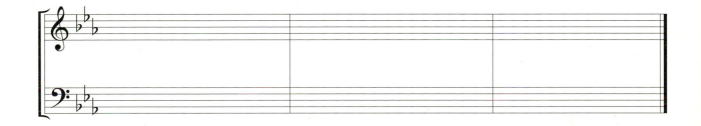

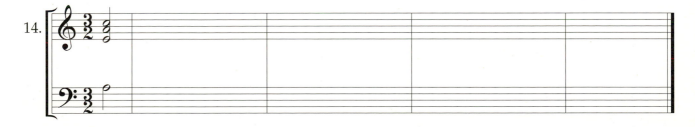

14.

a: i

Class: _____ Name: _____

Professor:

Harmonic Dictation: QUIZ NO. 1

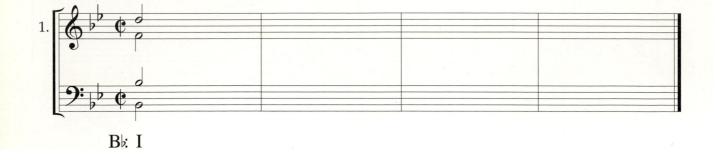

1. B♭: I

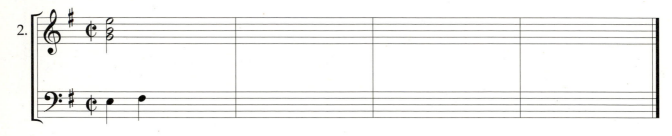

2. e: i

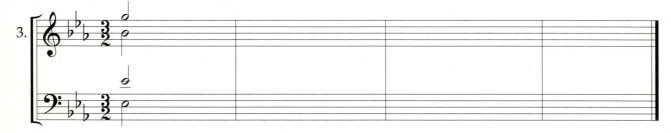

3. E♭: I

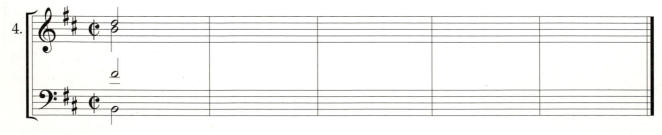

4. b: i

Class:

Professor:

Name: _____

5.

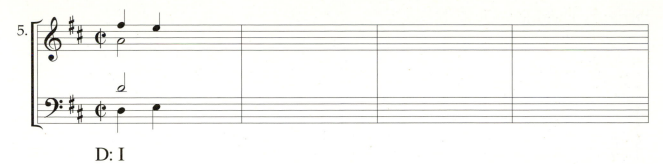

D: I

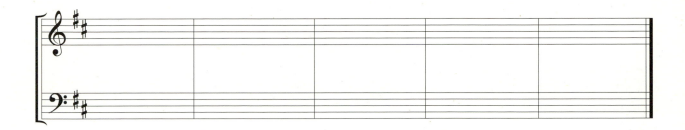

Harmonic Dictation: QUIZ NO. 2

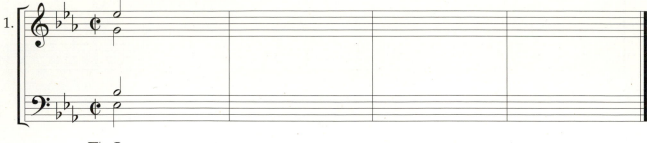

1.

Eb: I

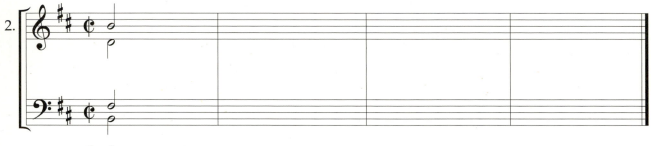

2.

b: i

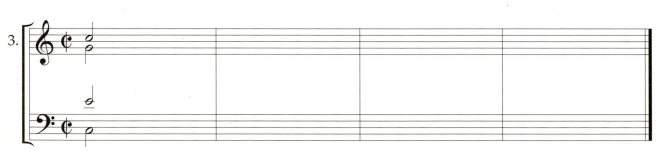

3.

C: I

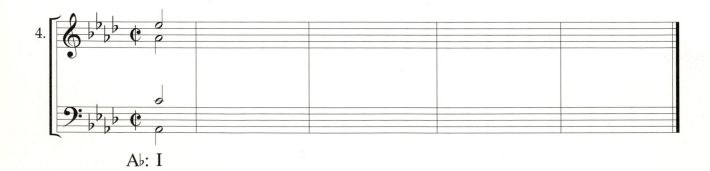

4.

Ab: I

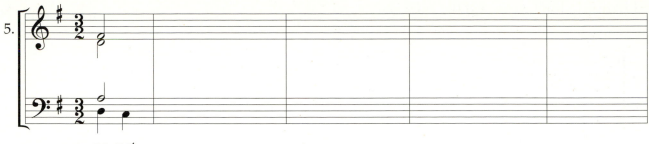

5.

G: V V$_2^4$

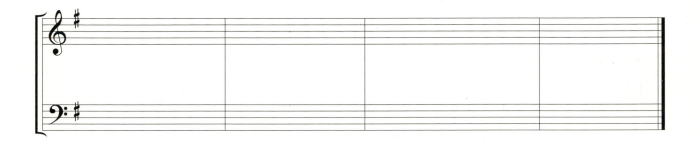

Harmonic Dictation: QUIZ NO. 3

G: I

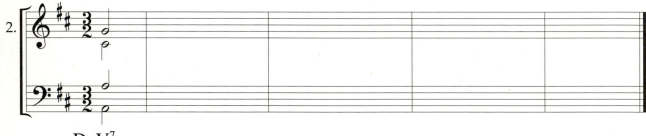

D: V⁷

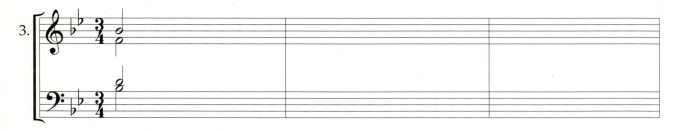

B♭: I

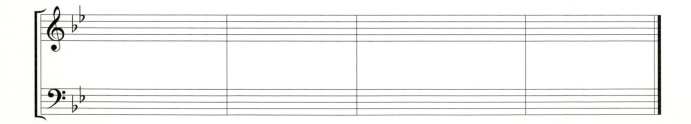

4.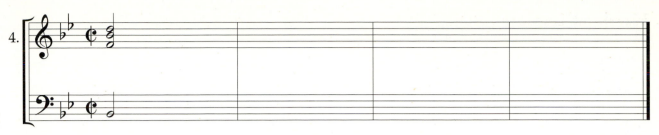

Bb: I

5.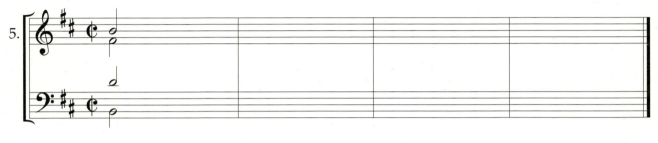

b: i

Unit 14

Examples from Music Literature

These exercises present actual musical examples for you to transcribe. All contain only the melodic and harmonic vocabulary studied so far and you should be able to transcribe each item completely. Listen to the example first. What is the texture? What kinds of cadences do you hear? Concentrate on individual lines and then listen harmonically. Isolate the altered chords. What are their functions? Is there decorative chromaticism?

1. Johann Sebastian Bach. *Herr, wie du willst, so shick's mit mir* (chorale)

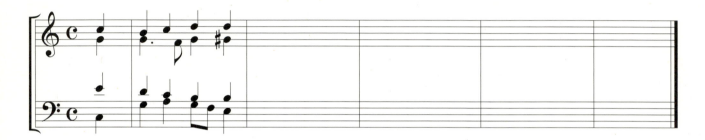

2. Johann Sebastian Bach. *Jesu, meiner Seelen Wonne* (chorale)

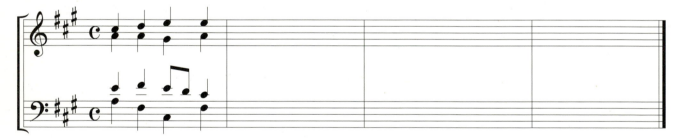

3. Johann Sebastian Bach. *Wer nur den lieben Gott läßt walten* (chorale)

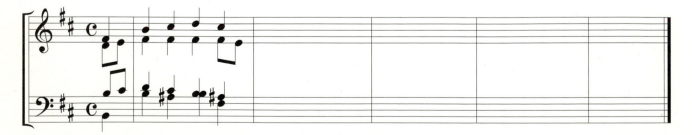

4. Johann Sebastian Bach. Minuet in G Minor

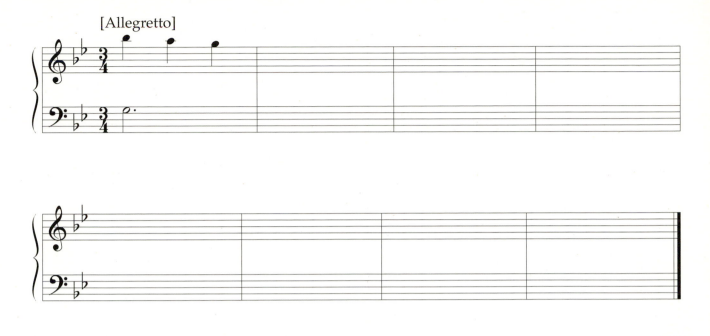

5. Edward MacDowell. *To a Wild Rose*, Op. 51, No. 1

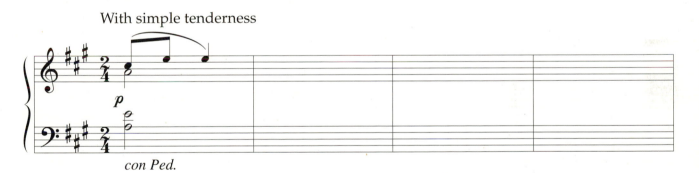

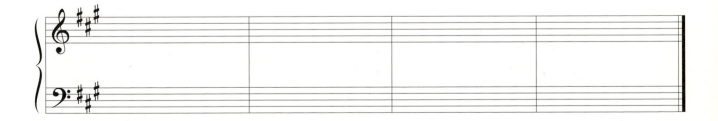

6. Carl Maria von Weber. German Dance

7. Frederic Chopin. Valse, Op. 69, No. 1

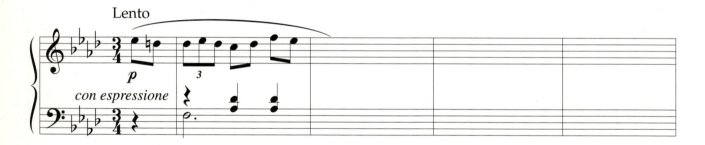

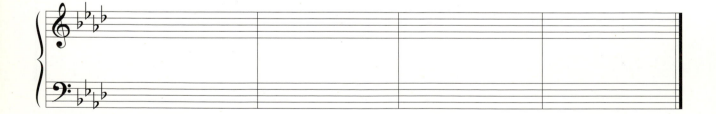

8. Wolfgang Amadeus Mozart. String Quartet, K. 158, mvt. I

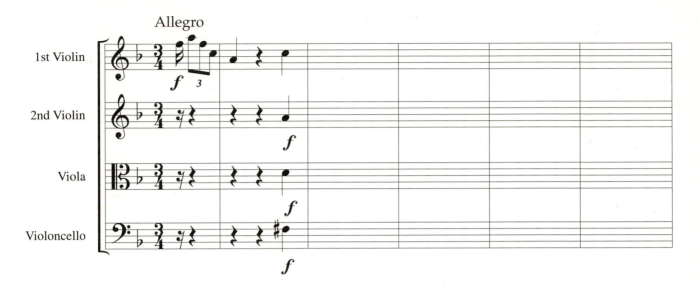

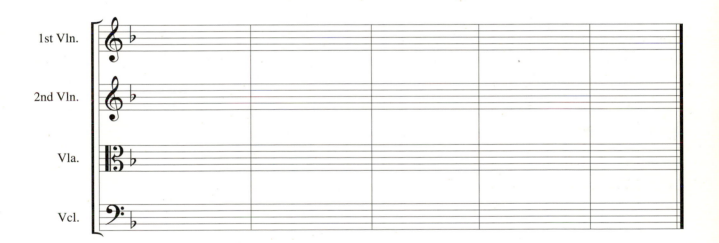

9. Joseph Haydn. Divertimento in D

Menuet - Allegretto

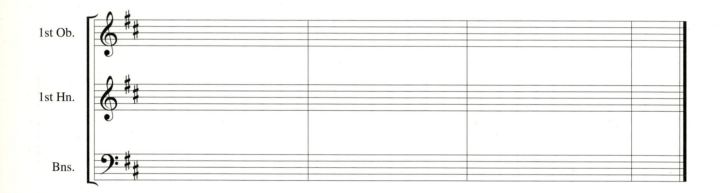

10. Ludwig van Beethoven. String Quartet, Op. 18, No. 6, mvt. I

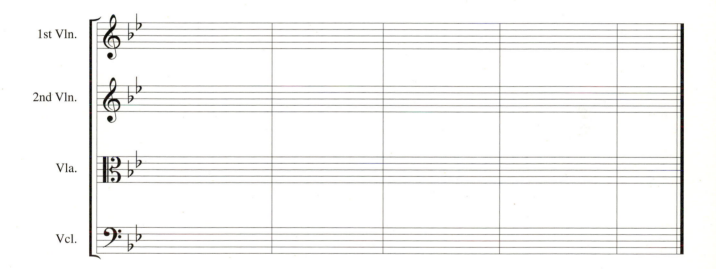

QUIZ NO. 1

1. Johann Sebastian Bach. *Jesu, meiner Seelen Wonne* (chorale)

2. Johann Sebastian Bach. *Es woll' uns Gott genadig sein* (chorale)

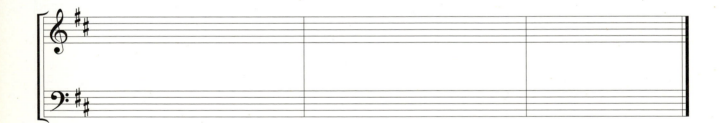

QUIZ NO. 2

1. Ludwig van Beethoven. *Romanze* from Sonatina in G

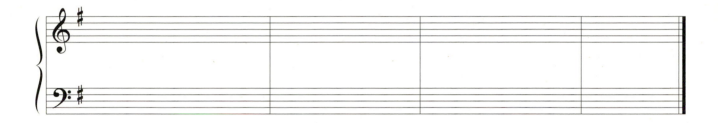

2. Frederic Chopin. Prelude, Op. 28, No. 7

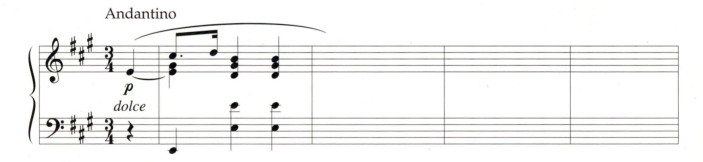

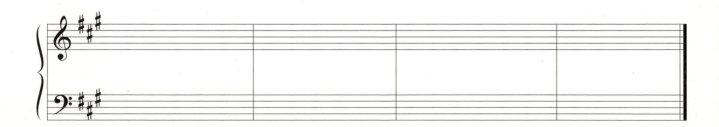

Name: _____

QUIZ NO. 3

Joseph Haydn. Divertimento in G, Hob. II:3

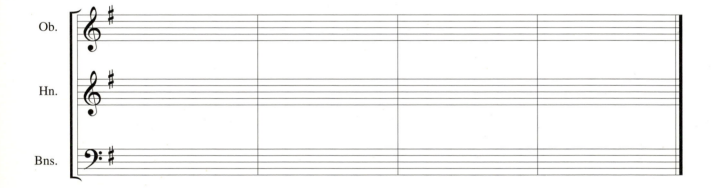

Unit 15

Melodic Dictation: Modulation to Closely Related Keys

Melodies

These exercises will challenge and develop your awareness of tonal centers. What is the original key? How is it established? Where does the key change? What devices are employed to effect the key change? Is the new key confirmed cadentially? Analyze the melody, using roman numerals. For examples of modulation to closely related keys in pieces by Bach, Diabelli, Haydn, and others, see Unit 17.

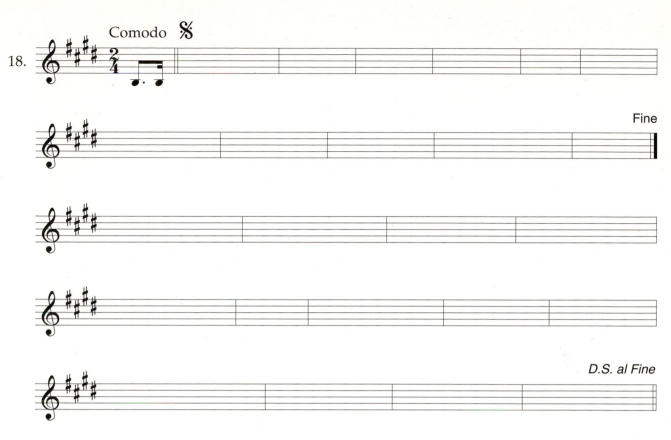

18. Comodo

Fine

D.S. al Fine

Melodic Dictation: QUIZ NO. 1

Melodic Dictation: QUIZ NO. 2

1. Doloroso

2. Allegro

3. Cantabile

4. Animato

5.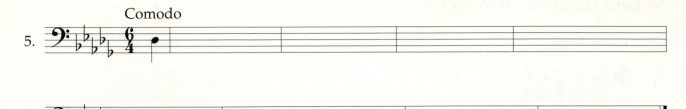

Comodo

Melodic Dictation: QUIZ NO. 3

Harmonic Dictation: Modulation to Closely Related Keys

Phrase-Length Exercises

> How is the first key established? Where does the key change? Is there a pivot chord? Is the new key confirmed cadentially? For examples of modulation to closely related keys in pieces by Bach, Diabelli, Haydn, and others, see Unit 17.

1.

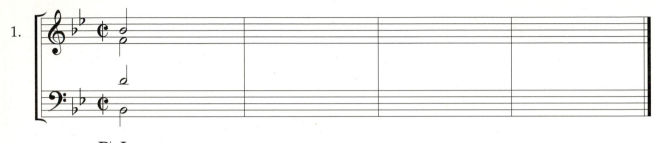

B♭:I

2.

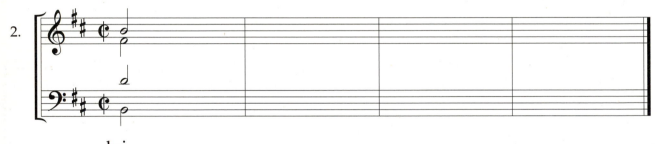

b:i

3.

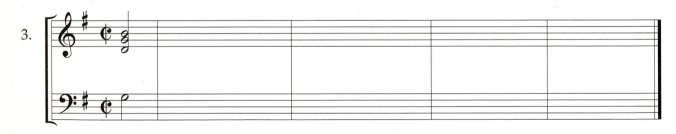

G: I

4.

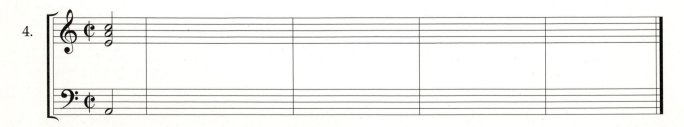

a: i

Class: Name: _____

Professor:

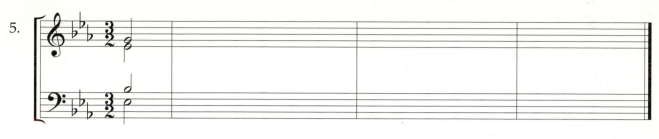

5.

Eb: I

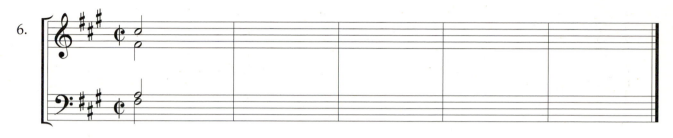

6.

f#: i

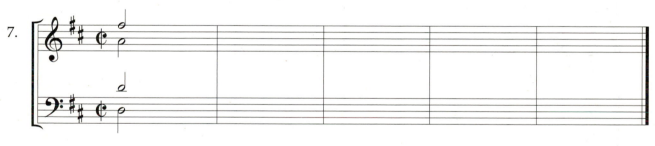

7.

D: I

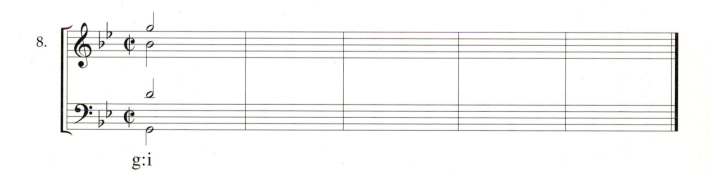

8.

g: i

9.

Ab: I

10.

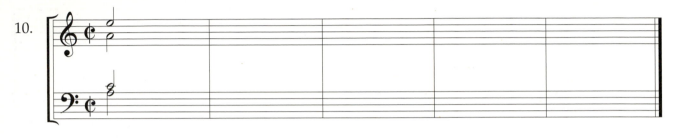

a: i

11.

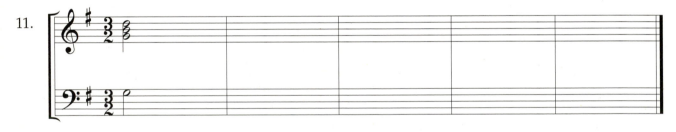

G: I

12.

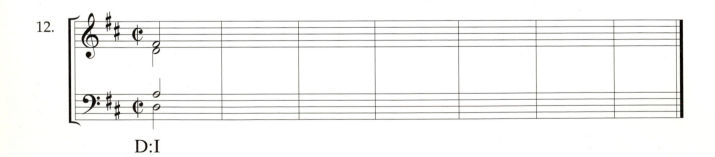

D: I

13.

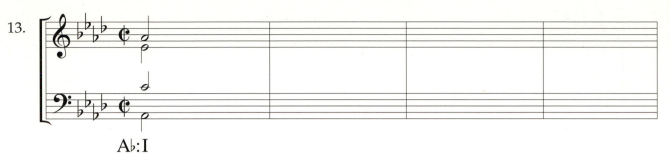

Ab:I

14.

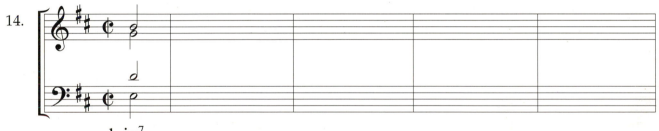

b:iv^7

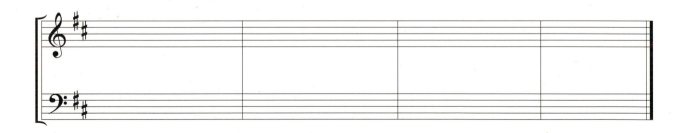

15.

A: I

16.

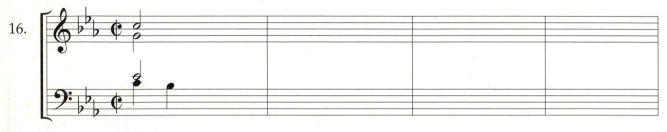

c: i

17.

f: i

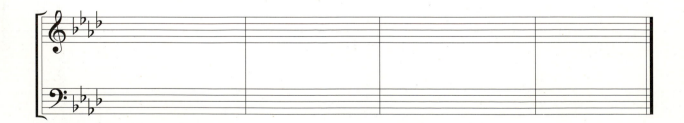

Class: _____ Name: _____

Professor: _____

Harmonic Dictation: QUIZ NO. 1

1.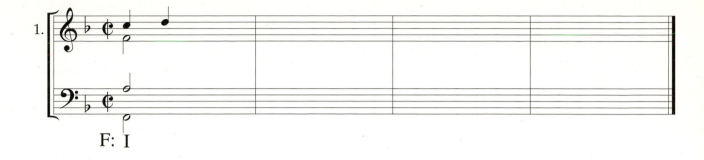

F: I

2.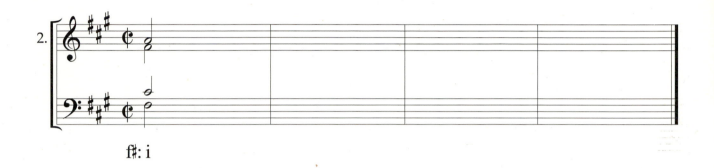

f♯: i

3.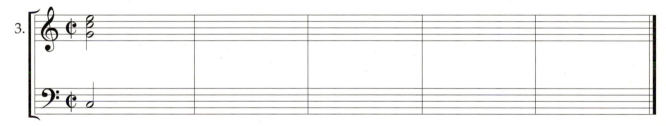

C: I

4.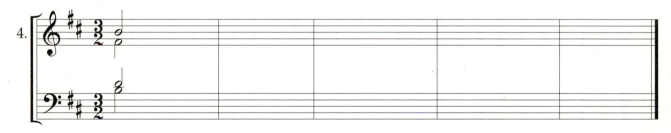

b: i

B♭: I

Class: _____

Name: _____

Professor: _____

Harmonic Dictation: QUIZ NO. 2

1.
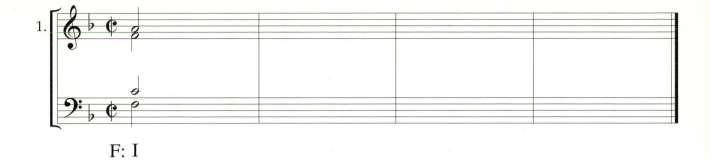

F: I

2.
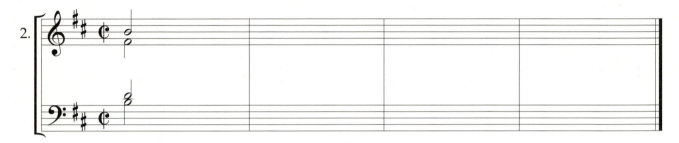

b: i

3.
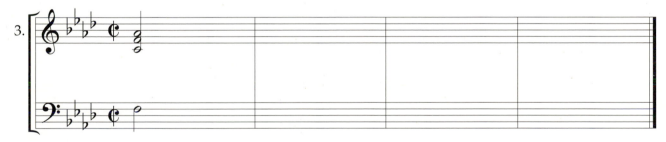

f: i

4.
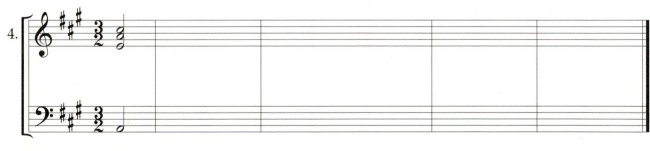

A: I

5.

         E♭: I

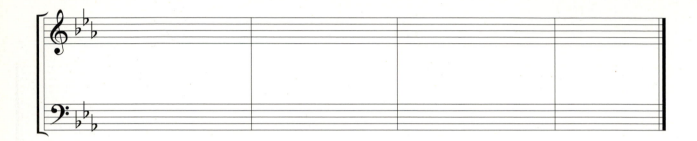

Class: _____ Name: _____

Professor: _____

Harmonic Dictation: QUIZ NO. 3

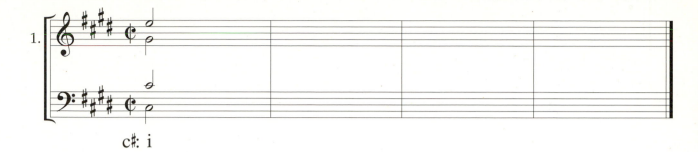

1.

c#: i

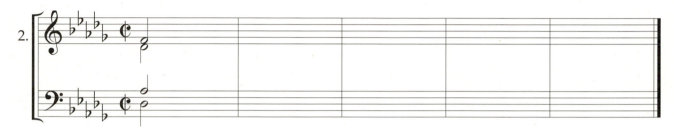

2.

D♭: I

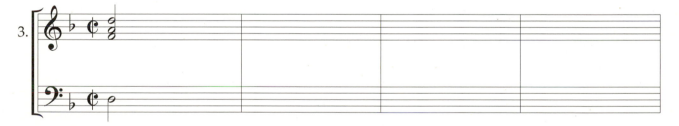

3.

d: i

4.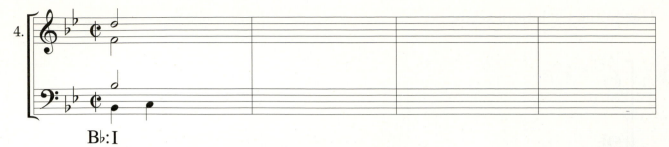

B♭: I

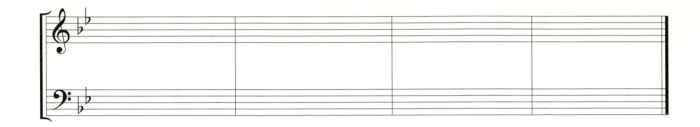

5.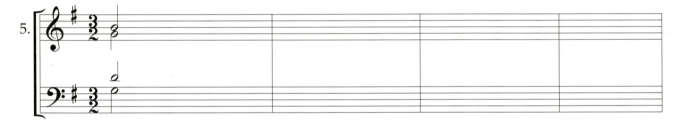

G: I

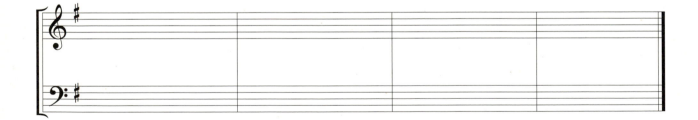

Unit 16

Rhythmic Dictation: Quintuple Meter

Listen to each exercise while counting or tapping the beat. Is the organization of beats 3 + 2 or 2 + 3? Does it remain the same throughout or does it vary? Do you feel the pulse at the beat level or do you feel alternations of simple and compound divisions? Try adjusting the tempo. Does the speed of the music affect your perception?

Preliminary Exercises

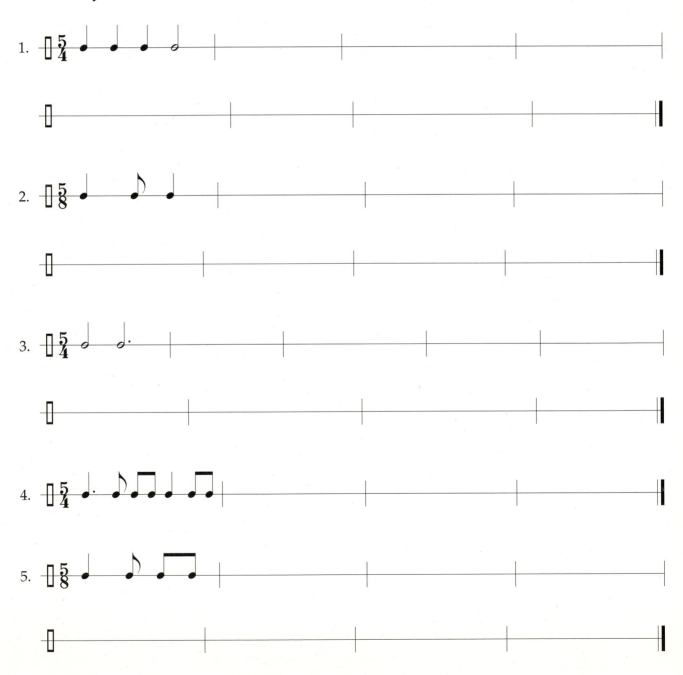

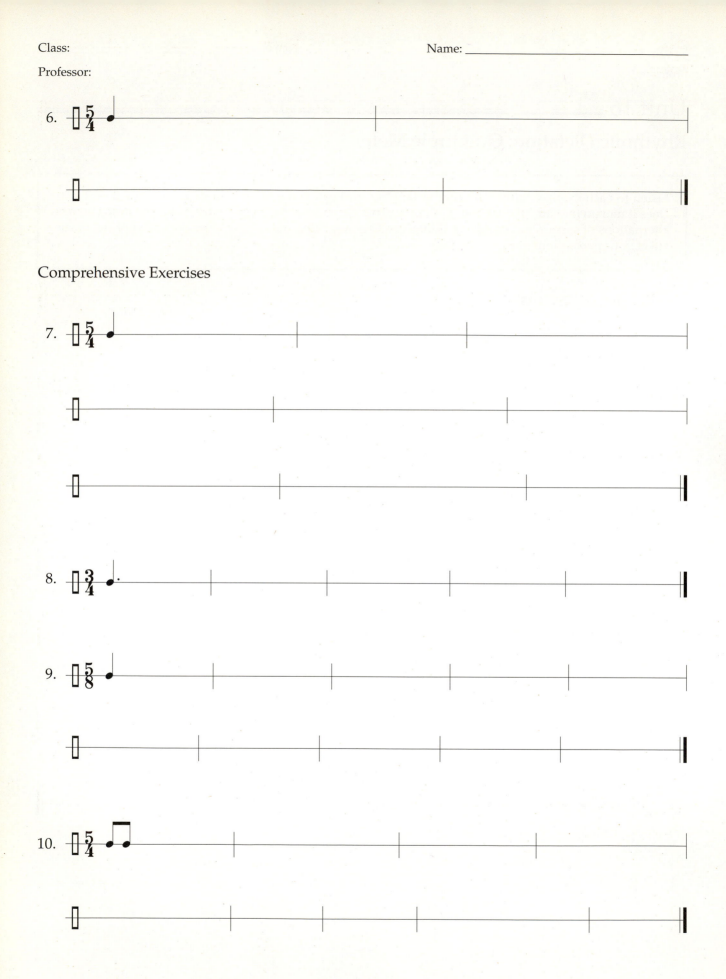

Comprehensive Exercises

16.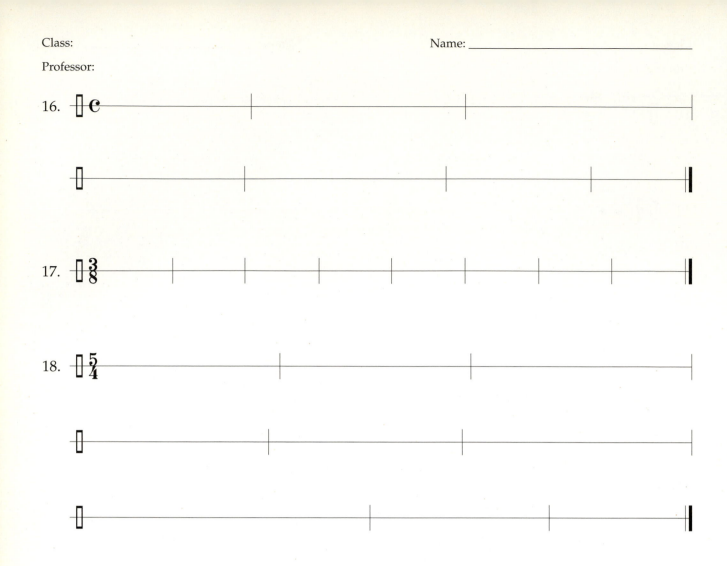

17.

18.

Name: _____

Rhythmic Dictation: QUIZ NO. 1

Rhythmic Dictation: QUIZ NO. 2

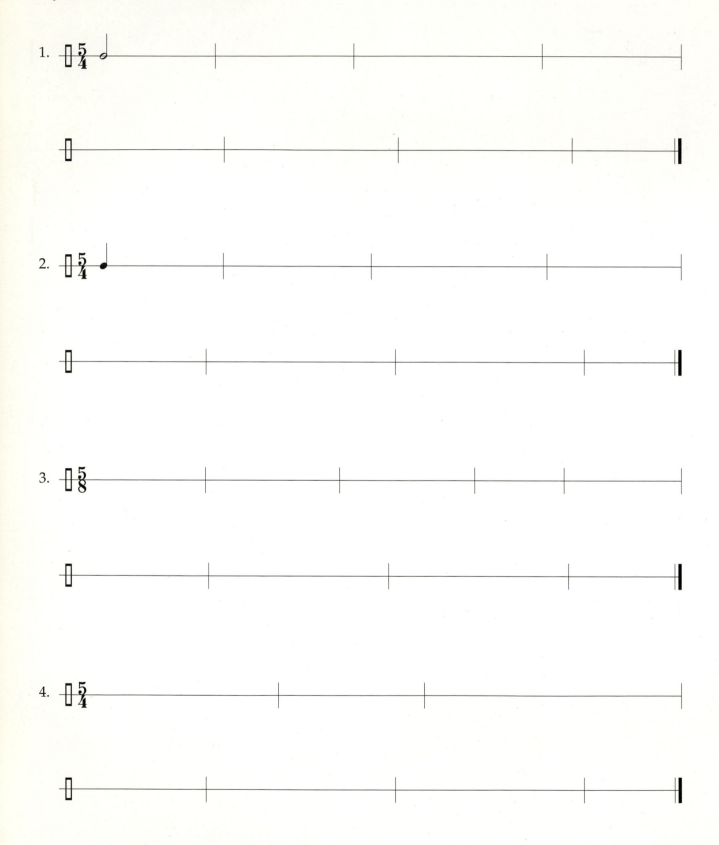

5.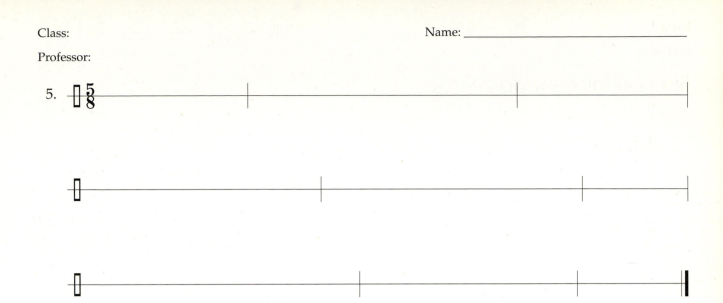

Rhythmic Dictation: QUIZ NO. 3

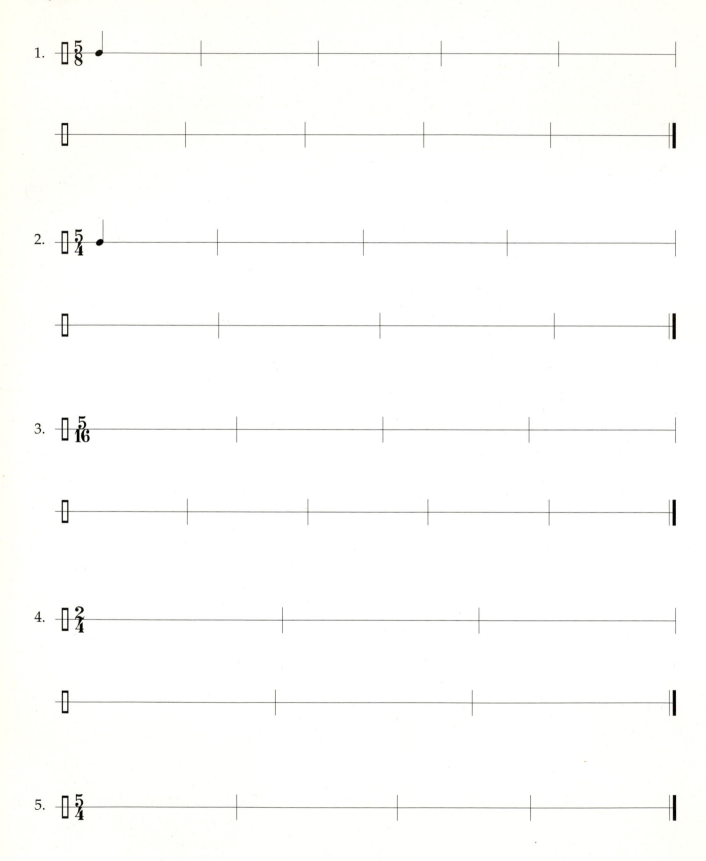

1. $\frac{5}{8}$

2. $\frac{5}{4}$

3. $\frac{5}{16}$

4. $\frac{2}{4}$

5. $\frac{5}{4}$

Melodic Dictation: The Neapolitan Sixth Chord, Augmented Sixth Chords, and Modulation to Distantly Related Keys

For examples of Neapolitan sixth chords, augmented sixth chords, and modulation to distantly related keys in pieces by Bach, Beethoven, and Schubert, see Unit 17.

Preliminary Exercises

6.

7.

8.

Class:

Name: _____

Professor:

Melodies

These melodies emphasize the altered scale degrees associated with Neapolitan chords (including ♭2) and augmented sixth chords (including ♯4 and ♭6). Where are altered chords implied? What scale degrees seem most implicative? What structural lines do the altered scale degrees and the notes of resolution form? Are there arpeggiations? Does the melody modulate? Determine the new tonic. How is it established? Is there a logical pivot point or common tone, or does the music shift abruptly into the new key?

Moderato

5.

Andantino

6.

Allegro marcato

7.

Allegretto

8.

Name: _____

Passionato

13.

Grazioso

14.

Fanfare

15.

Melodic Dictation: QUIZ NO. 1

Con passione

5.

Melodic Dictation: QUIZ NO. 2

Andantino

5.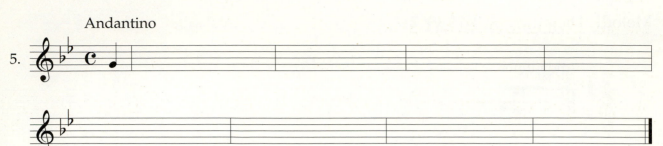

Melodic Dictation: QUIZ NO. 3

Amabile

1.

Grazioso

2.

Andantino

3.

4. Capriccioso

5. Comodo

Harmonic Dictation: The Neapolitan Sixth Chord, Augmented Sixth Chords, Enharmonic Modulation

Basic Progressions

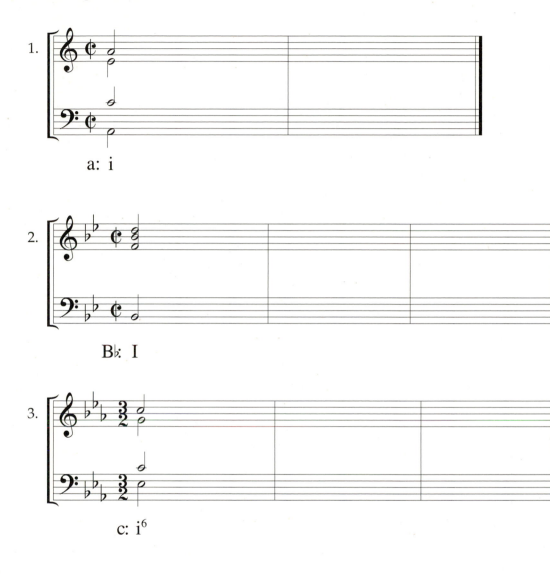

1. a: i

2. B♭: I

3. c: i⁶

4. G: I

5.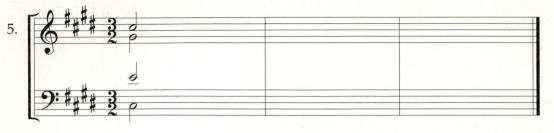

c#: i

6.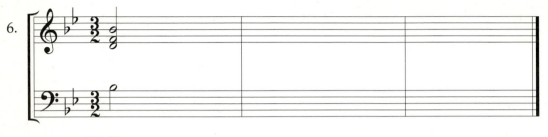

B♭: I

7.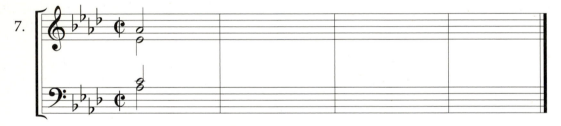

A♭: I

8.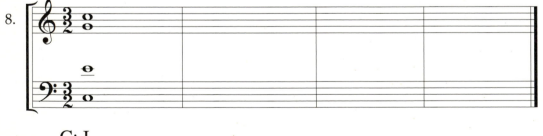

C: I

9.

E: I

10.

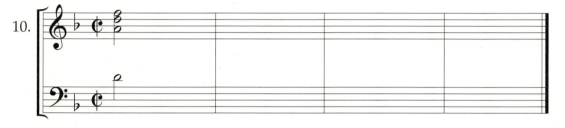

d: i

Phrase-Length Exercises

Drill on the Preliminary Exercises to establish the most common progressions using altered chords. Then listen to each phrase-length progression. Where do altered chords occur? Which voices have the altered scale degrees? Do the altered pitches resolve as expected? Do the phrases modulate? Concentrate on the way in which altered chords facilitate the modulation. For examples of Neapolitan sixth chords, augmented sixth chords, and modulation to distantly related keys in pieces by Bach, Beethoven, and Schubert, see Unit 17.

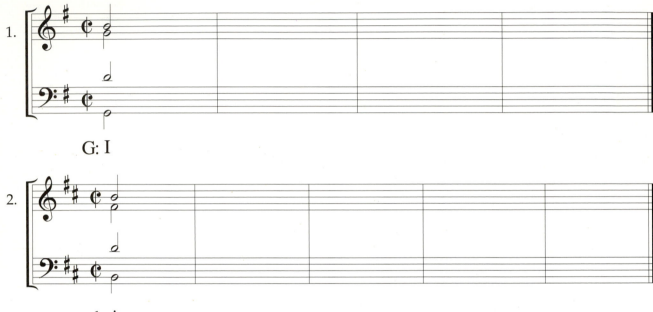

G: I

b: i

b: V♯

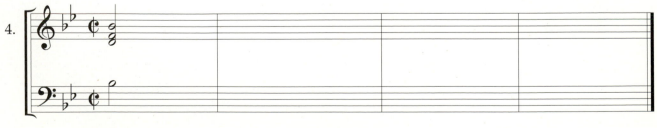

B♭: I

5.

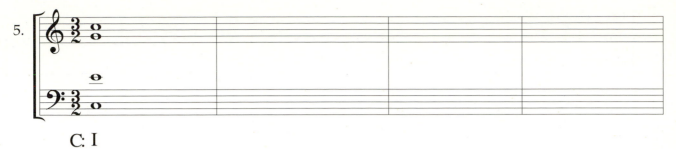

C: I

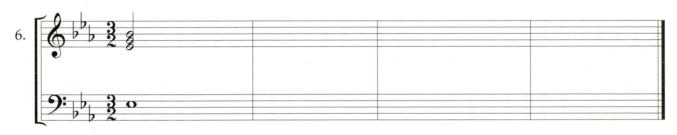

6.

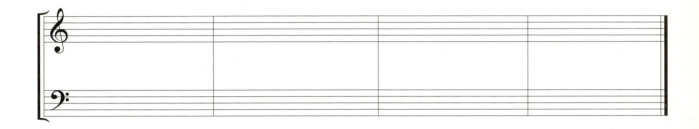

E♭: I

7.

F: I

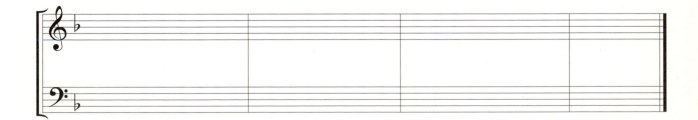

8.

B♭: I

9.

g: i

10.

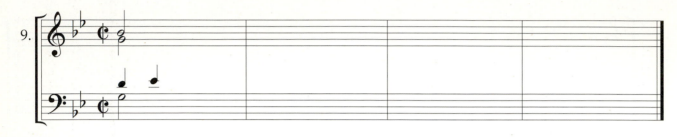

c♯: i

11.

G: I

12.

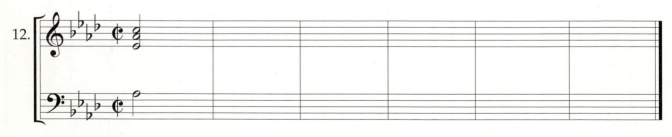

A♭: I

13.

C: I

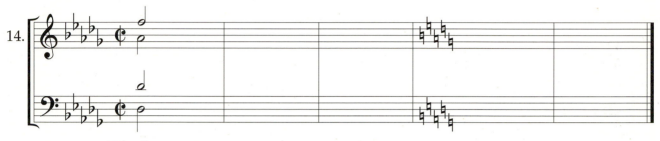

14.

D♭: I

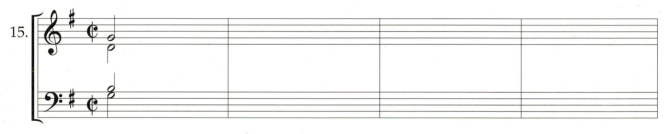

15.

G: I

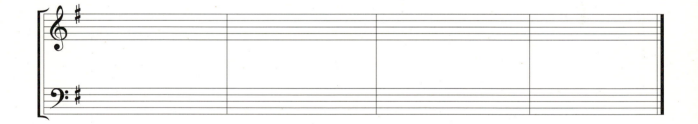

Class: _____   Name: _____

Professor: _____

Harmonic Dictation: QUIZ NO. 1

1.

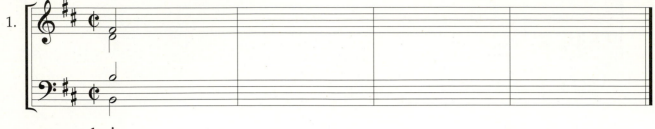

b: i

2.

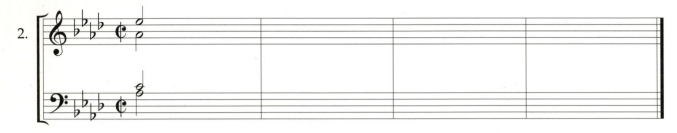

A♭: I

3.

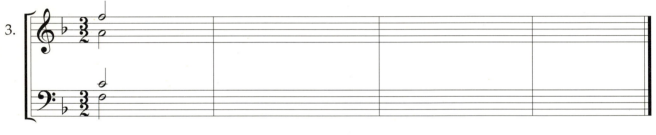

F: I

4.
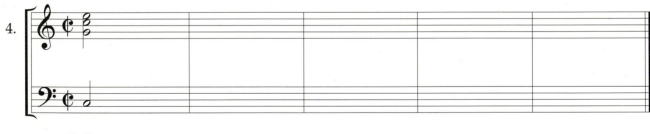

C: I

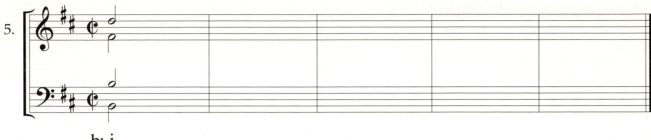

b: i

Harmonic Dictation: QUIZ NO. 2

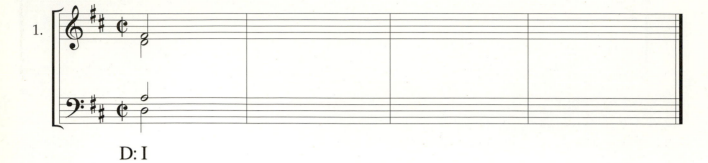

1.

D: I

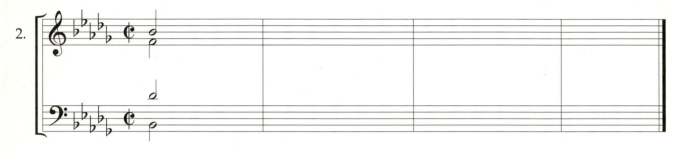

2.

b♭: i

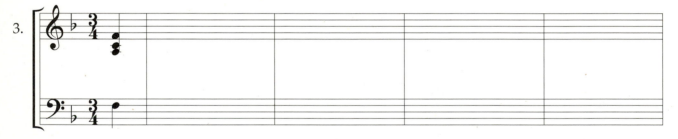

3.

F: I

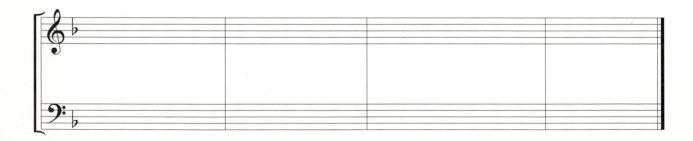

4.

f#: i

5.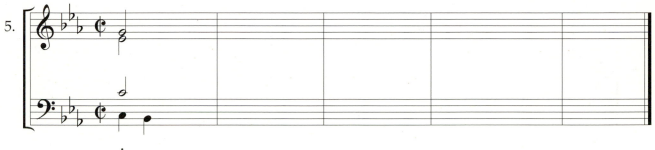

c: i

Harmonic Dictation: QUIZ NO. 3

1.

      f: i

2.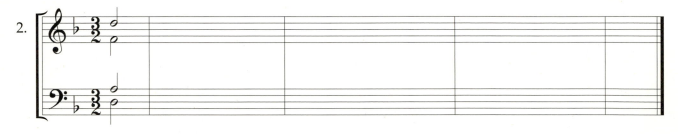

      d: i

3.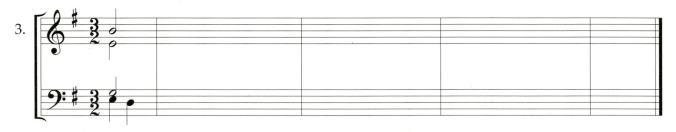

      e: i

4.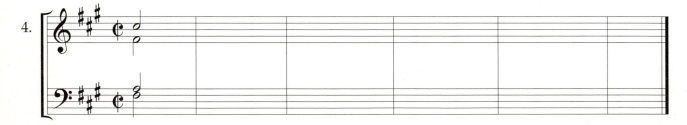

      f♯: i

5.

A: I

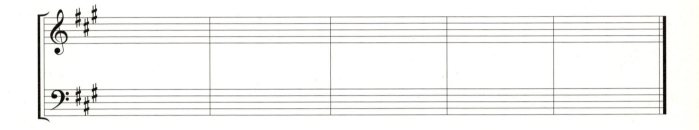

Unit 17

Examples from Music Literature

These exercises present actual musical examples for you to transcribe. All contain only the melodic and harmonic vocabulary studied so far and you should be able to transcribe each item completely. Listen to the example first. What is the texture? What kinds of cadences do you hear? Concentrate on individual lines and then listen harmonically. Isolate any altered chords. What are their functions? Does the music modulate? How are the keys established?

1. Johann Sebastian Bach. *Ach Gott, vom Himmel sieh' darein* (chorale)

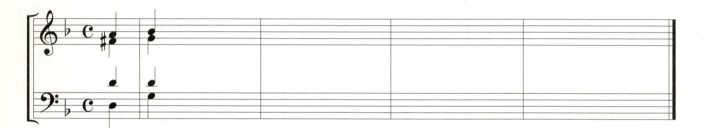

2. Johann Sebastian Bach. *Befiehl du deine Wege* (chorale)

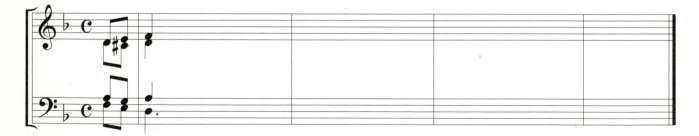

Name: _____

3. Johann Sebastian Bach. *Ach Gott, wie manches Herzeleid* (chorale)

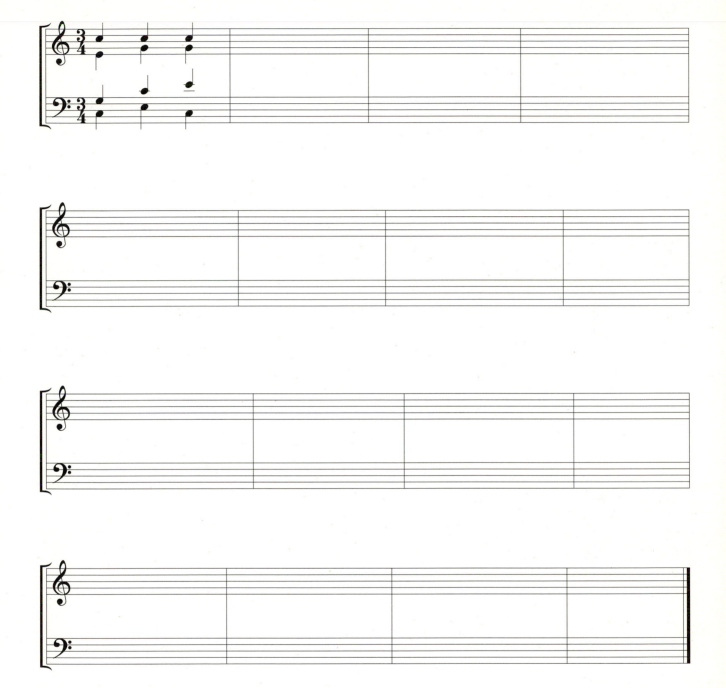

4. Johann Sebastian Bach. *Hilf, Herr Jesu, lass gelingen* (chorale)

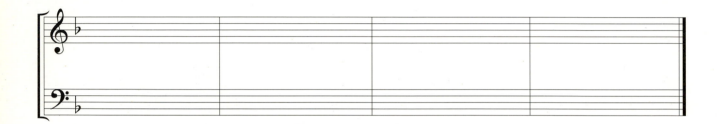

Class:

Professor:

Name: _____

5. Johann Sebastian Bach. Bourrée, French Overture

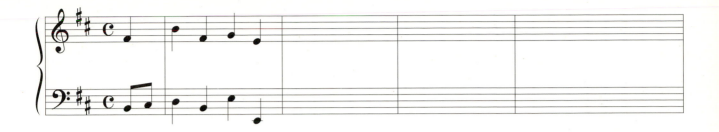

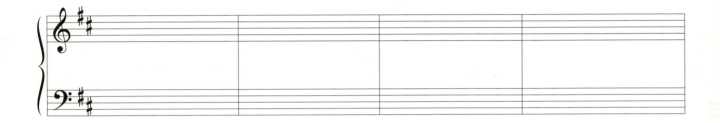

6. Jeremiah Clarke. Jigg

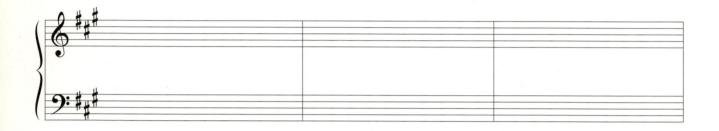

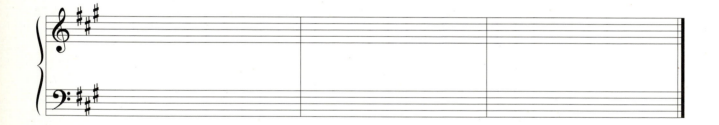

7. Antonio Diabelli. Rondino

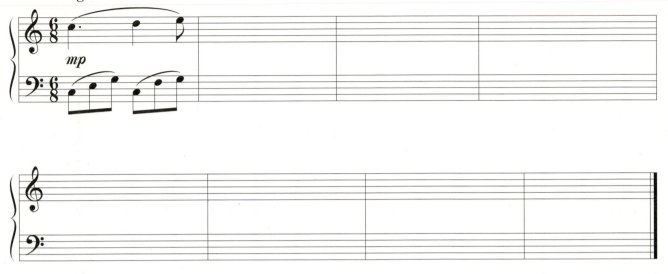

8. Joseph Haydn. Sonata, Hob. XVI:27, mvt. III

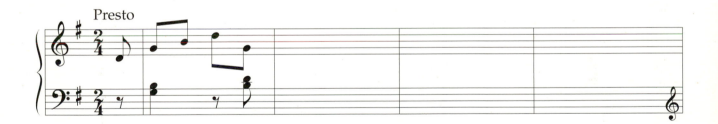

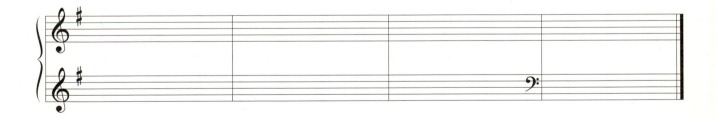

9. Ludwig van Beethoven. Bagatelle, Op. 119, No. 1

10. Ludwig van Beethoven. Minuet in G Major, WoO 10, No. 2

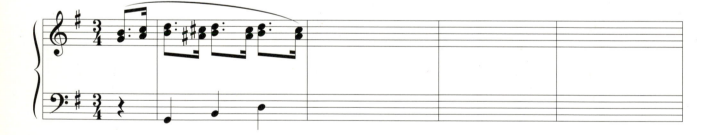

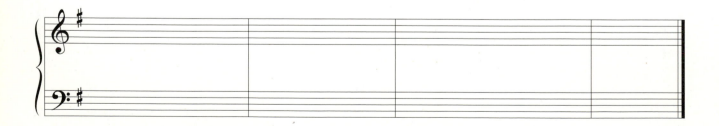

11. Mikail Ivanovich Glinka. Waltz, Op. 39, No. 15

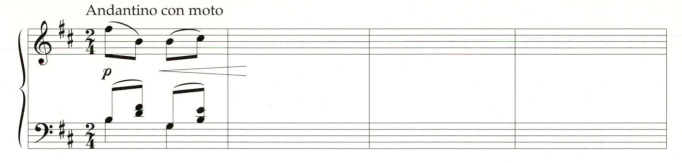

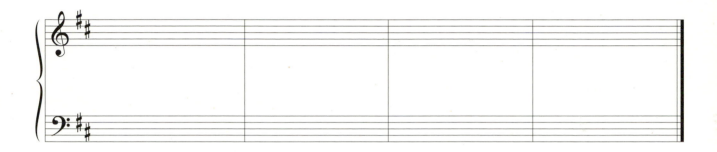

12. Franz Schubert. Scherzo in B-flat

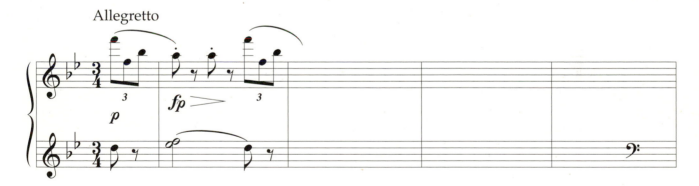

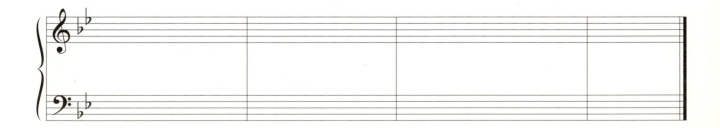

13. Joseph Haydn. Divertimento, Hob. II:18, mvt. III, Trio

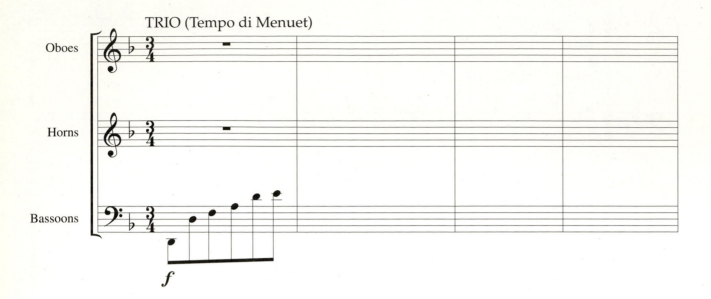

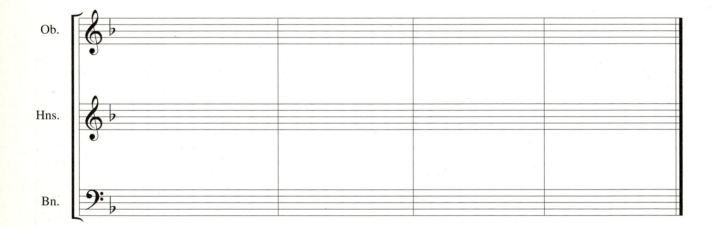

14. Ludwig van Beethoven. Quartet, Op. 18, No. 1, mvt. III

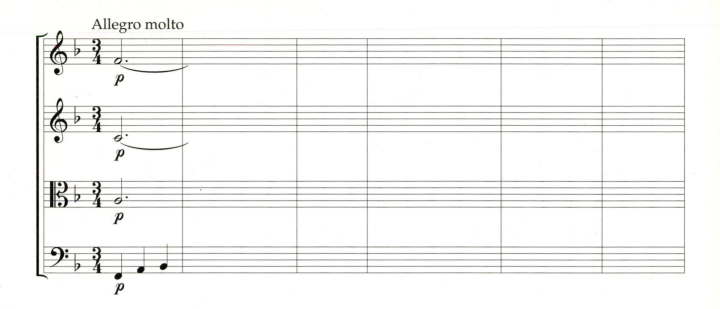

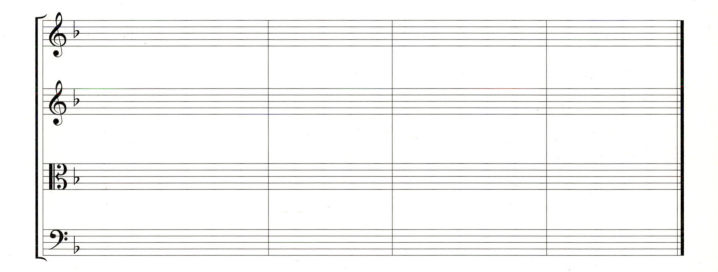

15. Ludwig van Beethoven. Quartet, Op. 18, No. 4, mvt. III

Allegretto

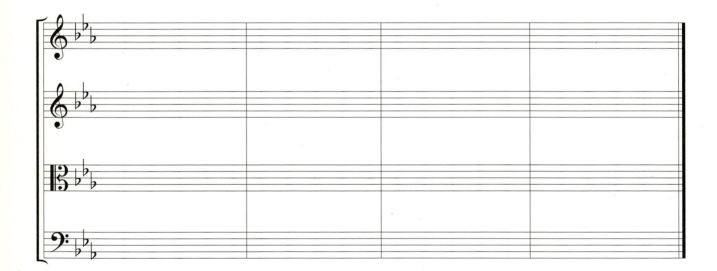

16. Ludwig van Beethoven. Quartet, Op. 18, No. 4, mvt. IV

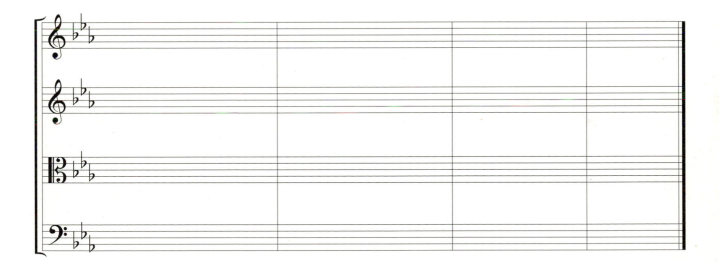

Name: _____

17. Wolfgang Amadeus Mozart. Quartet, K. 421, mvt. III

MENUETTO (Allegretto)

18. Wolfgang Amadeus Mozart. Quartet, K. 170, mvt. I

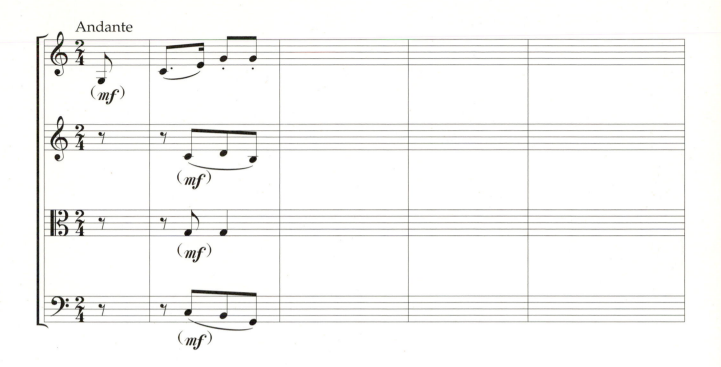

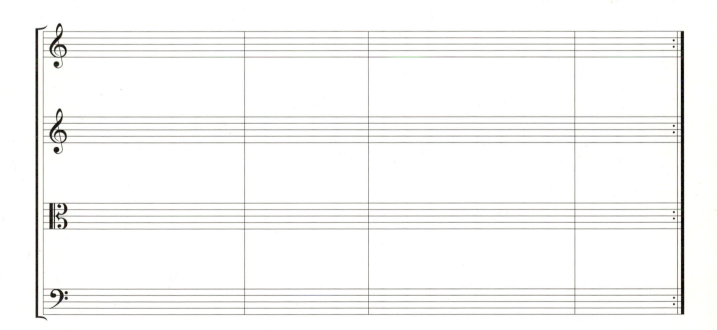

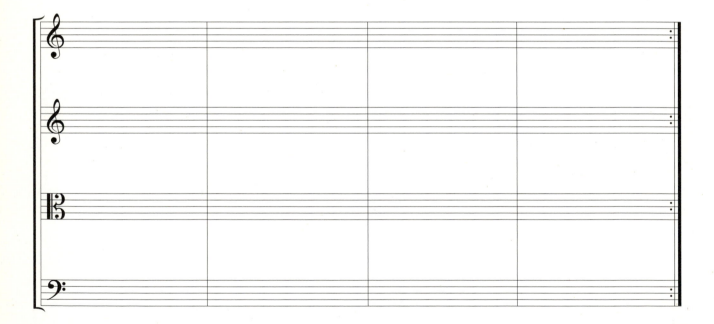

QUIZ NO. 1

1. Johann Sebastian Bach. *Befiehl du deine Wege* (chorale)

2. Domenico Scarlatti. Sonata, Longo 83

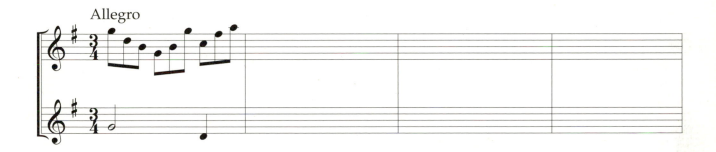

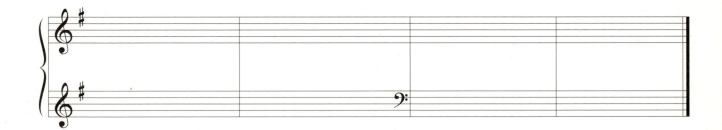

3. Joseph Haydn. Sonata, Hob. XVI:37, mvt. III

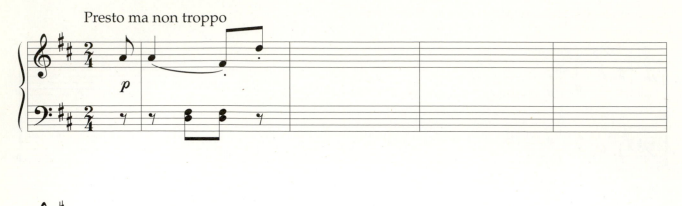

4. Ludwig van Beethoven. Sonata "Pathetique," Op. 13, mvt. III

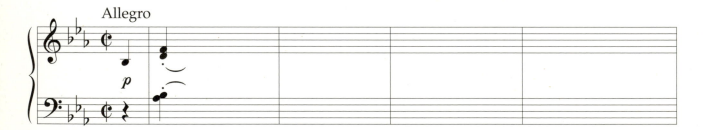

QUIZ NO. 2

1. Johann Sebastian Bach. *Meine Seel' erhebt den Herren* (chorale)

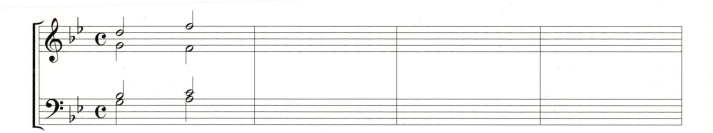

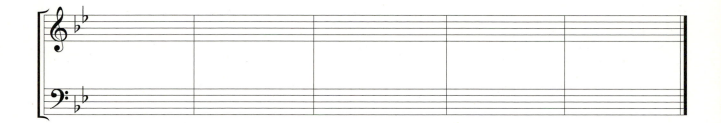

2. Ludwig van Beethoven. Sonata, Op. 14, No. 1, mvt. II

Maggiore Allegretto

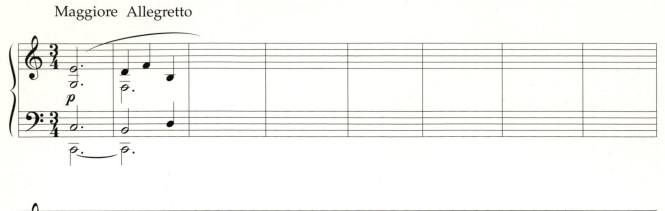

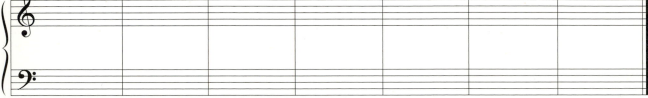

3. Johannes Brahms. Waltz, Op. 39, No. 15

Tempo giusto

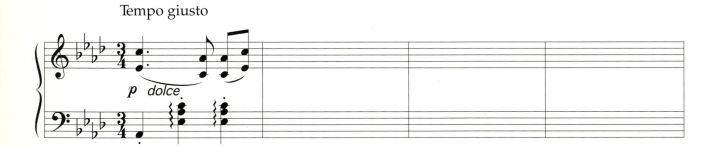

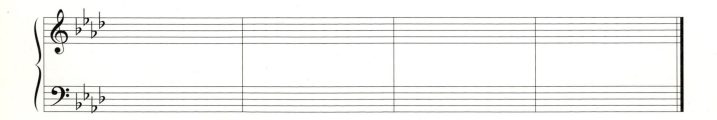

4. Ludwig van Beethoven. Quartet, Op. 18, No. 2, mvt. III, Trio

TRIO   Allegro

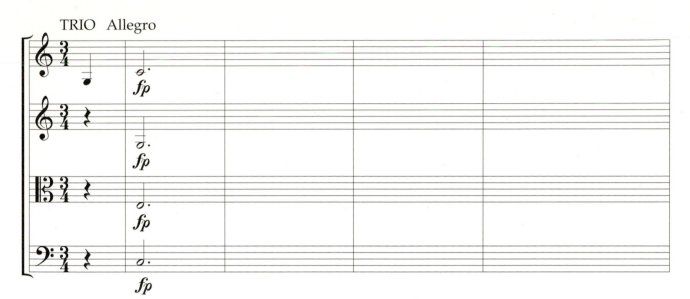

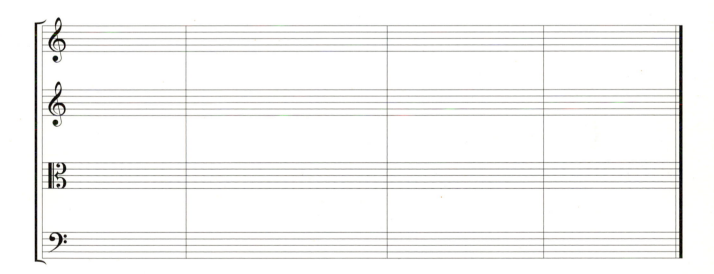

QUIZ NO. 3

1. Johann Sebastian Bach. *Jesu, meine Freude* (chorale)

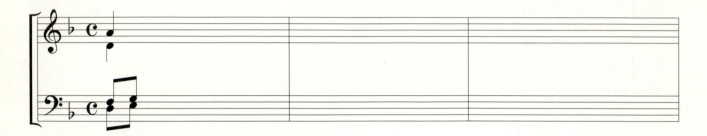

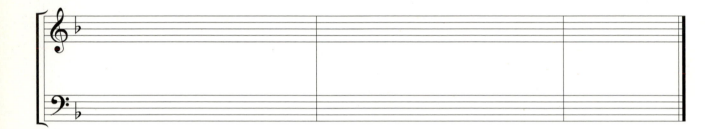

2. Robert Schumann. "Important Event," *Scenes from Childhood*, Op. 15, No. 6

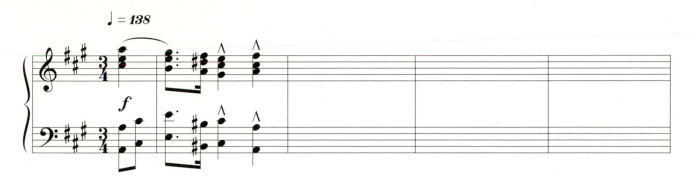

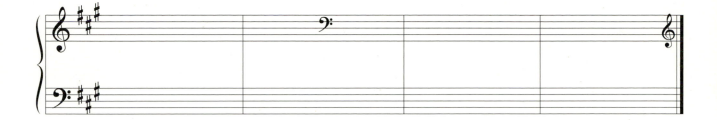

3. Edvard Grieg. Rigaudon, Op. 40, No. 5, Trio

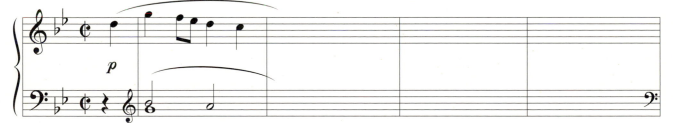

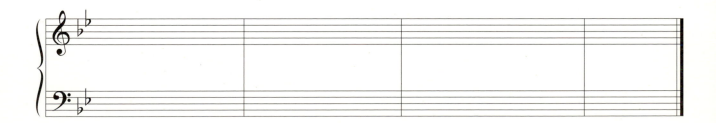

4. Ludwig van Beethoven. Quartet, Op. 18, No. 3, mvt. III

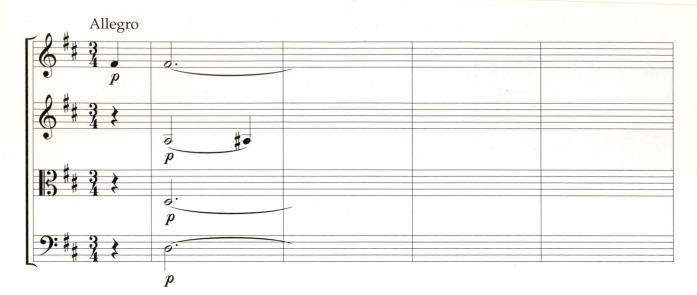

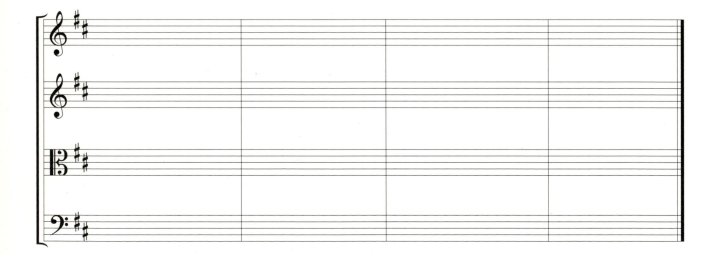

Unit 18

Rhythmic Dictation: Irregular Meters

Listen for the groups of two and three notes. Do they form a regularly recurring pattern? The meter signature itself should suggest the possible groupings. Once you have established this basic grouping, focus on the values within the groups. Are there subdivisions? Syncopations?

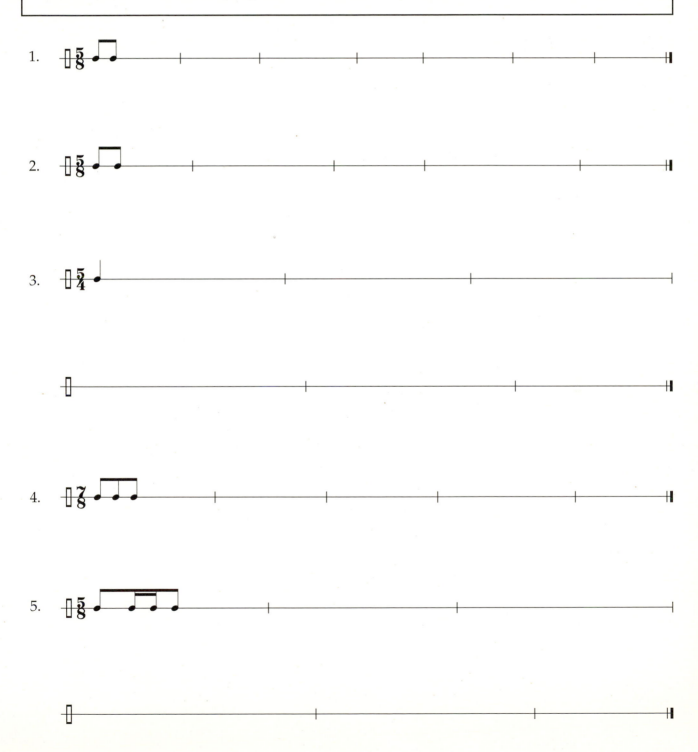

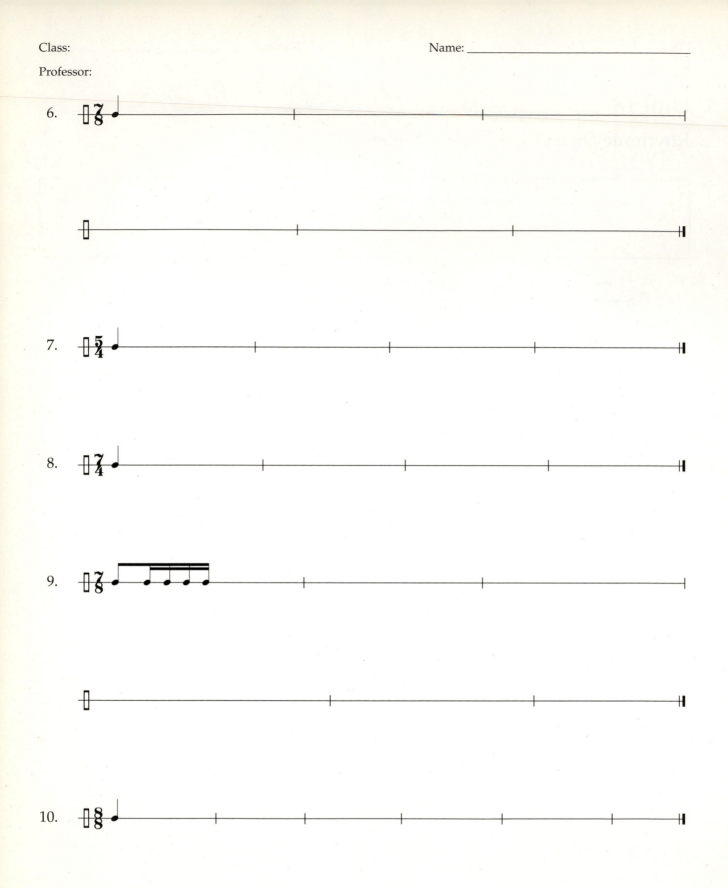

Name: _____

Rhythmic Dictation: QUIZ NO. 1

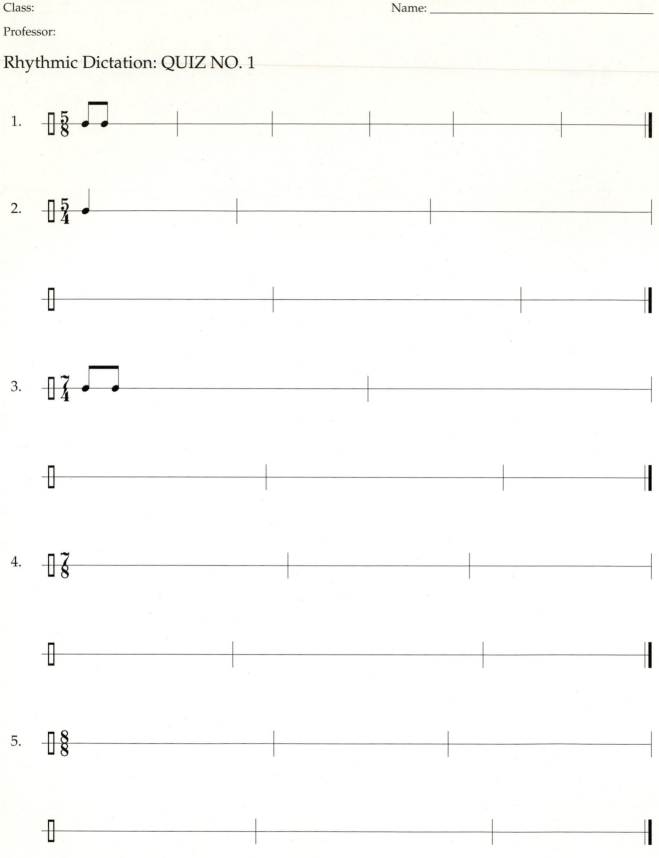

Rhythmic Dictation: QUIZ NO. 2

Melodic Dictation: Diatonic Modes

Review the church modes, concentrating on the location of the half steps (semitones). Then listen to each melody. Is the mode "major" or "minor"? Is there a whole step or half step from degree 7 to 8? From degree 5 to 6? From degree 1 to 2? Does the melody both begin and end on the tonic? How is tonic established? Try singing the scale to establish the mode. Examples of modal usage in pieces by Bartók and Bloch can be found in Unit 26, Part 1.

Con forza

5.

Cantabile

6.

Vigoroso

7.

Contempletivo

8.

13. Energico

14. Andantino

Melodic Dictation: QUIZ NO. 1

Moderato

1.

Marcato

2.

Doloroso

3.

Ritmico

4.

Amabile

5.

Melodic Dictation: QUIZ NO. 2

Harmonic Dictation: Diatonic Modes

Review the qualities of the triads and seventh chords in each mode. As you listen to the exercises, first establish the mode. Is it "major" or "minor"? What is the quality of the dominant or dominant seventh? What particular progressions most clearly establish the mode? Identify the tonic and the specific mode. A Roman numeral functional analysis for each chord is no longer appropriate. Examples of modal usage in pieces by Bartók and Bloch can be found in Unit 26, Part 1.

1.

2.

3.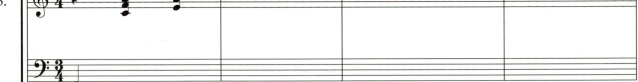

4.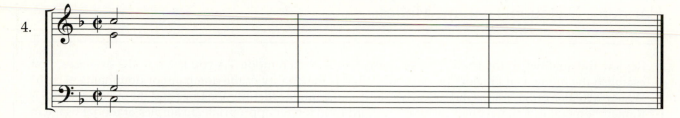

5.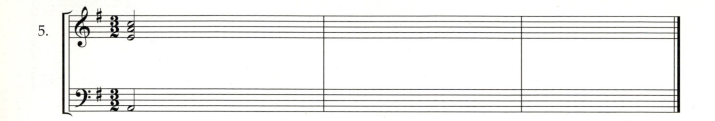

6.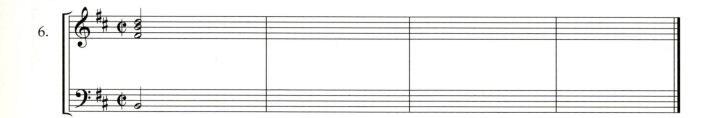

7.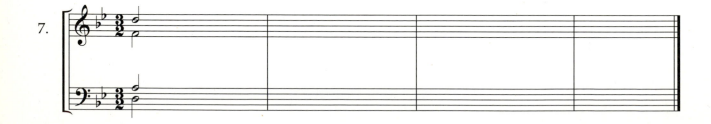

Class:

Professor:

Name: _____

8.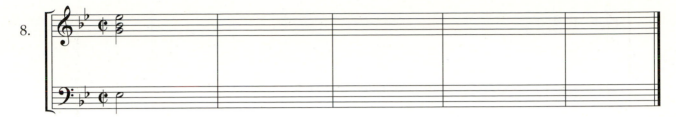

9.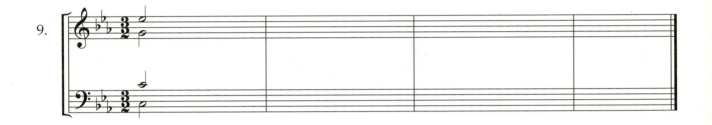

10.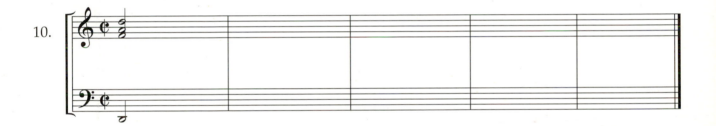

11.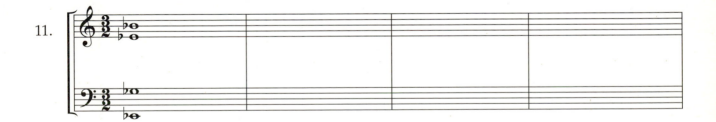

12.

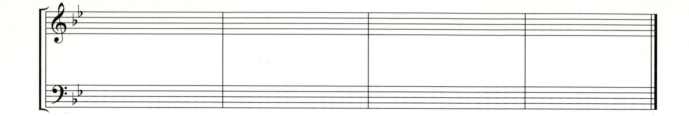

13.

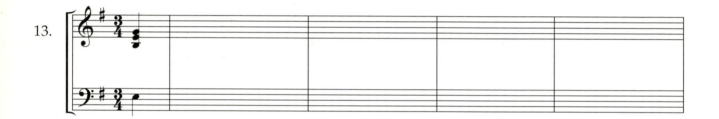

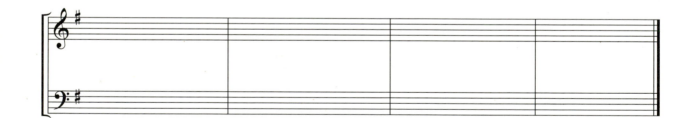

14.

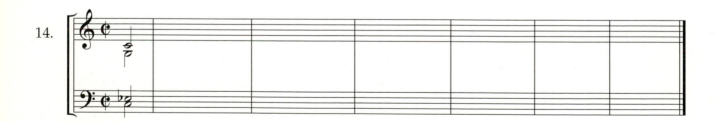

Harmonic Dictation: QUIZ NO. 1

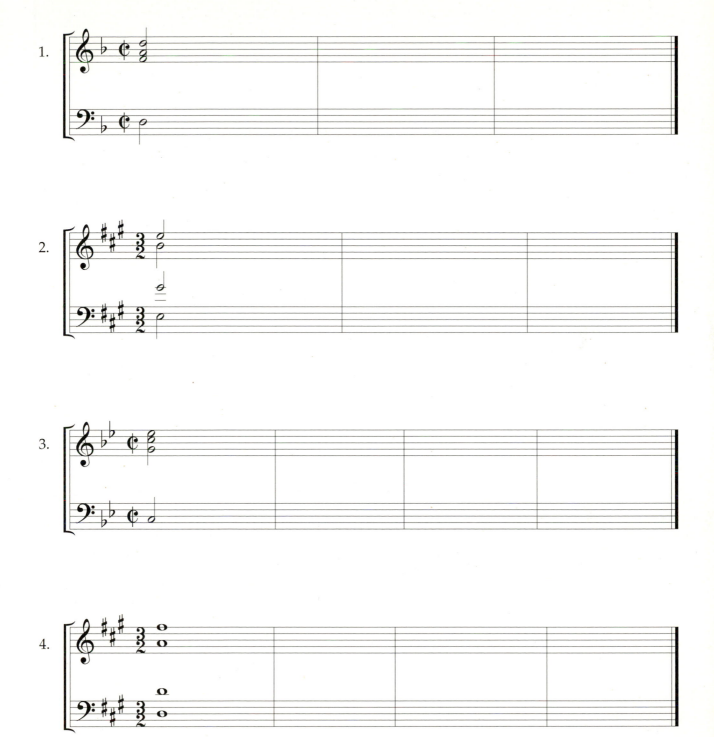

5.

Class:

Name: _____

Professor:

Harmonic Dictation: QUIZ NO. 2

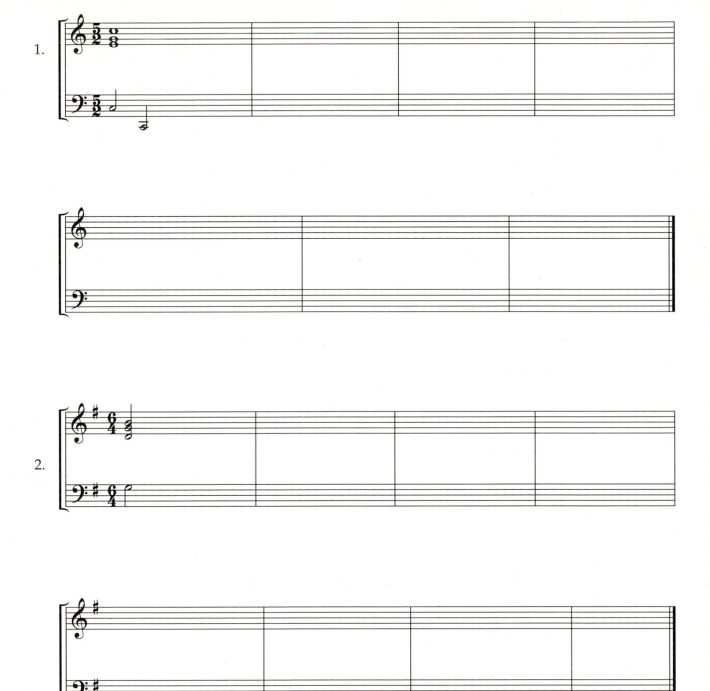

1.

2.

3.

4.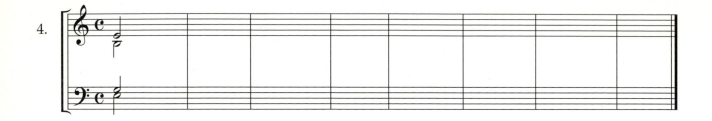

5.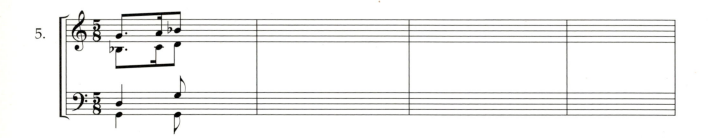

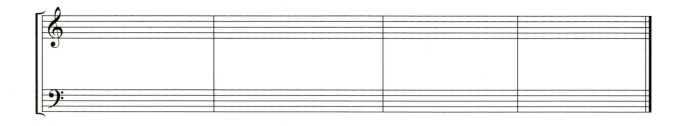

Unit 19

Rhythmic Dictation: Changing Meters

How does the pattern in each measure express the particular meter? Do recurring alternations of meters also show a recurring rhythmic pattern? How are cadences established?

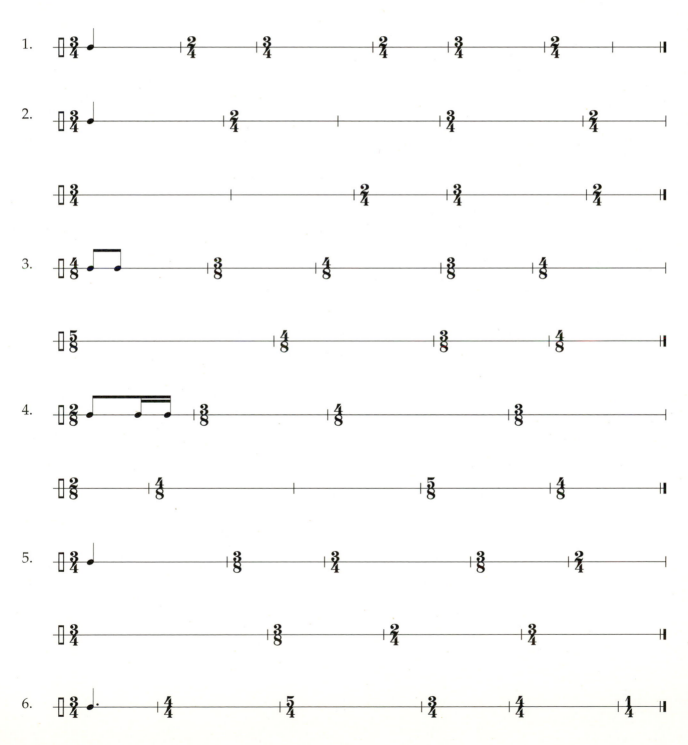

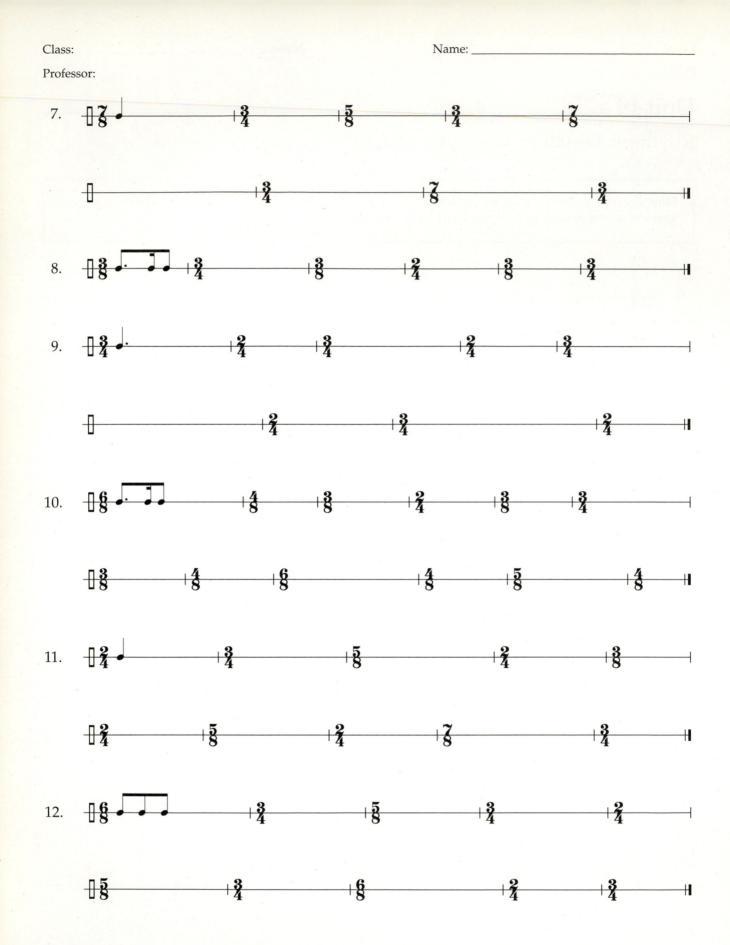

13.

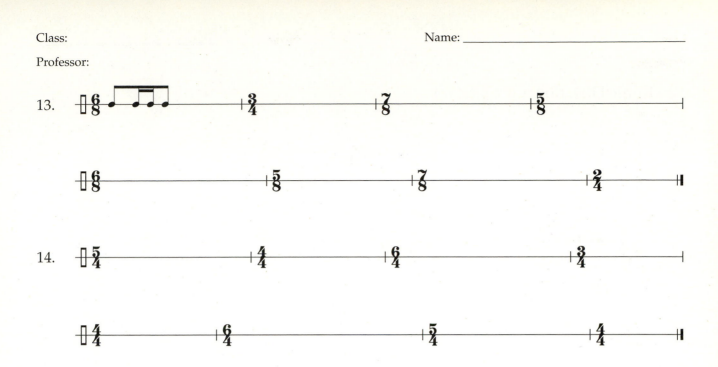

14.

Class:

Professor:

Name: ______________________________

Rhythmic Dictation: QUIZ NO. 1

1. 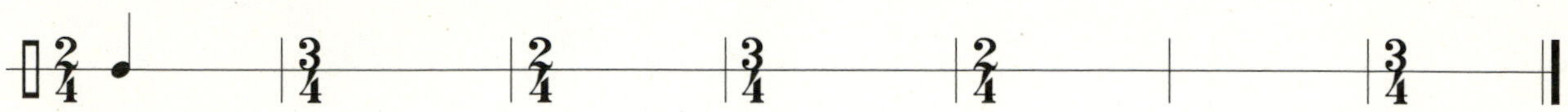

2. 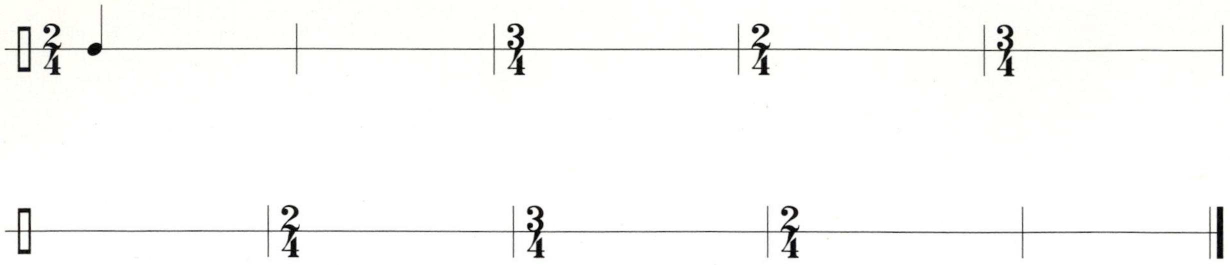

3. 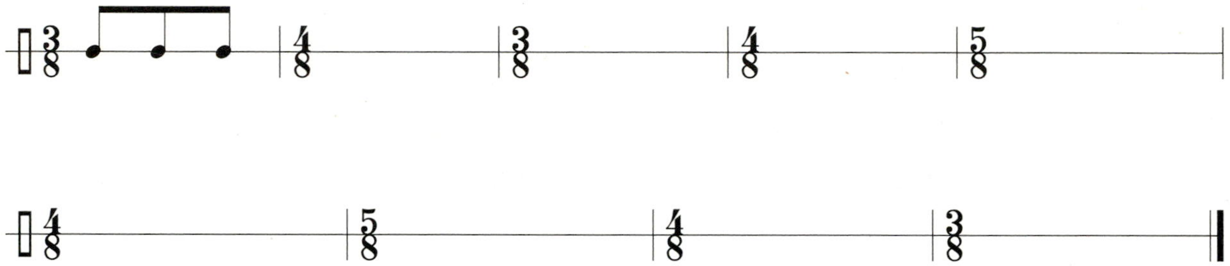

4. 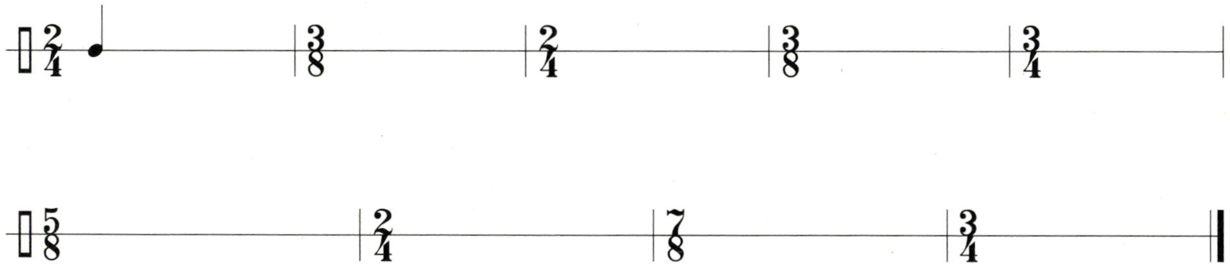

5. 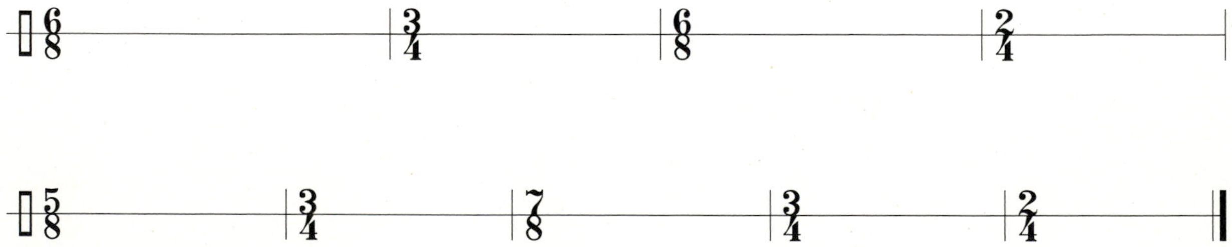

Name: _____

Rhythmic Dictation: QUIZ NO. 2

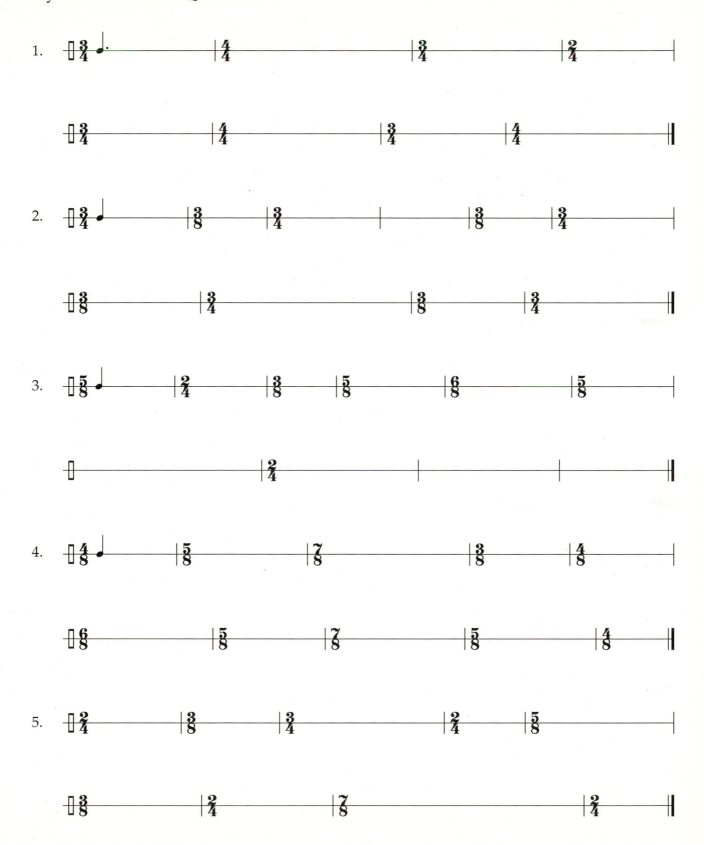

Part Music Dictation: Pandiatonicism

Focus on the individual lines. Is the motion conjunct or disjunct? Do you hear repetitions or *ostinati*, particularly in the lower voice? For an example of pandiatonicism in a piece by Stravinsky, see Unit 26, Part 1, no. 2.

Amabile

1.

Semplice

2.

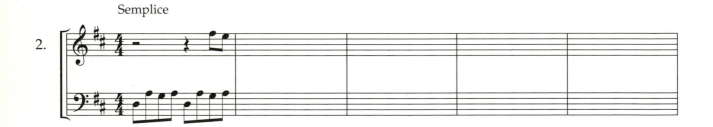

3.

Lent et grave

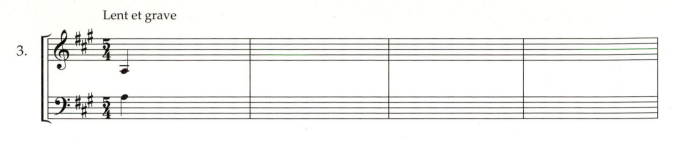

4.

Comodo

Modéré

5.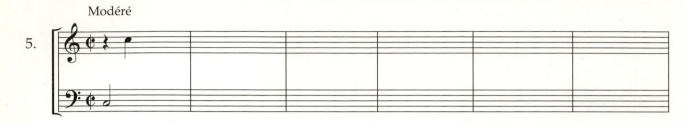

Grazioso

6.

Andantino

7.

Follow the structural lines formed by the highest and/or lowest pitches of the patterns found in the upper voice.

Allegro

8.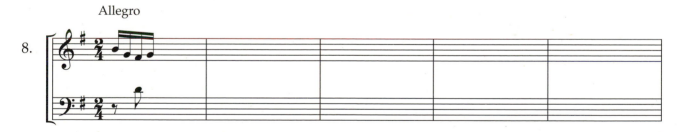

Follow the structural lines formed by the highest and/or lowest pitches of the patterns found in the upper voice.

9.

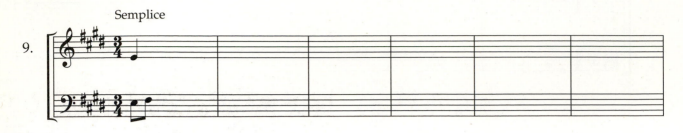

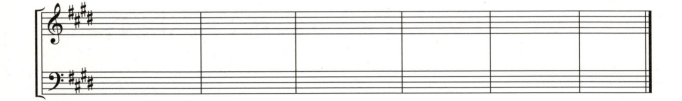

Listen for intervallic planing in one or both voices. What interval is being used?

10.

Class:

Name: _____

Professor:

Listen for intervallic planing in one or both voices. What interval is being used?

13.

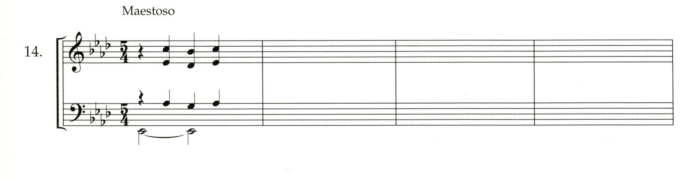

Listen for two textural elements. Focus first on the bass line. Then listen to the three upper voices. What technique is being used?

14.

Listen for two textural elements. Focus first on the bass line. Then listen to the three upper voices. What technique is being used?

Name: _____

Part Music Dictation: QUIZ NO. 1

Piacevole

1.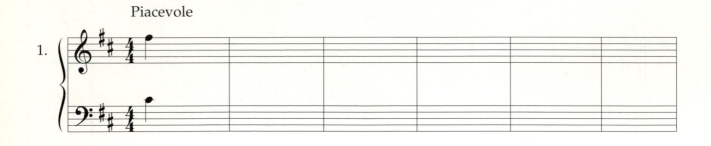

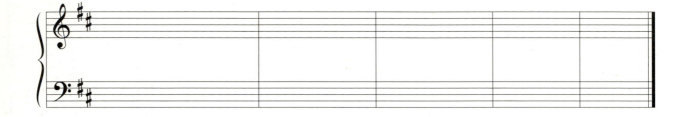

Andante

2.

Giocoso

3.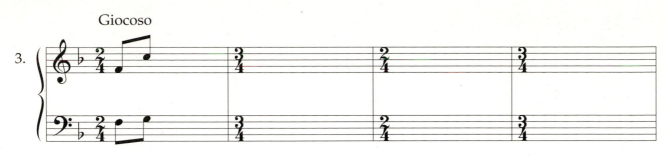

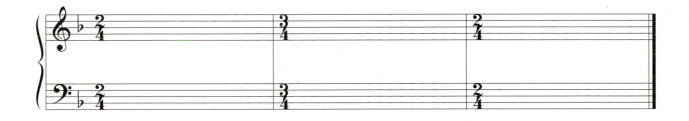

Sostenuto

4.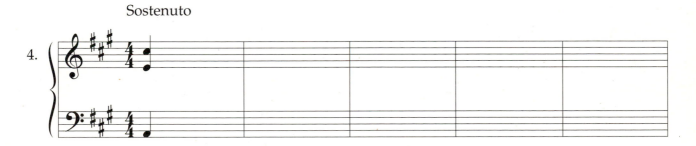

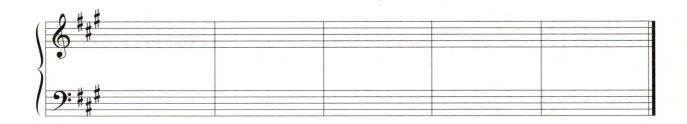

Fliessend

5.

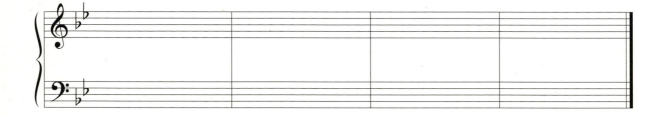

Name: _____

Part Music Dictation: QUIZ NO. 2

Tempo di Valse

1.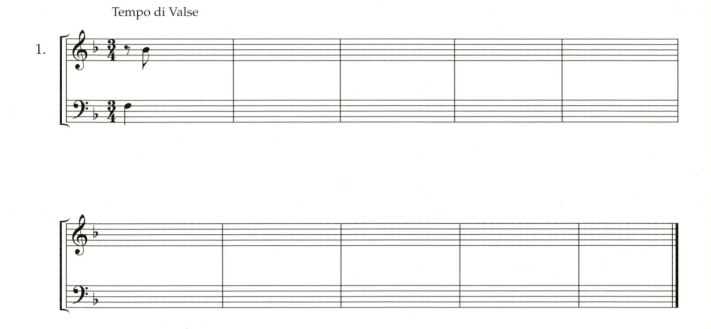

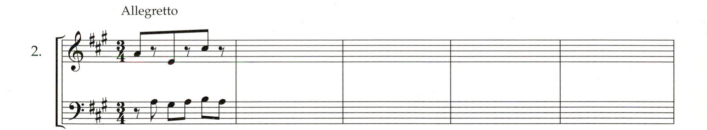

Allegretto

2.

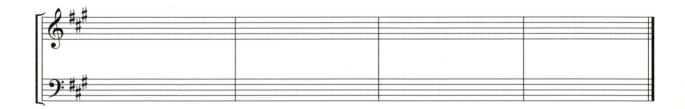

Berceuse

3.

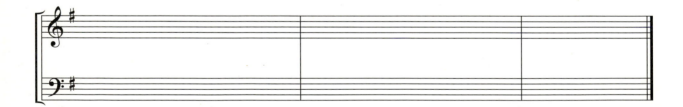

Moderato

4.

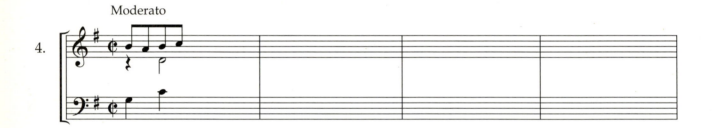

Moderato

5.

Unit 20

Rhythmic Dictation: Syncopation Including Irregular and Mixed Meters

Listen for syncopated accents occurring on weak beats or parts of beats. Does the syncopation occur at the beat level or at the division (or subdivision) level? Listen for uneven patterns of metrical accent that may suggest irregular or mixed meters. Recurring beat patterns such as 2 + 3 or 2 + 2 + 3 may occur. Some examples also employ triplets in simple meter or duplets in compound meter.

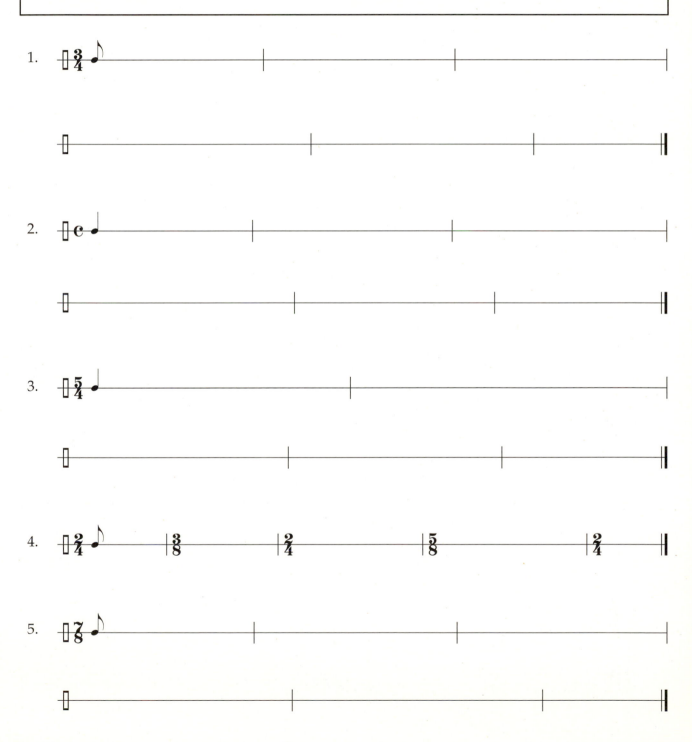

1.

2.

3.

4.

5.

11.

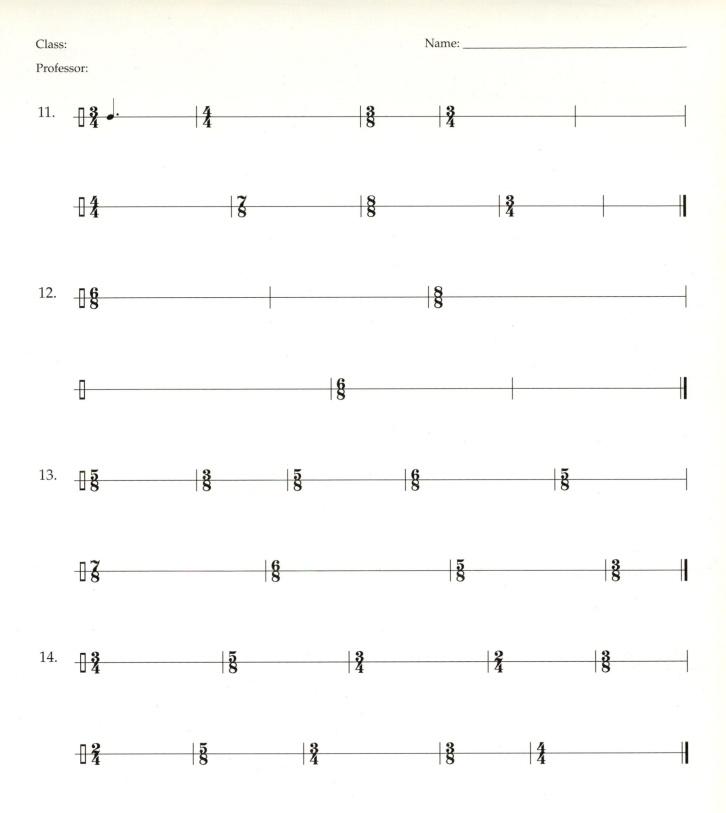

Rhythmic Dictation: QUIZ NO. 1

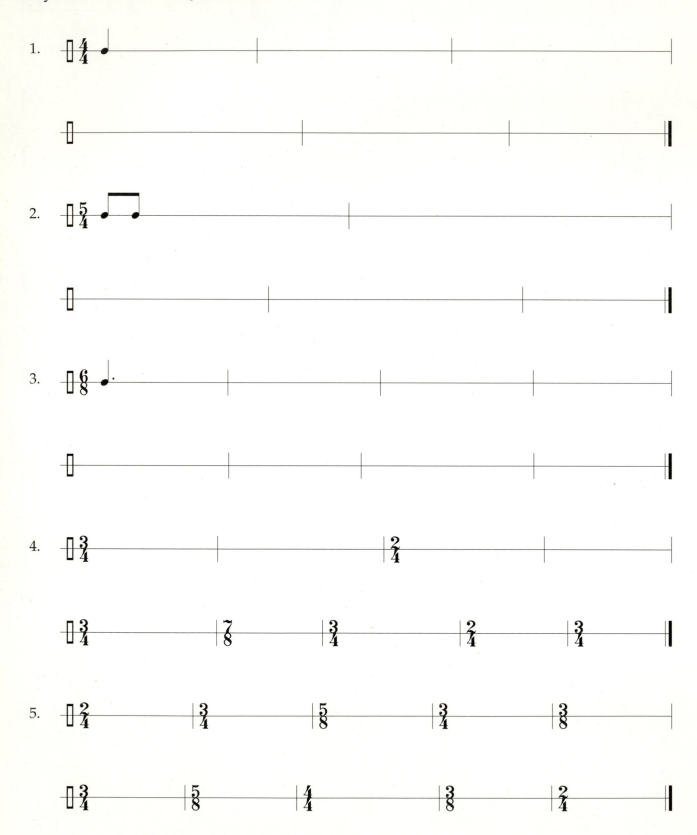

Rhythmic Dictation: QUIZ NO. 2

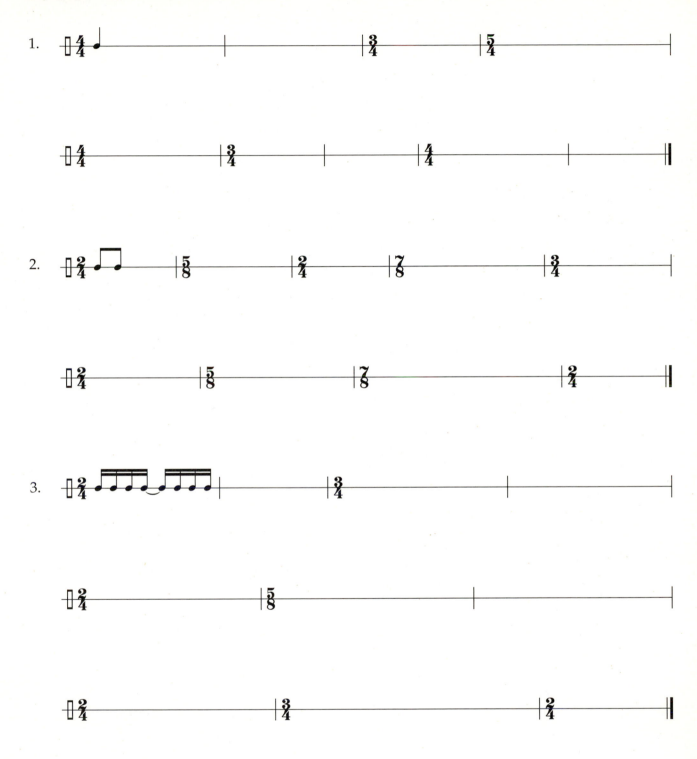

Name: _____

4.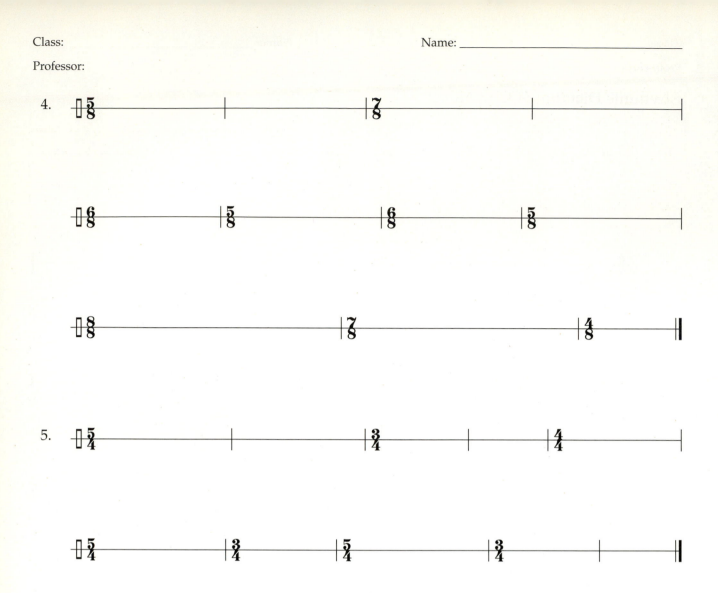

5.

Melodic Dictation: Extended and Altered Tertian Harmony

These exercises are more challenging. Is there a tonal center? How is it established? Isolate the arpeggiations. What is the quality of the chord? What position is it in? Are tall chords implied? What is their quality? Then focus on scalar passages. Is a conventional scale suggested? A church mode? Or is the pattern symmetrical or irregular? Examples of extended and altered tertian harmony in pieces by Debussy and Carpenter can be found in Unit 26, Parts 1 and 2.

Risoluto

13.

Comodo

14.

Melodic Dictation: QUIZ NO. 1

Serioso

5.

Class:

Professor:

Name: _____

Melodic Dictation: QUIZ NO. 2

Grazioso

1.

Moderato

2.

Moderato

3.

Scorrevole

4.

Tempo di valse

5.

Harmonic Dictation: Extended and Altered Tertian Harmony

These exercises present common, but often nonfunctional, progressions. Chordal extensions, such as the 9th, 11th, 13th, or added 6th are included. Focus on the qualities of each chord. Then work out the outer voices. Finally, fill in the inner voices. Chord symbols are now appropriate for analysis and should be placed above the treble staff as in sheet music or lead sheets. Examples of extended and altered tertian harmony in pieces by Debussy and Carpenter can be found in Unit 26, Parts 1 and 2.

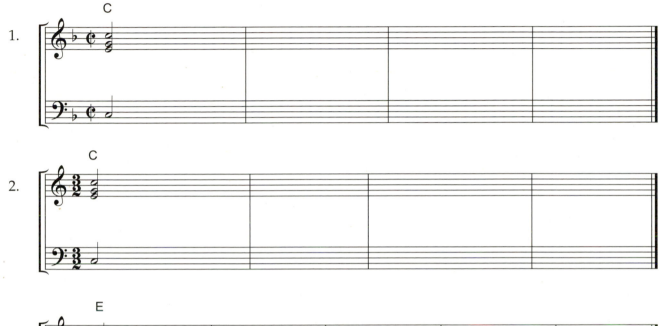

1. C

2. C

3. E

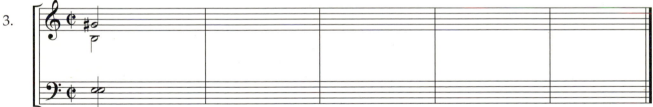

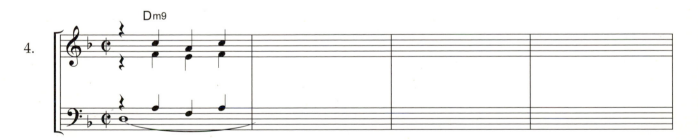

4. Dm9

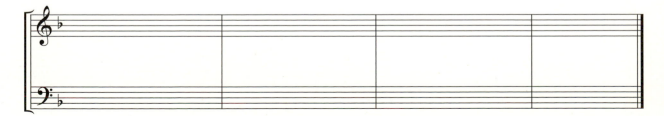

5.

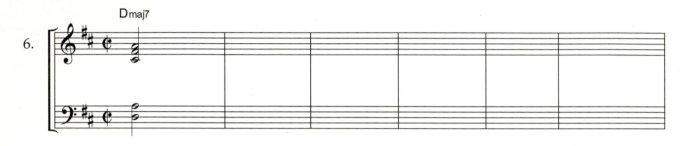

Several of the chords in the following exercise can be analyzed either as extended and altered dominants or as polychords. (See Unit 23.)

6.

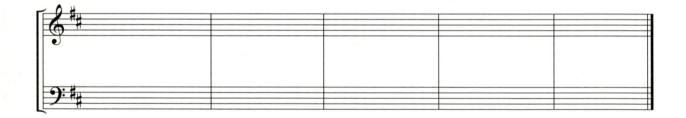

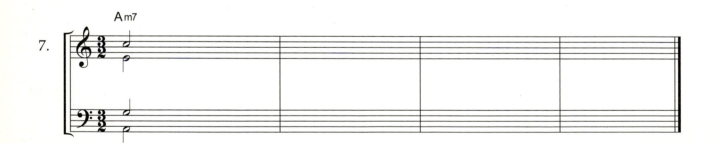

7.

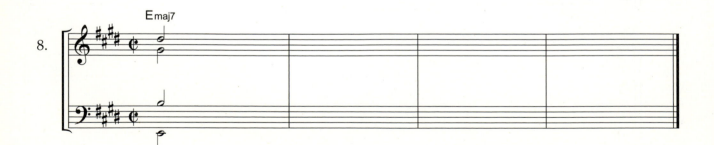

8.

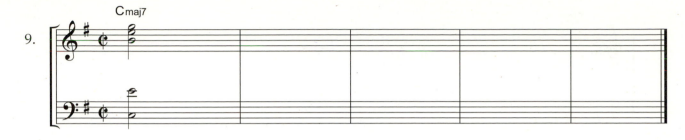

9. Cmaj7

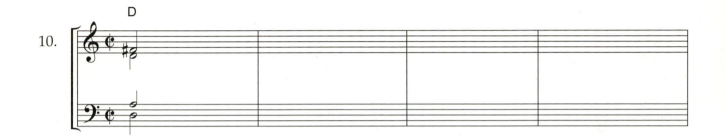

10. D

11. D7

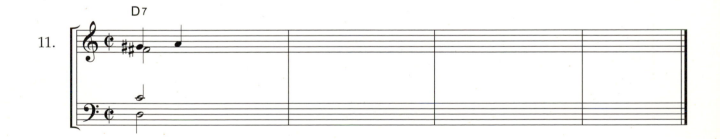

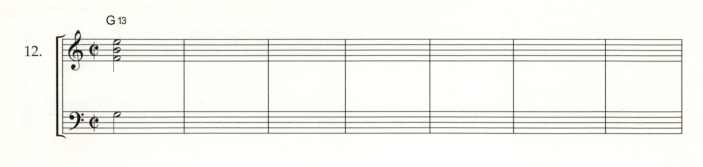

12. G 13

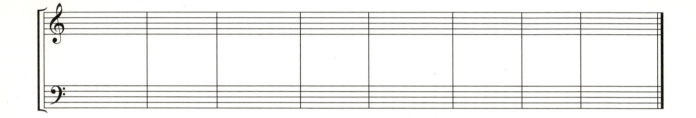

13. C maj7

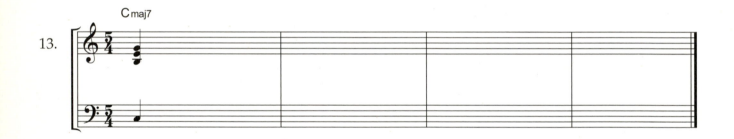

14. E

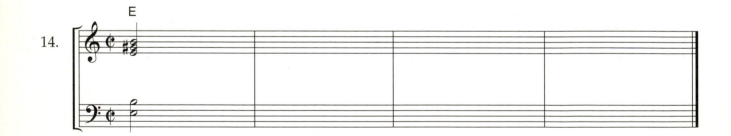

Harmonic Dictation: QUIZ NO. 1

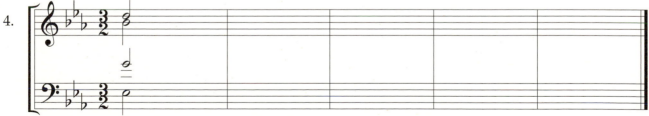

5.

Dmaj7

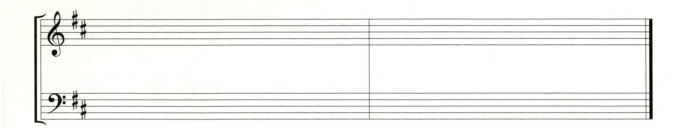

Harmonic Dictation: QUIZ NO. 2

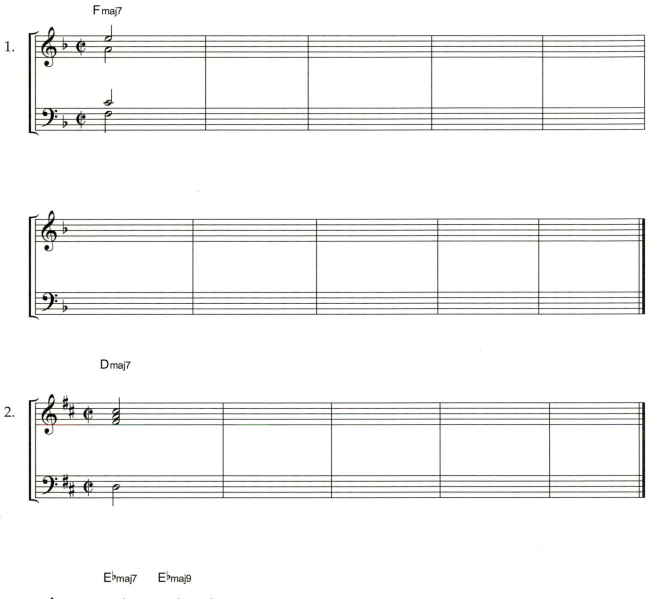

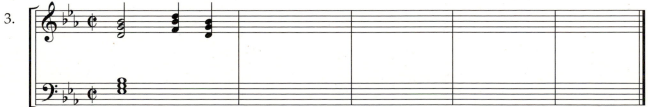

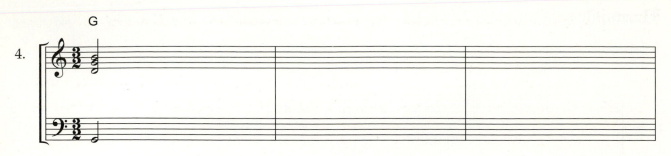

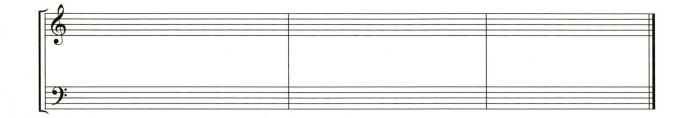

5.

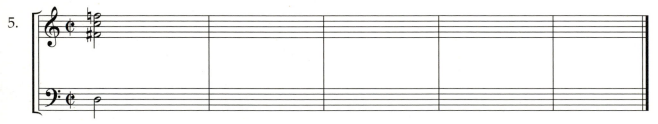

Unit 21

Melodic Dictation: Exotic Scales

Is there a tonal center? How is it established? What scale is present in each exercise? What are the characteristic intervals of the scale? Are they prominent in the melody? For examples of exotic and artificial scales in pieces by Debussy, Stravinsky, Bartók, Carpenter, and Lasala, see Unit 26, Parts 1 and 2.

Inscrutably

1.

Moderato

2.

Vigoroso

3.

Alla inglese

4.

Misterioso

9.

Gracieux

10.

Melancholique

11.

Moderato

12.

Gracioso

13.

Melodic Dictation: QUIZ NO. 1

Andantino

1.

Vif

2.

Moderato

3.

Im Volkston

4.

Andante tenebroso

5.

Melodic Dictation: QUIZ NO. 2

Con espressione

4.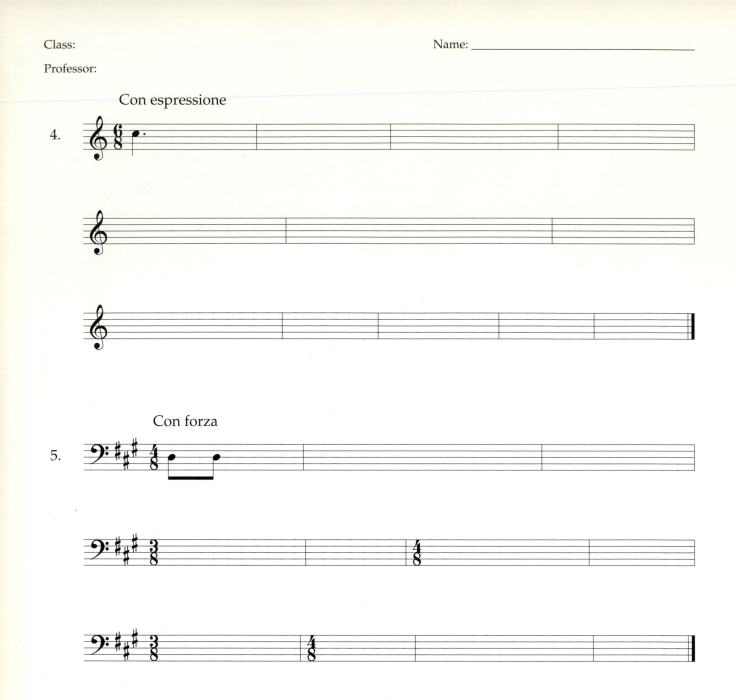

Con forza

5.

Part Music Dictation: Exotic Scales

Is there a tonal center? How is it established? What scale is present in each exercise? Do you hear repetitions of patterns? Ostinati? Imitation? What chord types are present? How are the chords connected? You do not need to provide a harmonic analysis. For examples of exotic and artificial scales in pieces by Debussy, Stravinsky, Bartók, Carpenter, and Lasala, see Unit 26, Parts 1 and 2.

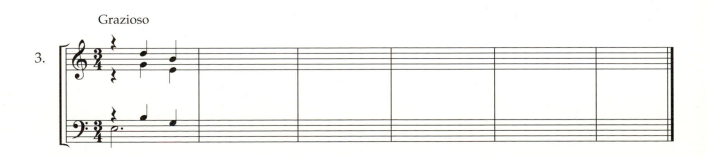

Assez lentment

4.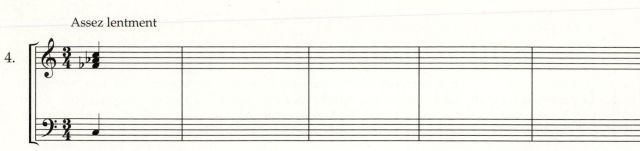

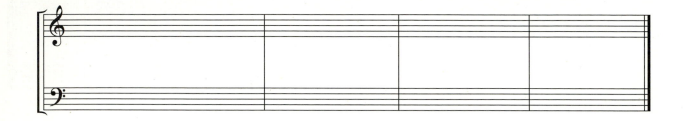

Comodo

5.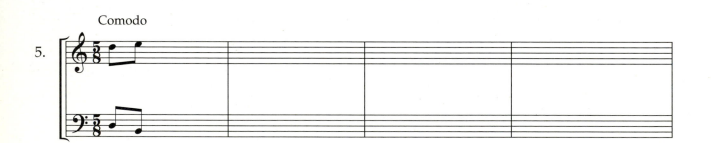

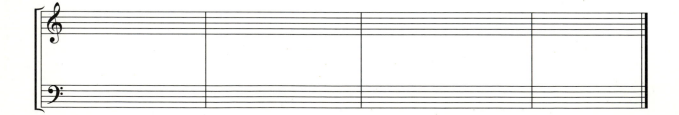

Class: _____

Professor: _____

Name: _____

Furioso

6.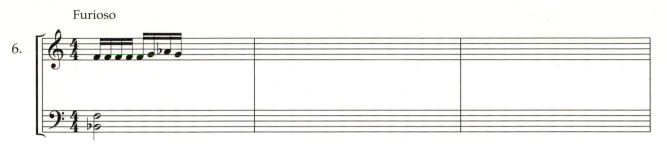

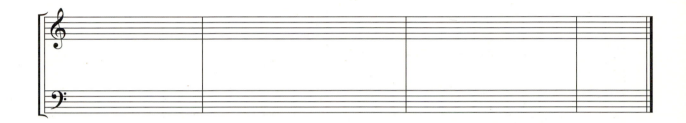

Semplice

7.

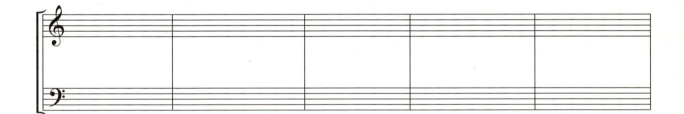

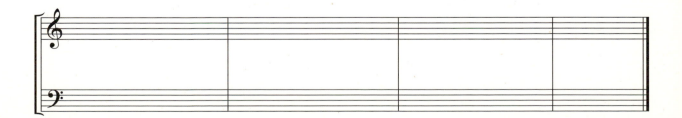

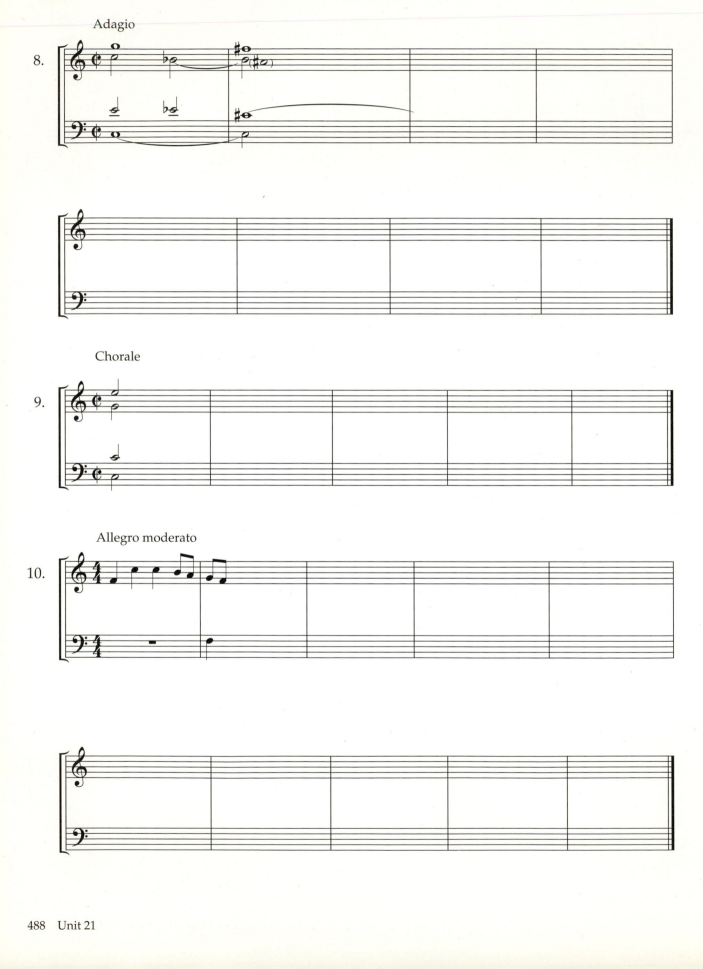

Part Music Dictation: QUIZ NO. 1

1.

Andantino

Lugubre

2.

Lebhaft

3.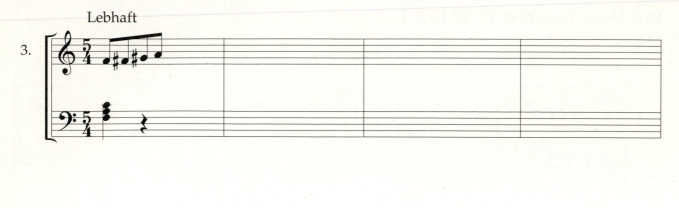

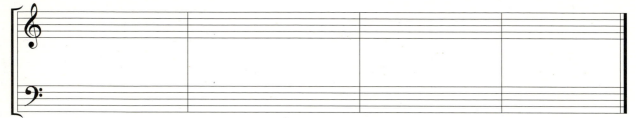

Name: _____

Part Music Dictation: QUIZ NO. 2

Scherzando

1.

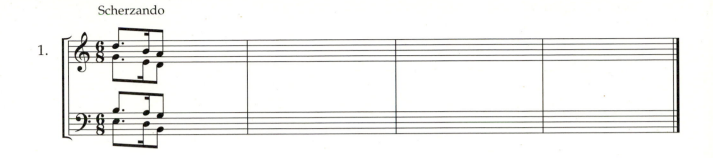

Moderato

2.

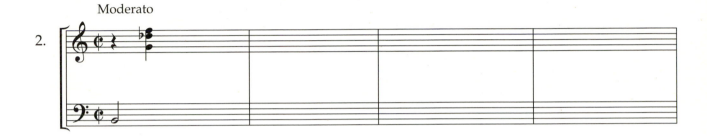

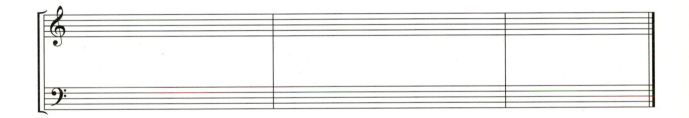

Tempo di Valse

3.

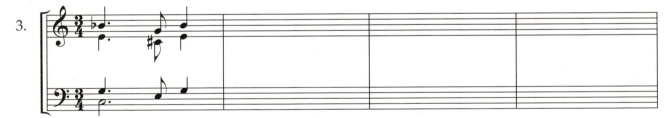

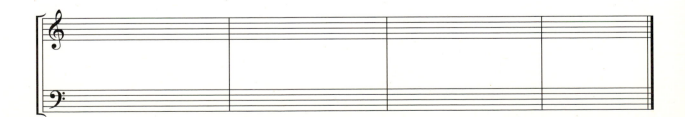

Unit 22

Melodic Dictation: Quartal Harmony

These exercises focus on patterns using fourths and fifths. Is there a tonal center? How is it established? Isolate the scalar fragments. What is the pattern of whole and half step? Are conventional scales suggested? Exotic or symmetrical? For examples of quartal harmony in pieces by Stravinsky and Debussy, see Unit 26, Part 1.

Nicht zu schnell

1.

Feierlich

2.

Sehr langsam

3.

Fanfaro

4.

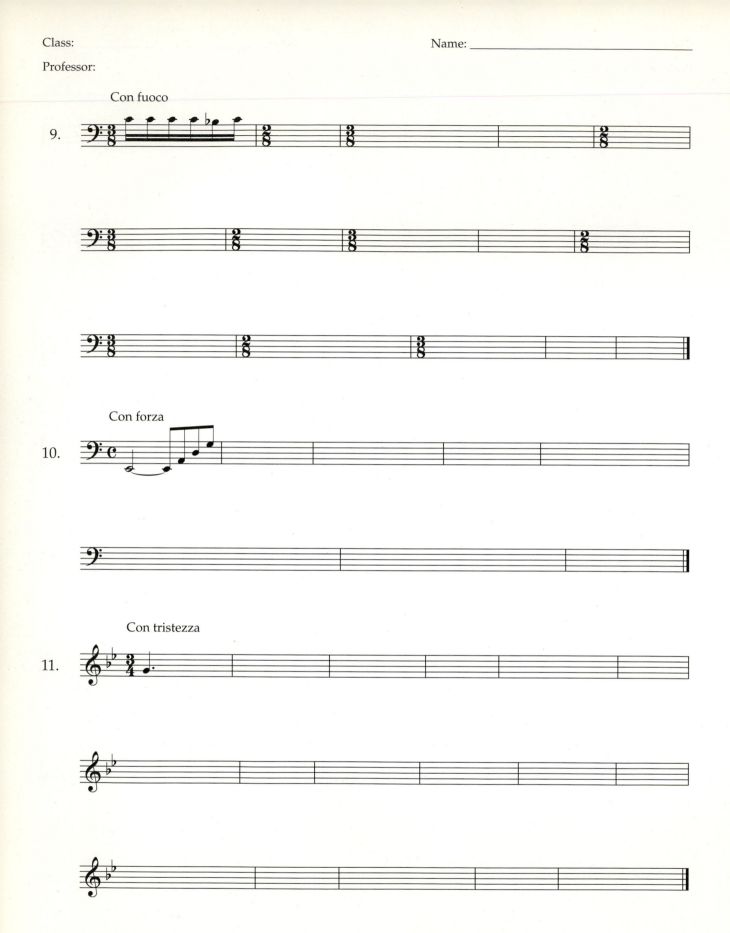

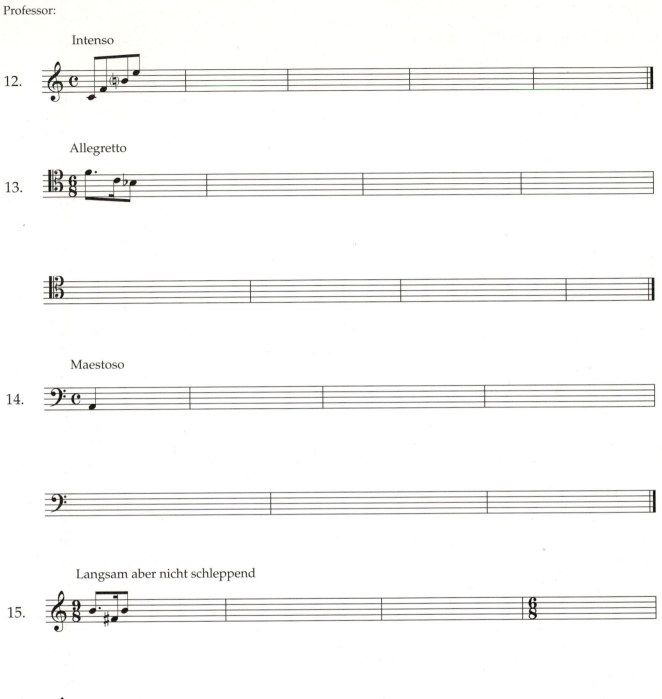

Melodic Dictation: QUIZ NO. 1

Melancholique

5.

Class: _____   Name: _____

Professor: _____

Melodic Dictation: QUIZ NO. 2

Con moto

1.

Commodo

2.

Pesante

3.

4. Scherzando

5. Giocoso

Part Music Dictation: Quartal Harmony

Is there a tonal center? How is it established? Concentrate on the individual voices. Do major or minor triads occur? Where? How are chords connected? You do not need to provide a harmonic analysis. For examples of quartal harmony in pieces by Stravinsky and Debussy, see Unit 26, Part 1.

Solenne

1.
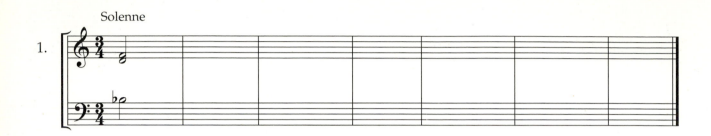

Semplice

2.

Lullaby

3.
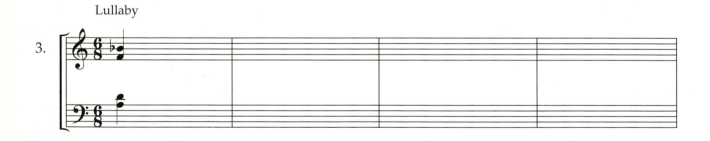

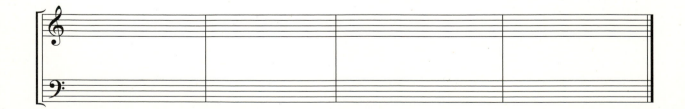

Etwas langsam

4.

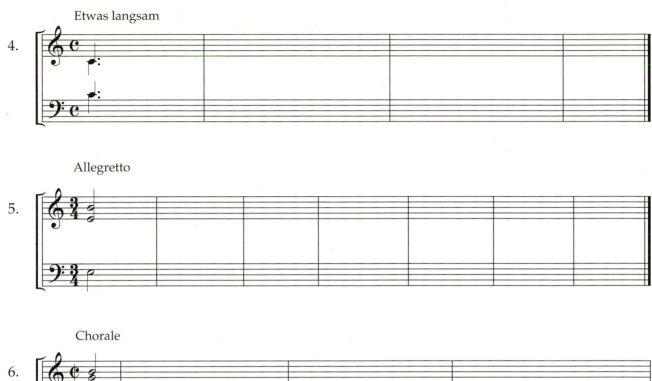

Allegretto

5.

Chorale

6.

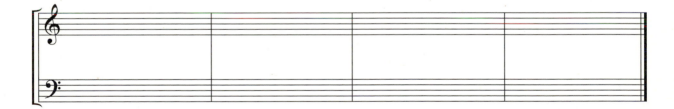

Moderato

7.

Class: _____   Name: _____

Professor: _____

Stately

8.

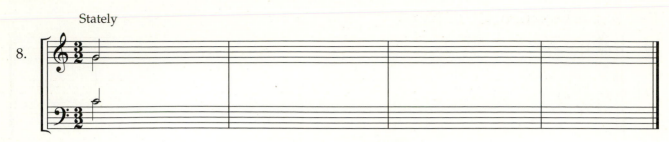

What technique is employed in the upper voices?

Molto sostenuto

9.

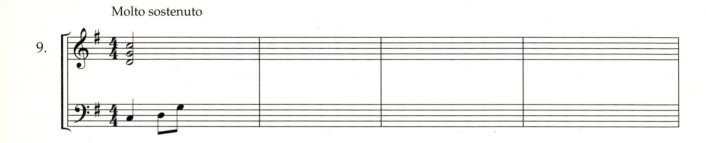

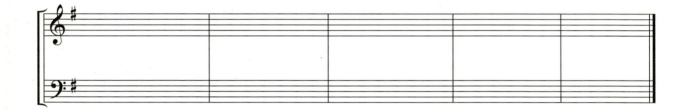

Breit

10.

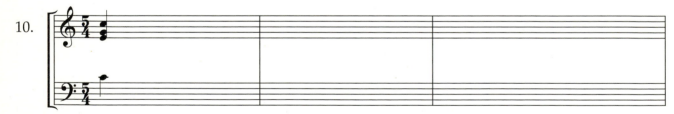

Part Music Dictation: QUIZ NO. 1

Lento

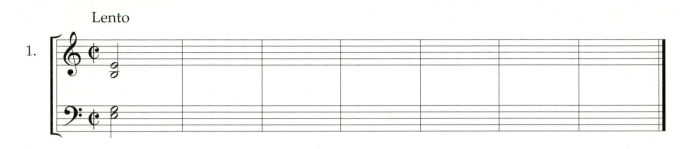

Maestoso

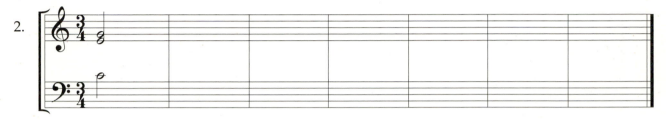

Comodo

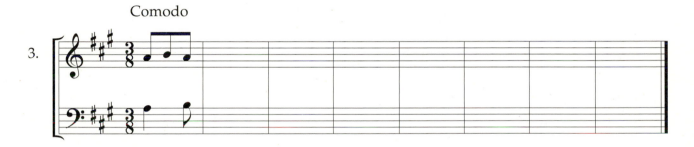

Larghetto

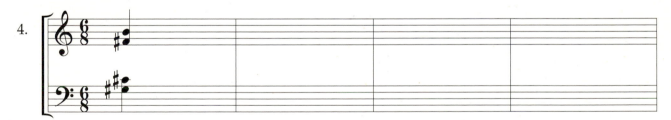

Maestoso

5.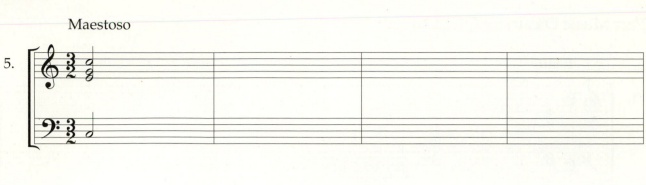

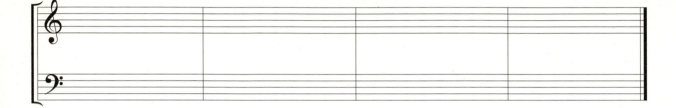

Part Music Dictation: QUIZ NO. 2

Moderato

1.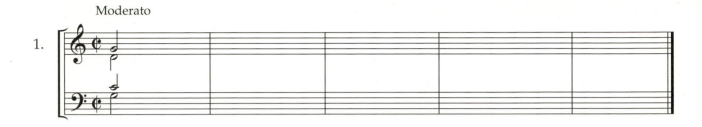

Con moto

2.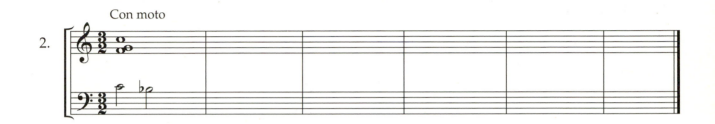

Andantino

3.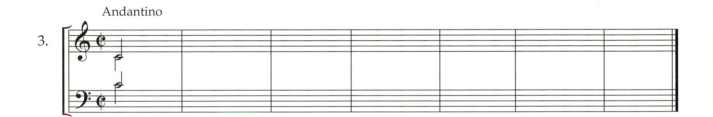

Amabile

4.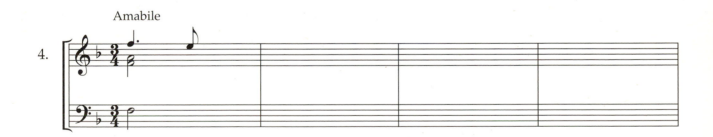

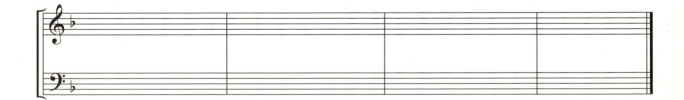

Festivo

5.

Unit 23

Part Music Dictation: Polyharmony and Polytonality

For examples of polyharmony and polytonality by Bartók, see Unit 26, Part 2.

What scale is suggested in each part? What device is employed in the lower voice?

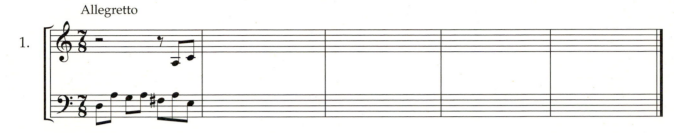

1.

What technique is being employed here?

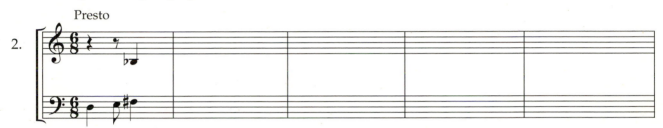

2.

Is there a tonal center? How is it established? What is the basic chord type?

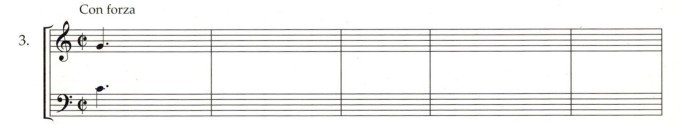

3.

Commodo

4.

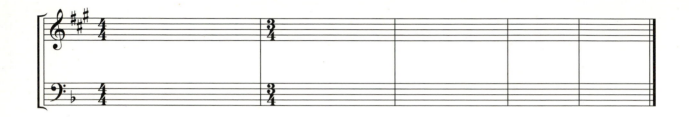

Sustained

5.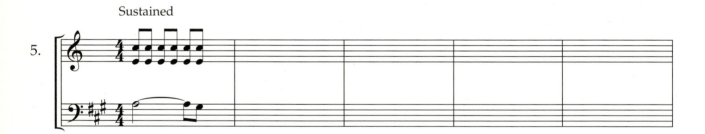

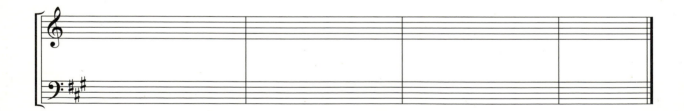

6.

Semplice

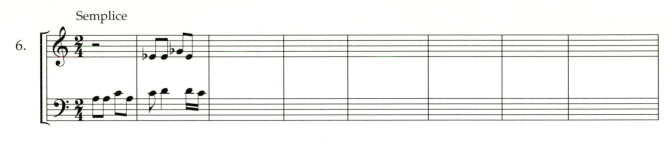

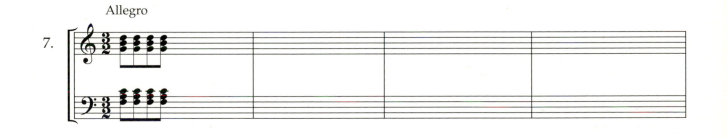

7.

Allegro

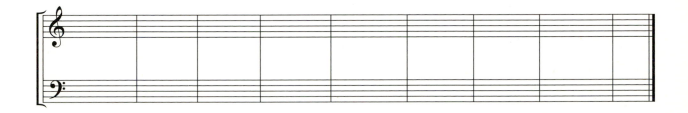

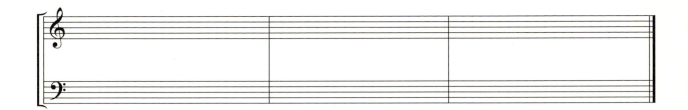

Maestoso

8.

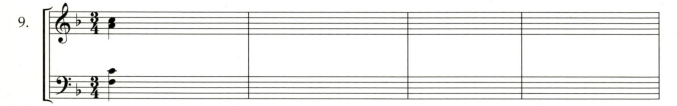

Rakishly

9.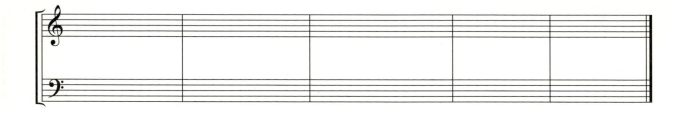

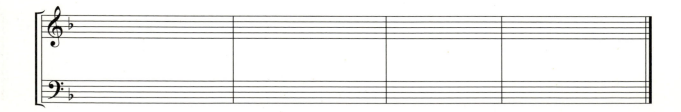

Allegro giocoso

10.
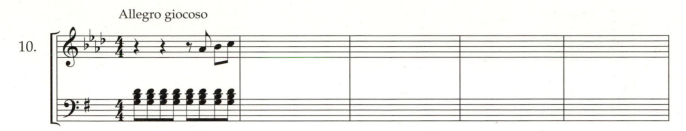

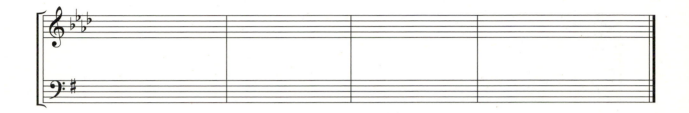

Lentemente

11.
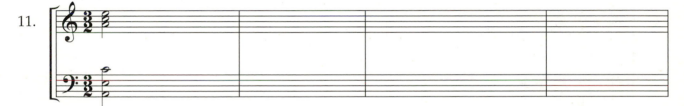

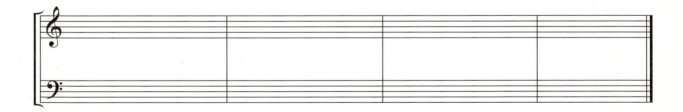

Vigoroso

12.

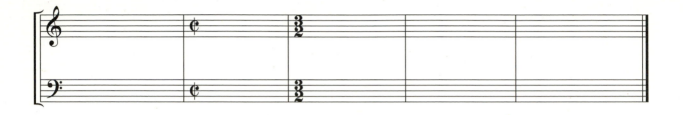

Nostalgico

13.
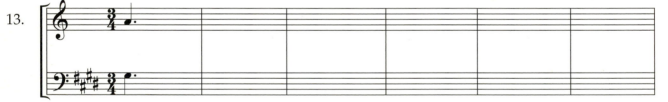

14.

Fanfare

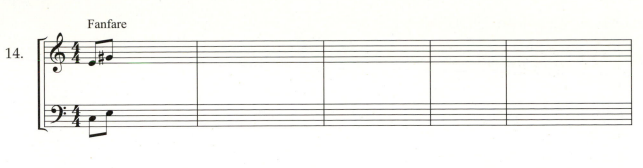

Part Music Dictation: QUIZ NO. 1

Piacevole

1.

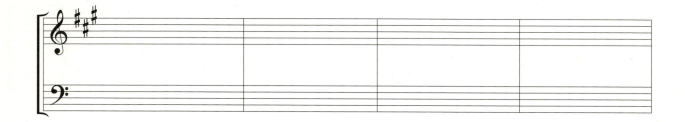

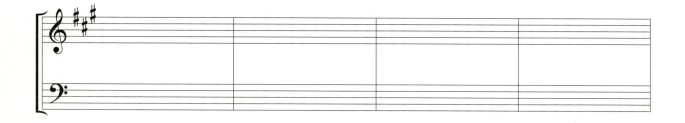

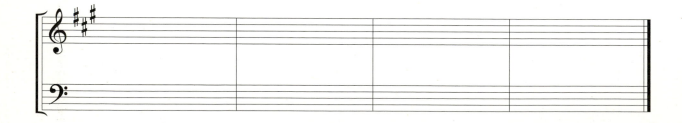

Grave

2.

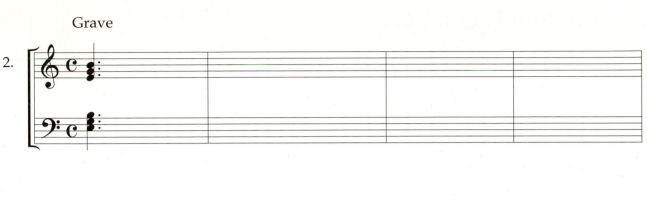

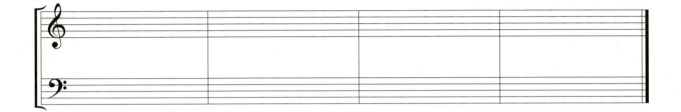

Allegro ma no troppo

3.

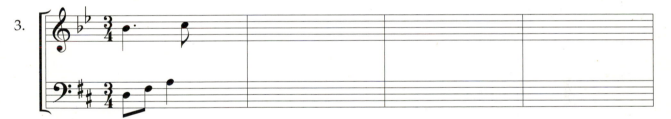

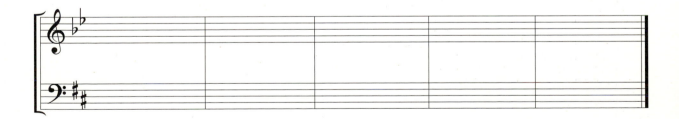

Vivace

4.

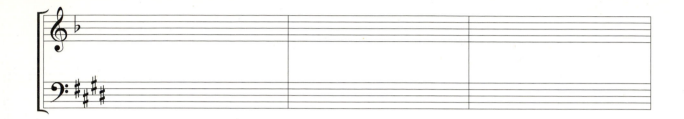

Allegretto

5.

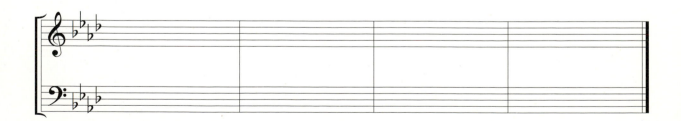

Part Music Dictation: QUIZ NO. 2

Moderato

1.
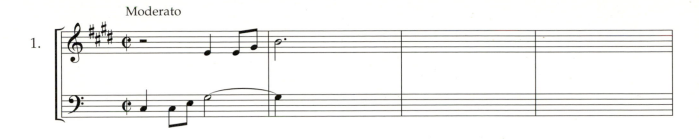

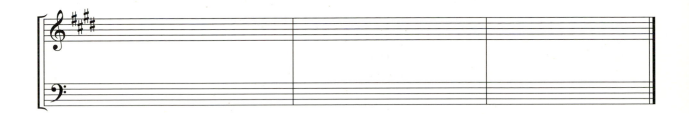

Tempo di Tango

2.
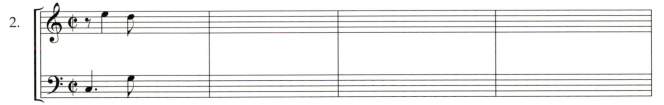

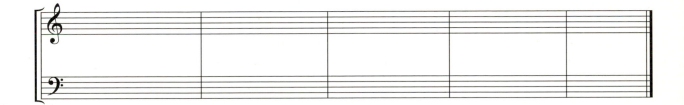

Maestoso

3.

Doloroso

4.

Majestically

5.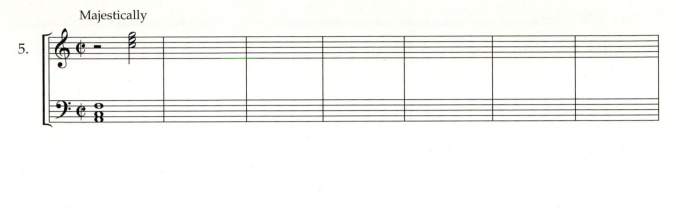

Unit 24

Melodic Dictation: Interval Music

Preliminary Exercises

These exercises will seriously test your ability to hear intervals! Focus on cells of three to four notes. Is there a pattern? Does this pattern recur? What is the interval connecting the recurrences (interval of transposition)? Are there permutations of intervals within the cell? Examples of interval music by Stravinsky, Bartók, Sessions, and Schoenberg can be found in Unit 26, Part 3.

In these next two examples, listen for the wedge shape.

Melodies

Are there obvious sets or cells? Do you hear recurrences or transpositions? Are there permutations of intervals within the cells? Examples of interval music by Stravinsky, Bartók, Sessions, and Schoenberg can be found in Unit 26, Part 3.

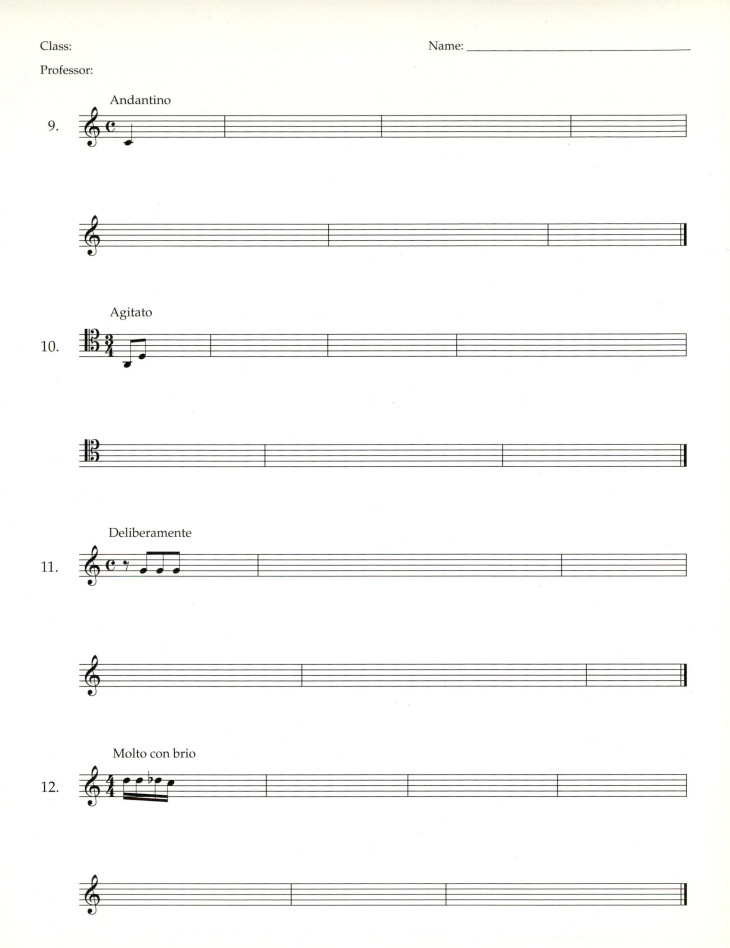

13.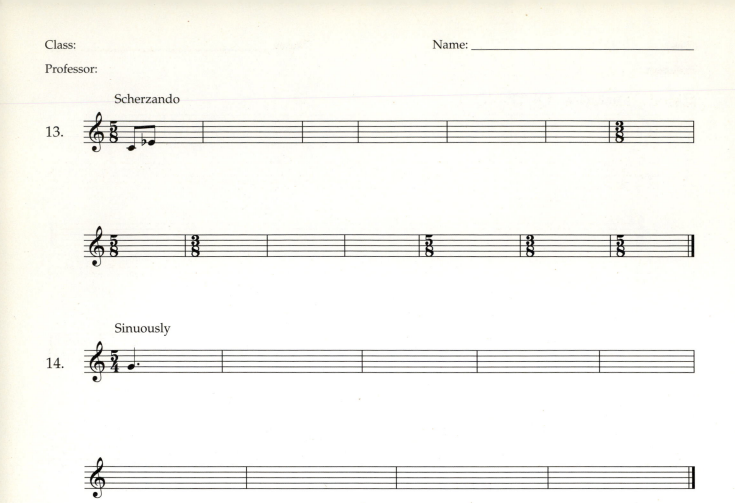

14.

Melodic Dictation: QUIZ NO. 1

Allegro ma non troppo

4.

Lugubre

5.

Melodic Dictation: QUIZ NO. 2

Scherzando

1.

Larghetto

2.

Strepitoso

3.

Agitato

4.

Moderato

5.

Unit 25

Melodic Dictation: Serial Music

Are there cells or sets within the rows? Are there any "anchors" such as repetition or recurrence of pitches or intervals in the same register to help you "solve" these exercises? Examples of serial music by Schoenberg, Dallapicolla, and Webern can be found in Unit 26, Part 3.

Melodic Dictation: QUIZ NO. 1

1. Fliessend

2. Allegro

3. Con espressione

Melodic Dictation: QUIZ NO. 2

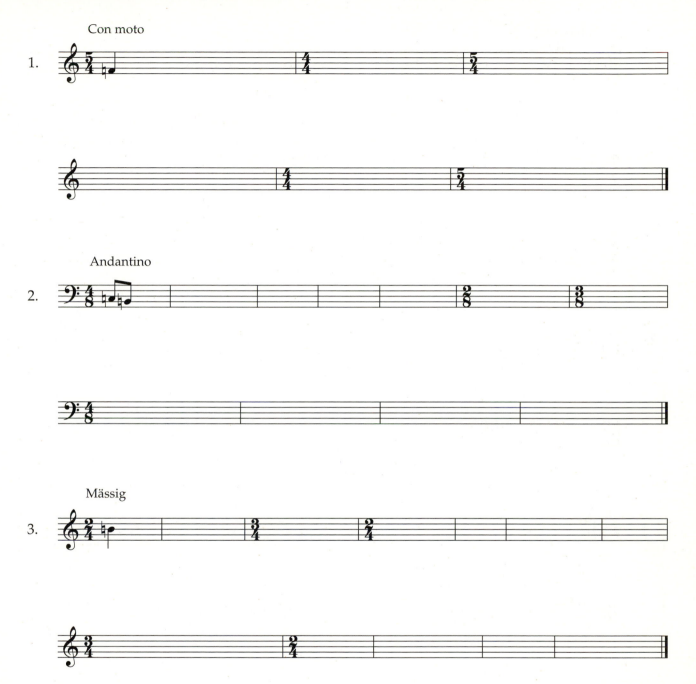

Unit 26

Examples from Music Literature

Part 1: Modality, pandiatoniscism, free tertian, jazz

These exercises present actual music for you to transcribe. All contain only the melodic and harmonic vocabulary studied in Units 18–25 and you should be able to transcribe each item completely. Listen to the example first. What is the texture? Concentrate on individual lines. What is the scale or mode? Then listen harmonically. What kinds of chord structures are employed? Are chords connected traditionally or is some contemporary device such as planing used? Is the music tonal? How is the sense of tonal center established? Are there obvious candences?

1. Béla Bartók, Evening in the Country

Lento, rubato

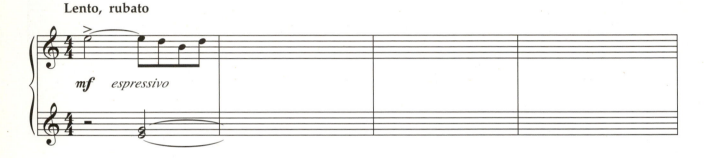

2. Igor Stravinsky, Vivo

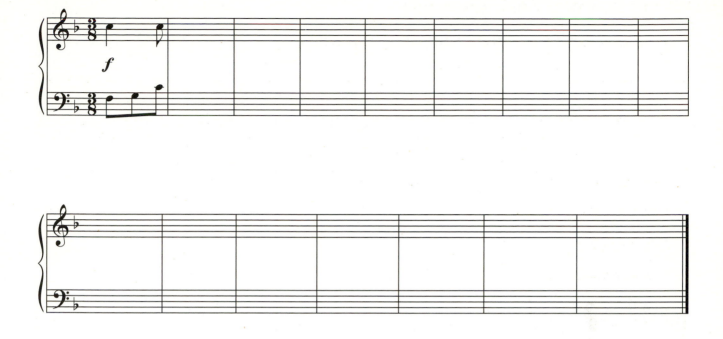

3. Ernst Bloch, Waves, mm. 71–78

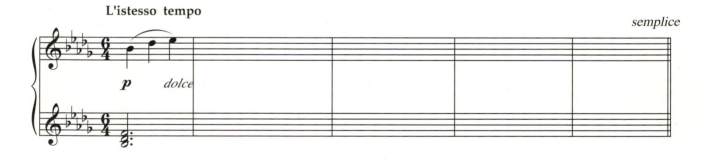

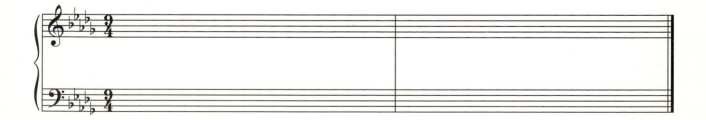

4. Claude Debussy, Prelude VIII, mm. 24–28

Très calme et doucement expressif

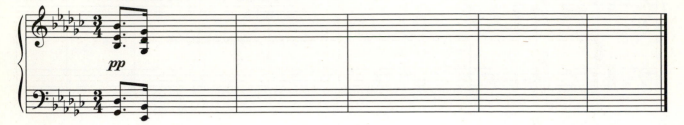

5. Claude Debussy, Sarabande, mm. 23–29

Avec une élégance grave et lente

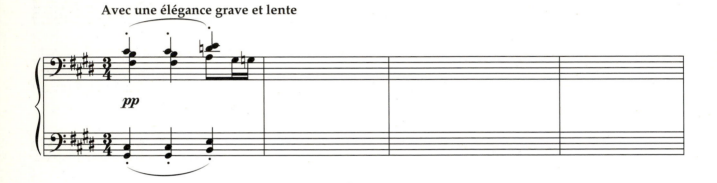

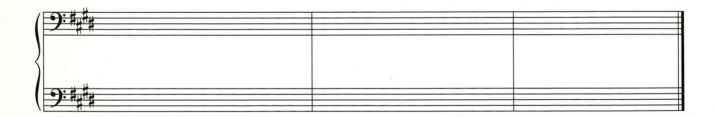

6. Igor Stravinsky, *L'Histoire du Soldat,* "Marche Royale"

QUIZ NO. 1

1. Carlos Chávez, Prelude No. 2

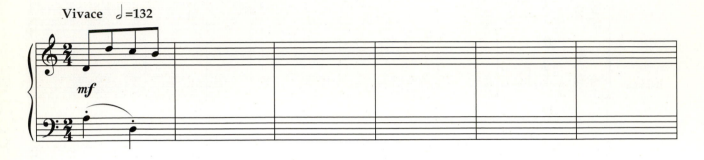

2. Claude Debussy, Rêverie, mm. 51–58

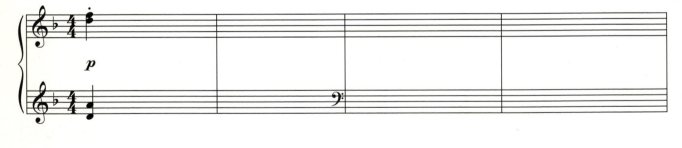

3. Igor Stravinsky, *L'Histoire du Soldat*, Petit Choral

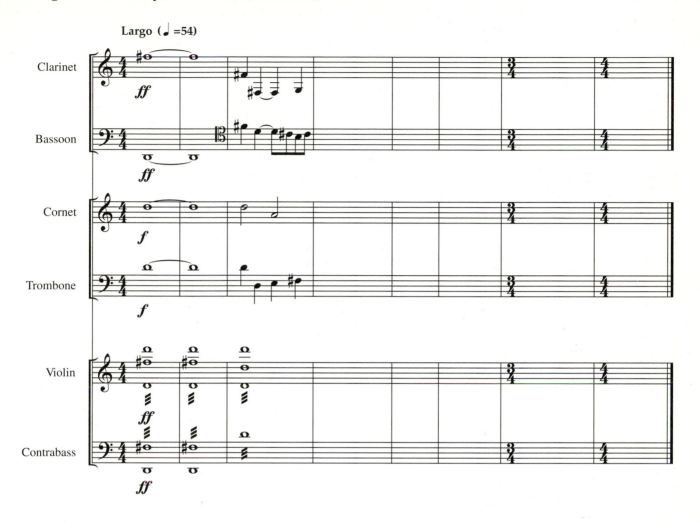

4. Bronislau Kaper, Green Dolphin Street

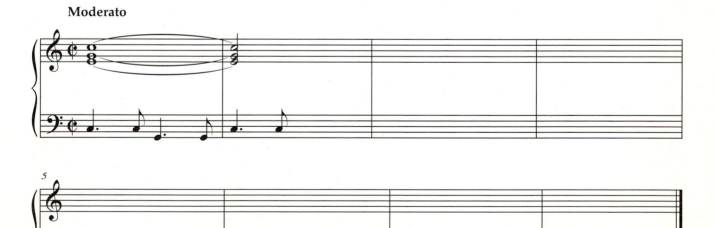

Part 2: Scalar and chordal techniques, polytonality

1. Béla Bartók, Forty-four Violin Duets, No. 33, Harvest Song

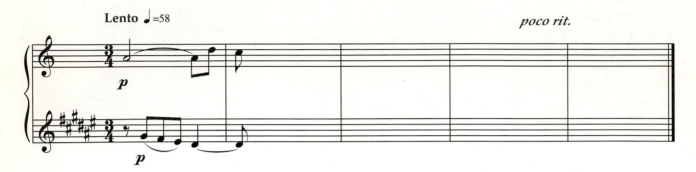

2. Bela Bartók, Sketches, II (See-saw . . .)

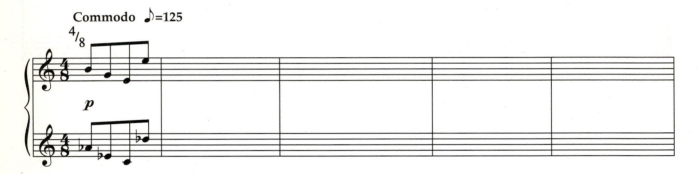

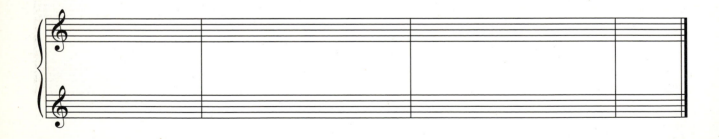

3. Béla Bartók, Sketches, V (Roumanian Folk Song)

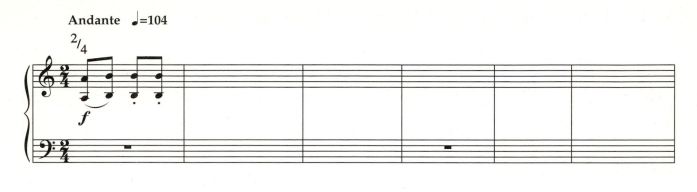

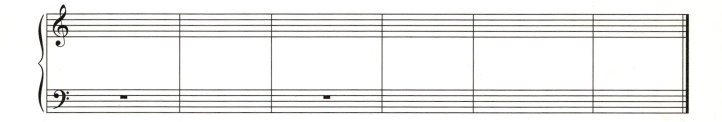

4. John Alden Carpenter, Danza, mm. 193–198

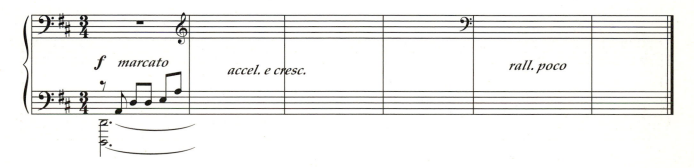

5. Ángel Lasala, Trío No. 1, I, mm. 77–82

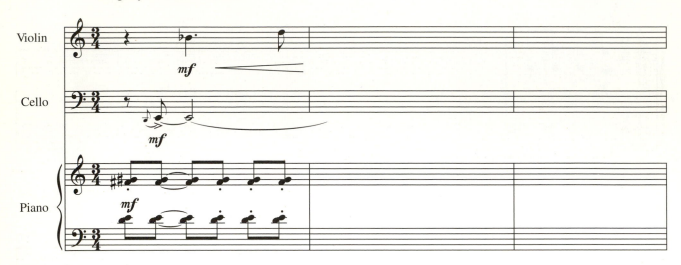

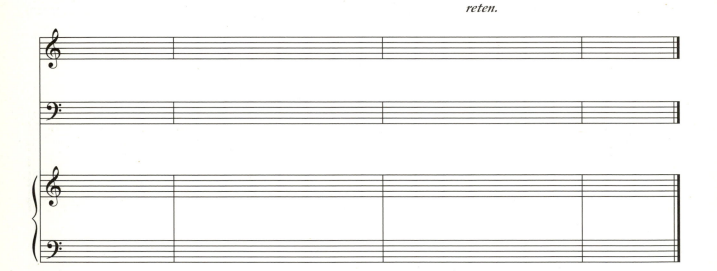

QUIZ NO. 2

1. Béla Bartók, Bear Dance

Allegro vivace

molto marcato

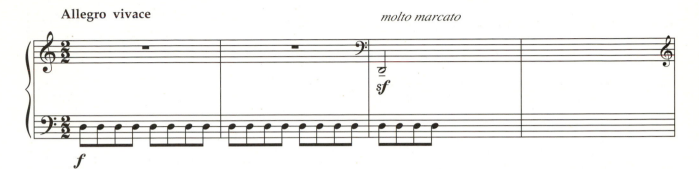

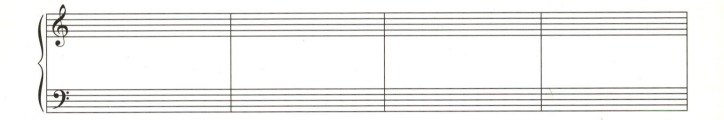

Part 3: Interval music, free atonality, and serialism

These exercises will require you to focus on hearing intervals. You may wish to review the interval exercises in Unit 1 and the web-based interval exercises. Listen for recurring motives of three or four notes. Is there evidence of twelve-tone serialism?

1. Igor Stravinsky, Symphony of Psalms, II

Tempo ♪=60

2. Béla Bartók, Music for Strings, Percussion, and Celesta, I

Andante tranquillo ♪=c.112–116

con sord.

3. Arnold Schoenberg, Three Songs

Etwas langsam (♩=76)

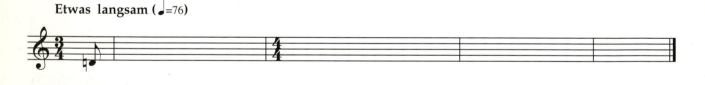

4. Luigi Dallapiccola, Goethe Lieder, Mvt. 2

poco rall.   **più tranquillo** (♩=54)

dolce; sost.

5. Roger Sessions, Sonata for Violin

Tempo moderato, con ampiezza e liberamente (♩=c.66)

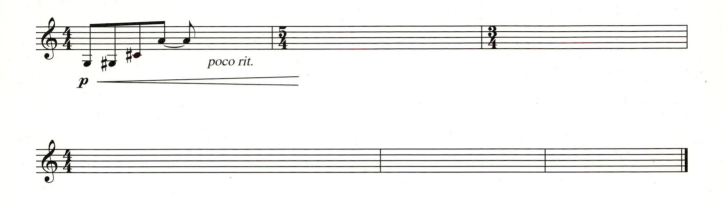

6. Arnold Schoenberg, Drei Klavierstück, Op. 11, No. 1

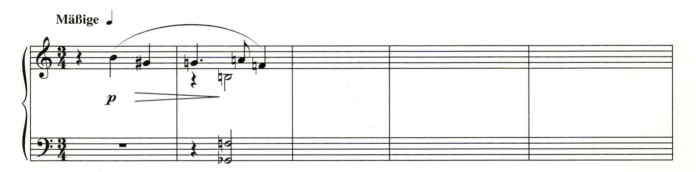

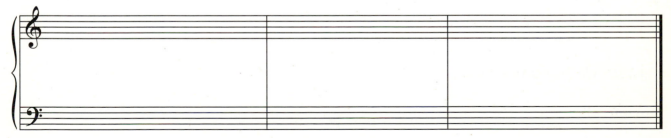

7. Anton Webern, Symphony, Op. 21, II, Variationen, Thema

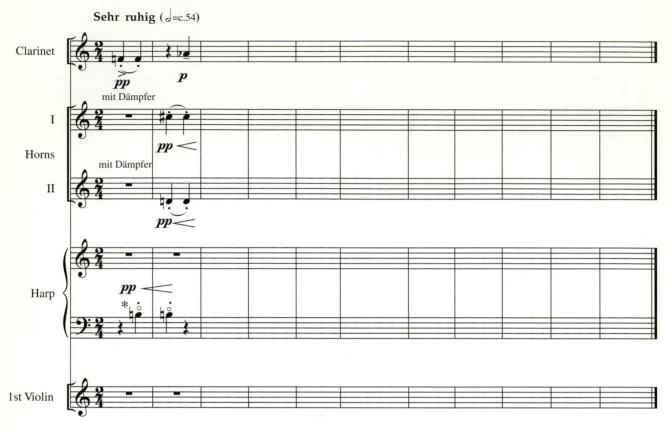

* The harmonics (○) in the Harp sound an octave higher than written.

QUIZ NO. 3

1. Edgard Varèse, *Octandre*, I

2. Ernst Krenek, *Suite for Violoncello Solo*

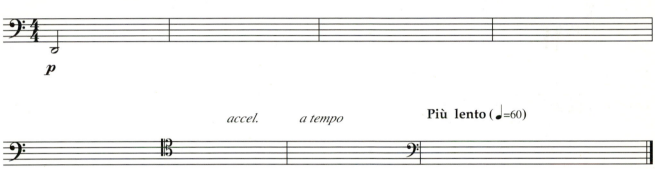

3. Luigi Dallapiccola, *Quaderno Musicale di Annalibera*, I

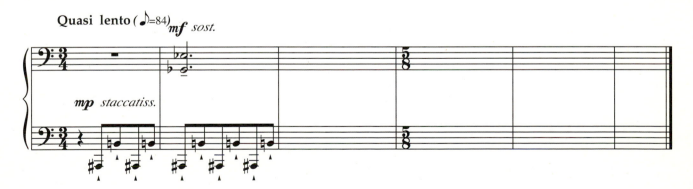